The American Exploration and Travel Series

MATT FIELD
on the
SANTA FE
TRAIL

TRAPPERS AND HORSES AROUND A FIRE

From a painting by Alfred Jacob Miller.

ELD

ON THE

SANTA FE

TRAIL

Collected by Clyde and Mae Reed Porter

*Edited and with an introduction and notes
by John E. Sunder*

NORMAN: UNIVERSITY OF OKLAHOMA PRESS

LIBRARY OF CONGRESS CATALOG CARD NUMBER: 60–7737

Copyright 1960 by the University of Oklahoma Press,
Publishing Division of the University.
Composed and printed at Norman, Oklahoma, U.S.A.,
by the University of Oklahoma Press.
First Edition.

To the memory of Clyde Porter,
who participated in the search for materials
which make up this volume
but did not live to see them published.

Acknowledgments

I wish to express my appreciation to the Missouri Historical Society in St. Louis for the use of Matt's original journal, supplemented by the intriguing Ludlow-Field-Maury manuscripts. Additional material and gracious assistance was given me by the librarians of the St. Louis Mercantile Library and the University of Texas. Since today's professional specialization encourages editors to seek a helping hand through the U.S. mail, those numerous correspondents who carefully answered my questions and made recommendations deserve thanks and are cited individually in the footnotes.

These acknowledgments, the title page notwithstanding, would be incomplete without a large measure of credit from me to the late Clyde Porter and his wife, Mae Reed Porter, whose collecting zeal in Western American history has put historians and the public in their debt.

Mrs. Norris Davis of Austin, Texas, supported by a generous grant from the University of Texas, typed this manuscript and helped edit the editor. I hope the footnotes equal in clarity and accuracy Matt's entertaining narrative.

John E. Sunder

Austin, Texas
January 15, 1960

ix

Contents

* The dates following article titles are not those on which the events described in the text occurred. These eighty-five articles, based upon Matt's memoirs and the journal of his tour to Santa Fe, were published in both the daily and weekly editions of the New Orleans *Picayune*, and the publication dates appear in parentheses in that order.

Contents

Illustrations

Editor's Introduction

A weary, wind-burned traveler from the plains stopped in Pollard's Hotel at Independence, Missouri, in the autumn of 1839. He had spent the summer on the Santa Fe Trail and in the settlements of New Mexico and in his journal had recorded his vivid, firsthand impressions of the Southwest. This promising young writer, Matthew (Matt) C. Field, returned West in 1843 and kept a second journal of his experiences. The two records, together with newspaper articles drawn from them, constitute a choice cut of early plains and mountain adventure. Although Matt was remembered in paint and print by his contemporaries, posterity overlooked his fine wit and creativeness and jostled to the literary side lines his history-packed narratives. His 1843 account, recently rescued from obscurity, was published by the University of Oklahoma Press and broke trail for the release of this, his earlier offering of 1839.[1]

Matt was only four years old when he and his family landed at New York shortly after the end of the War of 1812. His Irish father, a publisher of Roman Catholic books, had fled to London during the Hibernian turmoil of the late eighteenth century and, feeling insecure in England, "further escaped the sight of British oppression," as Joseph, one of Matt's three older brothers, related, by leading his family to America.[2] Matt was a bright lad with a weak constitution and, in his mid-teens, after a brief residence in Baltimore, was apprenticed to a New York jeweler to learn a physically undemanding craft. As an apprentice his mind

[1] Matthew C. Field, *Prairie and Mountain Sketches* (ed. by Kate L. Gregg and John Francis McDermott) (Norman, 1957).

[2] Joseph M. Field's memoir of Matthew C. Field, n.d., in Ludlow-Field-Maury Collection, Missouri Historical Society, St. Louis.

wandered freely from his detailed work to Joseph's success as an actor, and, having "a passion for the gems of Shakespeare much stronger than for those of India," he substituted the stage for broken watch fobs.[3]

A thespian's life, however, was not an easy one, particularly since Matt played supporting roles to stars Charles Kean, Ellen Tree, Junius Brutus Booth, and that "most admirable immitation [*sic*] of a spoiled Mastiff," Edwin Forrest.[4] Ludlow and Smith's theatrical company sponsored Matt for four years on the Mobile–New Orleans–St. Louis circuit, and Noah Ludlow, particularly, took a fatherly interest in his career. Matt opened in Montgomery, Alabama, in 1834, and the following year played Romeo, under his brother's watchful eye. When Ludlow and Smith had the unexpected opportunity to send a group to St. Louis for the winter season 1837–38, Matt was appointed "manager pro-tem" and opened his shivering company in the cold St. Louis Theatre. Financially, the season was a "heavy loss" to Ludlow and Sol Smith; to Matt, however, it was a lesson in experience.[5]

His health was fragile and did not improve with the uncertainties of stage life. When he returned to St. Louis in the spring of 1839, after a southern tour, he suffered from a gastric ulcer complicated by respiratory difficulties and was under medical care. Extremely worried about his health and his career, he questioned his professional ability—"I always fail in an exit; Tragedy, comedy, or farce, I can seldom make an effective *exit*"—lived frugally in a garret room, and husbanded his strength for performances.[6] During the day he wandered the city, at times alone,

[3] Noah Miller Ludlow, *Dramatic Life as I Found It* (St. Louis, 1880), 534.

[4] William G. B. Carson, "The Diary of Mat Field, St. Louis, April 2–May 16, 1839 (Part II)," *Bulletin of the Missouri Historical Society*, Vol. V, No. 3 (April, 1949), 181.

[5] Sol Smith, *Theatrical Management in the West and South for Thirty Years* (New York, 1868), 133; William G. B. Carson, *The Theatre on the Frontier* (Chicago, 1932).

[6] Carson, "The Diary of Mat Field, St. Louis, April 2–May 16, 1839 (Part I)," *Bulletin of the Missouri Historical Society*, Vol. V, No. 2 (January, 1949), 107.

at times with friends George Clark (son of William, the explorer), Edmund Paul (a Chouteau on his mother's side), and James Clay (son of "The Great Compromiser"); berated himself when he drank; watched his diet; delved into the local museum; and listened to western yarns.

Further complications involved two young ladies, Eliza Riddle, who later married Joseph, and Tullia Paul, both of whom rejected Matt's proposals. Such a blow was enough to drive any ardent suitor to choose between an actor's life and a frontiersman's free existence; and, since he was already disturbed, he set a "Day of Destiny," June 1, when he would decide upon the West, seminary study for the ministry, marriage, and the stage, or some possible combination of futures.

The West won: Matt prepared to leave for Santa Fe. He and a few friends planned to join a company of eighty traders outfitting in St. Louis for an early July departure from Independence.[7] Since he would cross into Mexican territory, he needed proper identification, yet evidently did not apply to the State Department for a passport. Until 1856, however, state authorities could issue similar documents. Either Matt secured his passport from the state of Missouri, or the governor of New Mexico granted a waiver through Don Manuel Álvarez, the American consul at Santa Fe, or through the Mexican vice-consul assigned to St. Louis.[8]

To outfit himself quickly, Matt sold his watch and chain; borrowed money from a St. Louis friend; laid in necessary foodstuffs, including a basket of champagne; and, through Ludlow and Smith, announced his theatrical swan song.[9] Although the critics

[7] *Daily Evening Gazette* (St. Louis), June 12, 1839.

[8] Gaillard Hunt, *The Department of State of the United States* (New Haven and London, 1914), 352; letter of Carl L. Lokke (Foreign Affairs Branch of the National Archives) to John E. Sunder, October 16, 1958; Register and Despatches of the United States Consul at Santa Fe, 1830–46, in General Records of the Department of State, Record Group 59, National Archives; *Daily Evening Gazette* (St. Louis), October 12, 1839.

[9] Matthew C. Field promissory note, June 12, 1839, and purchase receipts,

handled him roughly on occasion, his benefit performance on Tuesday evening, June 11, drew "a very respectable house." The audience turned out to honor Matt's likable, gentlemanly character as much as to applaud his talent and left him, as the press anticipated, with "something that shall sweeten his travels to the 'Far West.' " That night he played Bristles in *The Farmer's Story* and later in the evening delivered a "humorous and pointed" farewell address.[10]

With favorable river conditions the average steamboat churned upstream in seven days between St. Louis and Independence. Matt and his companions departed on either the *Naomi* (June 12), the *St. Peters* (June 19), or the *St. Lawrence* (June 21); but, whatever the steamer, his first newspaper article reveals the upriver trip was hectic. Ashore by June 27, he delivered an address "before an audience of 90 persons in the town of Liberty," lecturing them on literature and drama. After that formal curtsy to the arts, he joined his party at near-by Independence.[11]

The first seasonal Santa Fe trading companies had left Missouri weeks earlier, but apparently Matt's group—growing smaller every day—was unhurried.[12] Underway finally, his unorthodox party numbered only eighteen Americans and Mexicans—merchants and tourists—with a few wagons and a carefree spirit. In his journal Matt lists the seventeen men who accompanied him to the Southwest. Only five of them may be identified accurately: Bernardo, Capt. Branch, James Hasey, Josanasiah Luna, and Valintina. Of the others, possibly three materialize: Mr. Campbell, Jerry Folger, and Los E. Long. The remainder— Bell, Morris Boyles, Chas. Burrass, Charley, Wm. Decker, John Halbert, Letchworth, Salvadore, and Santa Simmons—are lost

June, 1839, in Ludlow-Field-Maury Collection, Missouri Historical Society, St. Louis.

[10] *Daily Evening Gazette* (St. Louis), June 11, 12, 1839; *Daily Missouri Republican* (St. Louis), June 10, 11, 1839.

[11] Portion of Matthew C. Field's address given at Liberty, June 27, 1839, in Ludlow-Field-Maury Collection, Missouri Historical Society, St. Louis.

[12] *Daily Missouri Republican* (St. Louis), July 11, 1839.

in the past, unless the future reveals them. Two of the nine, Salvadore and Santa Simmons, may be Mexicans, but the others are almost certainly Americans, perhaps Missourians.

Bernardo, the dying cook the expedition buried on the banks of the Arkansas, was mourned by Matt in his journal and a newspaper article. James Hasey is the "Lazy Hasey" trader who won respect by procrastination and extreme individualism. He, too, Matt enshrined in print. Josanasiah Luna is not a Puritan divine, as his name suggests, but is, instead, Don Antonio José Luna of Santa Fe. He was the thirty-one-year-old scion of a powerful New Mexican landholding family: "a man of affairs, wealthy . . . of marked intellectual power, sound judgment, and inflexible integrity of character."[13]

Although Captain Branch hides from history much of his career, some of his contemporaries mention the outline. Evidently he is the same "José de Jesús Branch" who was naturalized by the Mexicans on Christmas Day, 1829. His store in Taos boasted one of the few wooden floors in New Mexico—befitting his Virginian concept of civilization—and he ranked with the leading traders of the region. His family was in New Mexico, and he was going home when Matt followed his experienced trailsmanship to Santa Fe.[14]

The defeated Valintina who wrecked the carryall was Matt's boisterous eastern friend James Valentine. Since Jim was probably a New Yorker and a man of means, he may be the "James J. M. Valentine," a Fulton Street "counsellor" and the husband

[13] Ralph Emerson Twitchell, *The Leading Facts of New Mexican History* (5 vols., Cedar Rapids, 1911–17), II (1912), 492–93.

[14] Letter of Clyde H. Porter to Charles van Ravenswaay, June 18, 1956, among Incoming Letters, Missouri Historical Society, St. Louis; James Josiah Webb, *Adventures in the Santa Fé Trade, 1844–1847* (volume I of The Southwest Historical Series, ed. by Ralph P. Bieber [Glendale, 1931]), 93; Blanche C. Grant, *When Old Trails Were New* (New York, 1934). Captain Branch may be Alexander Branch, the trapper who was on the Upper Missouri in 1824.—Dale L. Morgan (ed.), "The Diary of William H. Ashley, March 25–June 27, 1825," *Bulletin of the Missouri Historical Society*, Vol. XI, No. 1 (October, 1954), 13.

of socially prominent Leonora Bailey, who was listed with at least five other James Valentines in the New York City directories of 1837 to 1840.[15]

Mr. Campbell straddles the thin line separating known and unknown. Although Matt tells us nothing of him, he may be Richard (José Ricardo) Campbell, the trader-traveler who reached New Mexico in the mid 1820's and was active for years in the Southwest. The elderly probate judge of Doña Ana County, New Mexico, in the fifties bore the same name and is probably the same man. Nonetheless, both Richard and Campbell are fairly common names, and the West is large enough to have accommodated several.[16]

Astride the same fence of identification are Jerry Folger and Los E. Long. Presuming that Jerry was one of the "fellow citizens" of St. Louis who were in Matt's company, he may be Jared W. Folger, the chair- and cabinetmaker who had a downtown warehouse at First and Olive.[17] Long's first name and middle initial are questionable in Matt's original journal. Los E. may be José, and José may be the Spanish substitute for something else, perhaps even for B. D. Long, the American wagon maker who had gone to New Mexico about 1830 and remained there to practice his craft.[18]

New Mexican political conditions were unsettled in 1839. Trade to Santa Fe, quite profitable in the twenties after Mexico's

[15] Letters of James J. Heslin (The New-York Historical Society) and Joseph L. Andrews (The Association of the Bar of the City of New York) to John E. Sunder, December 2, 1958, and January 5, 1959.

[16] Robert G. Cleland, *This Reckless Breed of Men* (New York, 1950), 264; Frank D. Reeves (ed.), "The Charles Bent Papers," *New Mexico Historical Review*, Vol. XXIX, No. 4 (October, 1954), 312; Twitchell, *Leading Facts*, II, 142–43.

[17] Charles Keemle, *The St. Louis Directory, for the Years 1836–7* (St. Louis, 1836), 9; Charles van Ravenswaay, "The Anglo-American Cabinetmakers of Missouri, 1800–1850," *Bulletin of the Missouri Historical Society*, Vol. XIV, No. 3 (April, 1958), 253, 255.

[18] Lewis E. Atherton, "Business Techniques in the Santa Fe Trade," *The Missouri Historical Review*, Vol. XXXIV, No. 3 (April, 1940), 340.

successful rebellion against Spain, had declined in the thirties. Governor Boggs of Missouri called attention "to the . . . depressed condition of the Mexican trade; which for . . . want of . . . aid from the General Government . . . [has] for several years past been gradually decreasing," yet it was not "almost extinct," as he added threateningly.[19] The trade remained profitable enough for several yearly caravans; although American traders complained freely of regulations, Indian troubles, the infrequent protection provided by the United States Army, and always of water, food, and the dirt and grime of the trail. Governor Manuel Armijo was accused of arbitrariness in imposing duties on American goods, was suspected of corruption in office, and provided a butt for accumulated hatreds. Matt heard his companions' complaints. He heard them not as a trader, however, and found most of the Mexican officials and much of Mexican society thoroughly enjoyable.

The caravan followed the well-known and established route from Independence southwestward across Indian country to Council Grove, Cotton Wood Grove, and the bend of the Arkansas. The north-bank river trail from that point crossed Walnut Creek and Pawnee Fork, brushed by the crossings of the Arkansas where some parties took the Cimarron Cutoff, and wound through Big Timber to the welcome gate of Bent's Fort on the Colorado plains near the mouth of the Purgatory. The party stopped briefly at Bent's, then turned southwestward again, traveling parallel to, but a few miles west of, the Purgatory. The trail brought them up and over Raton Pass and on to the headwaters of the Canadian, where the wagons continued south to join the main road to Santa Fe. Matt, following Captain Branch, took a more rugged trail through Cimarron Canyon and in the Taos Valley received his first impressions of Mexican culture.

---

[19] Governor Lillburn W. Boggs called attention to the trade in his second biennial message of November 20, 1838.—Leopard Buel and Floyd C. Shoemaker (eds.), *The Messages and Proclamations of the Governors of the State of Missouri* (16 vols., Columbia, Missouri, 1922–51), I, 362.

From Taos he journeyed to Santa Fe, part of the trail taking him through the narrow, winding upper Río Grande Valley, and at the capital immersed himself in Latin living. Snow and cold weather, however, made much of the Santa Fe Trail impassable in winter, and Matt, although pleased with his vacation, had to leave for home. He and another American, Dr. David Waldo, joined a company of Mexican merchants who had a military escort. They bumped along the dusty Cimarron Cutoff route beyond San Miguel to the Arkansas, where the escort took leave, and Matt, thinking himself a guide, led his party astray in the desert. Fortunately, he found the trail along the river, and the remainder of the trip to Independence, despite prairie fires, was less hazardous.

Five of the Mexican merchants continued in Matt's company on the steamer *Pizarro* from Independence to St. Louis, a month behind the twenty-wagon "annual Santa Fe caravan of traders," which had reached the settlements early in October with nearly one-fifth of a million dollars in Mexican specie.[20] At that time Missouri was sliding into depression, and specie was in demand to meet the hard-money policy of the state bank. Additional gold and silver coins, brought in by Matt's traveling companions, Don José Chávez and his friends, were spent during the winter in New York and Philadelphia for $75,000 in merchandise.[21] Early in June, 1840, the Chávez party set out to return home, just two weeks after "Mr. Messervey" reached Independence with the year's first expedition—some forty wagons—from Chihuahua and Santa Fe.[22]

Matt's journal, a brimming potpourri of material for newspaper articles, was tucked away in his trunk aboard the *Pizarro*. The pencil-written account was more than a mere source of articles, however: it was and remains an unusual bit of Western Americana. Since most of it is verse—the heroic couplet—it is a

[20] *Daily Missouri Republican* (St. Louis), October 4, 5, November 12, 1839.
[21] *The Daily Picayune* (New Orleans), June 12, 1840.
[22] *The Weekly Picayune* (New Orleans), May 25, 1840.

rare, perhaps unique, record of events on the trail kept by an actual participant.[23] Other western travelers have quoted the poets in their diaries or have incorporated in their narratives a few lines of impromptu verse, but have any equaled Matt? His 108-page journal, about the size of *The Reader's Digest,* is bound with marbled cardboard covers and may deceive the casual viewer, since it begins and ends in prose, yet it encloses a poetic heart.

A budding poet when he left for Santa Fe, Matt—Don Mateo Campo to his friends—returned a confirmed one. He was not a lonely bard, however, since the decades from 1820 to 1860 were ones in which most American newspapers carried "Original Contributions" from local writers. With or without editorial encouragement, our aspiring Shakespeares and Miltons contributed to the press their " 'choicest thoughts' " and " 'moonshine madness.' "[24] Matt had more solid fare to offer, although there is no clear indication that he intended to publish his entire journal. Albert Pike's western verse suggests the content of Matt's but does not equal it in quantity. Matt's lines center on the "loadstone" Santa Fe, as the poet A. E. Trombly called it, and were the product of a human "iron filing" drawn to it across the plains.[25]

Matt realized the opportunity almost immediately to publish newspaper articles drawn from his journal. The New Orleans *Picayune* hired him as an assistant editor early in the winter of 1839–40 and serialized his accounts as "Sketches of the Mountains and the Prairies." These "fanciful relations of real incidents," the press added, "although written to amuse . . . contain useful information" on Mexican culture and the Santa Fe trade. A few of the sketches were "somewhat longer than usual," but the *Picayune* anticipated correctly that the public would love

[23] Letter of Robert R. Hubach to John E. Sunder, October 20, 1958.

[24] David Donald and Frederick A. Palmer, "Toward a Western Literature, 1820–1860," *Mississippi Valley Historical Review,* Vol. XXXV, No. 3 (December, 1948), 420.

[25] Albert Edmund Trombly, *Santa Fe, Santa Fe* (Prairie City, Illinois, 1941), 7.

them long or short. Other newspapers copied the series, usually without giving credit to Matt, and the fat of plagiarism crackled in the fire.[26]

The series ran for nearly two years, from 1839 to 1841, and, although all the stories are fascinating reading, included a few particularly remarkable and historically valuable accounts. Matt's description of "Pueblo De Leche" is the best available and was reprinted by *The Colorado Magazine* (1937) along with his sketches of "Big Timber" and "Robbery of Fort William."[27] His interpretation of the Crow festival, despite some highly questionable features, is an actor's recognition of "primitive Indian Drama" and would do credit to modern anthropology. The "Battle of the Ranch," "Señora Toulous," "A Sunday in San Miguel," and "The Lost Track," to select arbitrarily a few articles from many, carry the ring of proven metal and are a historian's delight.

Matt had a strong humanitarian streak in his character and writing. The wild horse, buffalo, prairie dog, grizzly bear, and even the lowly mouse were part of his broad interest in life, caught his attention, and were handled skillfully in his narrative. Generally, he pitied the wild creatures killed by his party on the trail, because he felt a universal kinship between man and lesser life. Also, since he had an amateur interest in geology and paleontology, his work refers speculatively to the mastodon, violent natural upheavals, and prehistoric seas. Man, however, whether Indian, traveling companion, merchant, or trapper, always occupied the center of his thoughts and accounts; and Matt's accurate observations of New Mexican life hint that perhaps the Americanization of New Mexico was more a Latinization of the American.

[26] *The Daily Picayune* (New Orleans), January 23, May 5, 1840; *The Weekly Picayune* (New Orleans), December 16, 1839.

[27] "Sketches of Big Timber, Bent's Fort, and Milk Fort in 1839," *The Colorado Magazine*, Vol. XIV, No. 3 (May, 1937), 102–108. LeRoy R. Hafen may have been the editor of the article.

Joseph Field and Charles Keemle took Matt into partnership on the new St. Louis *Weekly Reveille*, a strongly literary newspaper, and encouraged his natural writer's talent. He fancied himself a bit of a playwright—two years earlier he wrote a "caricature of Cinderella" called *Schinder El'ler; or the Doctor and the Little Dutch Sleeper*, which was produced in New Orleans—and put his satire to good use in dozens of short poems for both the *Reveille* and the *Picayune*.[28]

Twentieth-century critics find a librettist's talent rather than poetic genius in his compositions. According to Field family tradition, however, Poe and others of Matt's day found much commendable in his work.[29] We may grant that his lines sing "with a light and lively Irish lilt in rhythm," glitter "with sparks of wit," and glow "with humor"; but historians using his journals and articles must beware of poetic license and the overwritten.[30]

Shortly before Matt's death, Carey and Hart of Philadelphia projected a volume of verse entitled *Poems of Phazma* under his pseudonym, with an introduction by Joseph Field. The *Reveille*, as a co-operative gesture, republished selections from his work to keep his name before the public until satisfactory arrangements could be made with the publishers. Despite the low publication cost of much less than one dollar a copy, the project failed.[31]

Matt, in precarious health after a "severe attack" in the summer of 1844, traveled eastward that fall to sail from Boston on a health-giving cruise. His "ancient prediliction for water"—note how his 1839 journal swims with watery references—convinced

[28] Matt's name appears in the "editors and proprietors" column of the St. Louis *Weekly Reveille* from July 15 to November 11, 1844. See *The Weekly Picayune* (New Orleans), March 21, 1842, and Ludlow's *Dramatic Life*, 533, for references to *Schinder El'ler*.

[29] Lilian Whiting, *Kate Field, a Record* (Boston, 1899), 4.

[30] *Globe Democrat* (St. Louis), August 13, 1944.

[31] Prospectus for *Poems of Phazma*, January 1, 1849, and letter of Carey and Hart to N. M. Ludlow, April 21, 1844, in Ludlow-Field-Maury Collection, Missouri Historical Society, St. Louis; *Weekly Reveille* (St. Louis), March 30, 1846.

him his vigor might be restored at sea. Before sailing, he stopped at Buffalo to meet an old childhood acquaintance, George Jamieson. Together they visited Niagara Falls, where Matt, breathing painfully, insisted upon hoisting his frail body, a "mere shadow," George said, over the rocks. Returning to Buffalo, Matt boarded a train for Boston.[32]

Friends in Boston, unable to discourage his plans, saw him aboard the bark *Huma* bound for Mobile and New Orleans. On the second day out, November 15, he died quietly and quickly and was buried at sea. Joseph Field explained the burial as "fulfilling a wish [Matt] had expressed in one of his poems"; but Ludlow, realistic rather than romantic, stressed that the warm weather made necessary immediate burial since the ship was several days from Pensacola, the next port of call.[33] Cornelia and the Field children, in Mobile awaiting Matt, remained there, sheltered by the Ludlows, after the family tragedy.

In the columns of the *Reveille*, Joseph eulogized " 'poor Matt' —our weak, sick brother," and the influential *Daily* (St. Louis) *Missouri Republican* remembered Matt "as a most estimable gentleman." An ambitious artist, James Carson, painted and publicly exhibited a portrait copied from an 1843 daguerreotype of Matt in mountain costume.[34] Matt's friends were full of pleasant reminiscences of him, but none mentioned the final irony of his death: at last he had made a thoroughly dramatic *exit*, and the play was complete.

In preparing Matt Field's journal and newspaper articles for publication, I have attempted to keep editorial changes within

[32] *Weekly Reveille* (St. Louis), March 24, 1845, quoting a letter of George Jamieson to the *Knickerbocker Magazine*.

[33] Joseph M. Field's memoir of Matthew C. Field, n.d., in Ludlow-Field-Maury Collection, Missouri Historical Society, St. Louis; Ludlow, *Dramatic Life*, 535; *The Daily Picayune* (New Orleans), December 3, 1844; *Weekly Reveille* (St. Louis), December 23, 1844.

[34] *Weekly Reveille* (St. Louis), December 23, 1844, March 31, 1845; *Daily Missouri Republican* (St. Louis), December 16, 1844.

the text at a minimum. Misspelled, repeated, and wrongly used words (both English and Spanish) have been corrected only as needed for clarification. Kept in the text are archaic spellings, slight misspellings, grammatical errors, variants of words, and mispunctuation which would cause no confusion. Likewise, Spanish names and phrases have been translated in the text, within brackets, only for clarity. More lengthy explanatory material is included in the footnotes. In Matt's first journal entry, he mentions having lost his Spanish grammar. It is obvious, as one reads farther, that the author has written Spanish and Indian words and phrases as he heard them spoken; e.g., *Governor Amijo, Camanche.* When these words are consistently and frequently used, they have been noted only occasionally in the text. No attempt has been made to change Matt's own accenting of Spanish words.

The *Picayune* articles are arranged according to the occurrence of events in the text during the journey to and from Santa Fe. However, a few of the articles are not tied down to a definite place or time, and, to handle those, I attempted to scatter them throughout the others.

MATT FIELD
on the
SANTA FE
TRAIL

I

Matt Field's Journal
July 15–October 30, 1839

Cotton Wood Grove, Missouri Territory,
200 Miles from Christian Habitation,[1] *July 15, 1839*

The Prairies! The wild Desert plains! After 15 days travel, here we are in a little paradise, a grove of tall trees, through which runs a beautiful stream of water over a pebble bottom. Flower and shrub in luxuriant profusion greet the eye and the cool breeze playing among the rustling leaves, adds variation to the songs of birds while the murmuring stream keeps up a running accompaniment. "Cotton Wood Grove" is far pleasanter and more beautiful than Council Grove[2] and after days of travel over burning plains with nothing but grass and sky to meet the weary vision, the finest pulsations of the heart are awakened at sight of this real oasis in the Desert. Yesterday in pursuit of an antelope I lost my Journal up to this date which I was in the habit of carrying always about me, also my Spanish Grammar in which I had become very agreably [*sic*] interested. My very good Friend *Charles Burross*

[1] By action of Congress, approved June 30, 1834, "all that part of the United States west of the Mississippi, and not within the states of Missouri and Louisiana, or the territory of Arkansas, and, also, that part of the United States east of the Mississippi river, and not within any state to which the Indian title has not been extinguished . . . [was regarded as] Indian country." Technically, Matt's reference to "Missouri Territory" is not accurate, yet the area was referred to commonly as Indian territory, Western territory, or even Oregon territory.—*The Statutes at Large of the United States* (17 vols., Boston, 1845–73), IV (1846), 729; John B. Wyeth, *Oregon* (volume XXI of Reuben G. Thwaites [ed.], *Early Western Travels, 1748–1846* [32 vols., Cleveland, 1904–1907]), 50. For the location of Cotton Wood Grove see article footnotes 28 and 29.

[2] See article footnote 23.

rummaged his trunk and found this old Blank Book for me, and now I begin again. My last Journal was exactly a month old and contained minute notes of our whole travel since the day we left St. Louis. and there it lies for the wolves and antelopes, and they may swallow all my lies. Yesterday I slept in the noon day sun— no covering but my hat. I dreamt that I met *Charley Fisher*, and he told me my Brother *Joe* was dead. Last night I dreamed I was preparing for an evening party—all night long I was comb-ing my hair and titivating.[3] It is now evening—since we left the *Cotton Wood* we have traveled 15 miles over the most desolate prairie we have yet seen—we met water now and then in holes— tasteless & warm. We are fagged and weary—we see antelopes, but cannot get near them. The Flies are very furious—a green fly, nearly as large as a Bee that *bits* [*sic*] the horses till the blood streams down their neck and sides. There are grasshoppers as large as my thumb—Lizards are also very numerous. The Sun is down—The waggons [*sic*] are coming up.

July 16th The "Sand Hills"[4] are in sight, looking like a marble city in the distance. The sun is an hour high and our course is di-rectly West—before us, or rather between us and the horizon float a few scattered clouds—desolate wanderers like ourselves. The sunlight falls upon them and their shadows fling a dim veil before the sky untill [*sic*] they fall upon the earth, and darken here and there wide spots of the prairie green. And this is the only variety in the lonely prospect—clouds in the sky—Shadows on the earth. How like the ocean! How very like the ocean! And yon "Sand Hills"—how much they resemble a distant view of land! At times, a few days ago, we would have now and then views of distant and scattered trees, and these would rise on the sight and fade away again most veritably like ships at sea. and these rolling heaves of the prairie—they are so much like the swelling waves of the Sea, that the ocean is constantly in my

[3] Dressing up.
[4] See article entitled "The Sand Hills."

4

mind. The Ocean! The grand, The Boundless, The magnificent! Was not these vast prairies once thy Bed? Why are they so like thee? Thou great emblem of Eternity!

No traces have ever been found of The *Tower of Bable* [*sic*]. I observe in many places masses of imbedded stone, bearing some traces of regularity. Why might not this be the great plain which the ambitious men of old selected on which to mount their ladder to the heavens?—This spot, where the horizon touching the earth around makes heaven appear nearer to our sublunary sphere? Here may have gathered the nations together in their strength— here myriads of men worked as with one hand, and in their pigmy pride sought to pull down the glory of the great power that made them—till the loud voice of his thunder broke from the clouds they sought to reach, and his avenging lightning came forth blasting the uplifted hand of impiety, and crumbling its work to dust; scattering the nations and confounding their tongues, and changing this fertile earth into a vast ocean of desolation! *It may be!* It is past 9 A.M. The waggons are crossing a very difficult Mud hole, and here we breakfast.

The Prairies

[*Wednesday, July 17*]
Alone! Yet not alone, for still
In hollow roll—on sloping hill
Insect and bird with happy voice
Greet the Sun's light, live & rejoice!
Yet this as sky o'er Desert sleeps,
What solumn [*sic*] wonder o'er me creeps!
No part of man hath ever been
Where mine now treads the prairie green
The nimble footed Buck & Roe
The Antelope[5] and Buffalo,

[5] At one time millions of pronghorn antelope inhabited the plains, but by 1920 only a few had escaped the hunters. Since they were inordinately curious

Alone are Monarchs of the land
Where now in lonely awe I stand!
And now at noon we pause for rest,
Yon stagnant pool must yield us drink,
Where the frog builds his slimy nest
And the Lizard creeps through the miry stink.
The Waggons form their firm coralle [*sic*]
For foes and mules a rampart wall.
And now the Spanish Judge[6] is seen
Scraping aside the mantle green
Of the dark pool to dip his can
And rob the snakes to nourish man.
The steel is struck, the fire is burning
And now the coffee mill is turning.
And Bacon simmering in the pan
Tells that the cooking has began.
Beneath the shade of an umbrella,
Stuck firmly in the yielding ground,
Your poet like a prudent fellow
Lies to indite his *lies* profound.
His head reclined upon his saddle
Where presently he'll ride astraddle.
His rifle lying by his side,
Which went off once, but nothing died.
His shot pouch and his powder horn
Speak danger to some Deer forlorn,
Some Buffalo or other brute
At which he shortly means to shoot.
But stay—Behold the Dinner Table,

animals, they were taken, many times, by trickery—the large, branching horns
of the male antelope no defense against man's rifle. Today the pronghorns are
protected by conservation laws and the herd is increasing.—*American Wild Life
Illustrated* (comp. by the Writers' Program of the Work Projects Administration
in the City of New York) (New York, 1949), 28–31.

[6] Quite possibly Don Antonio José Luna. See the introduction for his biographical sketch.

A table cloth of Dimmeist [?] Sable,
No other than a Buffalo robe
Spread on the earth a tabl [*sic*] good,
Covered with cups & plates & tin
To hold our meat & coffee in.
And there's *fat* Bacon fried in *fat*,
And *Hoe Cake*[7]—What do you think of that!
And, By my appetite! Who could
Believe *hoe cake* could smell so good?

[*Thursday, July 18*]
The Sun is sixty minutes high
The wet grass is getting quickly dry
The mules, unstaked, are running loose—
Except the poets, silly goose!
Who dreamt so sound he could'nt wake
But slept and left his horse at stake.
Now they are bridging o'er the stream
To pass across each loaded team
Throwing in heavy brush and grass
To bear the waggons as they pass,
To keep the skittish mules from falling
And guard the sinking wheels from stalling.
And Double teams they still require
To drag the Waggons through the mire.
Behold with what a fearful pitch
The lumbering waggon jumps the ditch.
See how the frightened mules are staring
Hear the whips crack, and Drivers swearing.
"Get up! Go on! Gee! Dam [*sic*] you, haw!"
Crossing the Little Arkansas![8]

[7] The hoecake or hoe cake was made of corn (Indian meal) and baked on a hoe, originally, in the ashes or before the fire.

[8] The Little Arkansas, a notable landmark on the trail, flows southeast approximately midway between McPherson and Ellinwood, Kansas, and enters the Arkansas at Wichita. The trail crossed the smaller stream's upper reaches.

2 o'clk. P.M. Upsets! Breakdowns! Stops & Disasters!
No subjects, all are Kings and masters.
Where all are great and none are small
The Devil soon will carry all
And so to all our hearts content
To Hell the Carry all[9] wast sent.
Down went the wheel and out went "Jim"
And the trunks went tumbling after him.
And as poor Jim must bear the blame
The spot shall ever bear his name
So where the driver lost his seat
We christen *"Valentine's Defeat!"*
The "Sand Hills" near the Arkansas,
Where now sojourn the friendly *Kaw*,[10]
Seems like a marble city, seen
Through intervening forests green,
And at the sight fond feelings stir
The bosom of the wanderer.
Feelings of home, companions kind,
Kindred, and dear ones left behind.
So like a city seems the view,
You scarce can believe it is not true.
And every little town delight
Springs into memory at the sight.

The sun was half an hour from setting
When we were wondrous busy getting
Over "Owl Creek"[11] a nasty pool—

9 For the full story of the carryall see the article entitled "Valentine's Defeat."

10 The Kaw (Kansa or Kansas) Indians, by treaty with the United States in 1825, surrendered much of their Kansas land claim. They were assigned a rectangular reservation beginning twenty leagues up the Kansas River at the site of Topeka. Although Matt did not pass through the reservation, he probably met Kaw settlers near by.—William F. Zornow, *Kansas* (Norman, 1957), 43–44.

11 Matt is referring to one of the small watercourses between the Little

Pretty good water if 'twas cool
But in these plains our parching two lips
Must sigh in vain for "Bogarts" Julaps [*sic*].[12]
Here we first saw the Buffalo tracks
The Beautiful brutes with broken backs, & C.

[*Friday, July 19*]
Sleeping beneath a waggon in
A blanket or a buffalo skin
With thousands of musquito's buzzing
Is not the sweetest kind of dozing.
And then just as our eyes are closing,
Towards the morning, damp and chill
The dew comes down to plague us still.
And when at last sleep seals our eyes,
Day comes to tell us we must rise
Pilgarlic Poet, when awake,
Saddled his horse and drew his stake,
Then turned something to do or say,
When Pony Pegasus walked away.
And poor pilgarlic ran a race
Or [*sic*] foot to give his horse a chase.
Through the high grass chill & wet
Two miles ere he could mounted get.
"Cow Creek"[13] next crossed and barred our way,
And here we had the Devil to pay,
The mud, as soft as new made mush,
Required such loads of grass & brush,

Arkansas and Cow creeks. See article footnote 15 for the modern names of those
small streams.

[12] "Bogart's billiard saloon [in New Orleans] was a great resort for [river]
pilots in those days. They met there about as much to exchange river news as to
play."—Mark Twain, *Life on the Mississippi* (Montreal, 1883), 178.

[13] (Big) Cow Creek and Little Cow Creek, near Lyons, Kansas, were on a
difficult section of the trail. They flow northwest to southeast, join near Saxman,
Kansas, and enter the Arkansas at Hutchinson.

That even *Jim* at last gave o'er,
And swore point blank he'd work no more!
He had toted grass, and done his best,
And others now might do the rest.
Napoleon, when he crossed Bernard,[14]
Perhaps met nothing half so hard—
Nothing of which historians speak—
As getting over "Big Cow Creek"!
And *getting over* is'nt *all*,
Besides the *Large*, there's several *Small*,
And a small Cow Creek tho' but a *Calf*,
Beats the Old *Cow* sometimes by half.
But here we are all snug and over,
And set down for the night in clover,
And snug beneath the Waggon writing
Sits Poor Pilgarlic, verse inditing
While the musquitos drink his blood
And swear no doubt his rhyme is good.
Beautiful are the prairie flowers,
Beautiful in the noon tide hours
When a passing cloud goes flitting o'er them
And flings a shadowy veil before them.
Beautiful in the morning light
When the dew drops shine like crystals bright.
But ah! most beautiful are they,
When plucked and bound in a bouquet,
Christened and kissed—a gentle guest
To wear all day about my breast.
"Cow Creek!" and yet, no Buffalo;
And Nineteen days from Independence,

---

[14] Napoleon's crossing of the St. Bernard Pass into Italy occurred in May, 1800. Actually, he crossed the mountains with the rear guard of his army; not on a choice stallion, but on a mule led by a local peasant. Other generals had made longer and more perilous marches, yet they "lacked both Bonaparte's eye for theatrical effect and incomparable talent for self-advertisement."—*The Cambridge Modern History* (13 vols., Cambridge, England, 1934), IX, 60.

And Buffalo tracks where e'er we go,—
I wonder where they could have went hence!
Tomorrow night we'll have to *guard*,
3 hours on duty—rather hard,
But quite as pleasant to be fighting,
As lying for musquito biting.
Tomorrow we'll have Buffalo
And then right merrily we'll go!

[*Saturday, July 20*]
Nights mantle hung o'er half the world,
Pilgarlic in his blanket curled,
Lay snug beneath a waggon snoring
When heavy clouds set up a roaring,
And down the rain came swiftly pouring.
This made each sleeper round in the camp
Jump from their [*sic*] blankets rather damp,
And plainly proved musquito netting
Is no sure guard against a wetting,
However it may serve to keep
Sharp insects from us when we sleep.
Next morn at breakfast—*Jim* & *Jerry*
Laughed till they made the whole camp merry
Telling the horrors of the night,
The pain of each musquito bite
The rain that never seemed to stop,
But poured a pint in every drop.
"Oh" said Jim, "My God 'Twas awful"
As industriously he stuffed his craw ful [*sic*].
At 2 o'clock we reached "Round Mound,"
Alias "Plum Point," where plumbs abound.[15]

[15] Plum Point (Plum Buttes), between Cow and Walnut creeks, was reached a short distance east of the great bend of the Arkansas. Matt misleads his readers by calling the Point "Round Mound." Round Mound, another well-known location on the trail, is a "spur" of the Don Carlos Range in northeastern New Mexico. It was located to the left of the outgoing trail in the Ute Creek area near Farley, New Mexico.

And plumbs we eat—tho' hard and green,
They were the best here to be seen
And here we saw the foot prints new
Of a Buffalo—and soon in view
Deep in a hollow, clear and full,
Through a glass we saw a nobl [*sic*] Bull
And swift and eager for the chase
The new fledged hunters joined the race.
We lost the Bull when from the mound,
We took the low and rolling ground,
But travelling round a hill or two,
His eminence appeared in view
Above a hillock moving slow,
We saw his back as he grazed below.
Cautiously now we moved along,
So silently the zephyr's song
And the young insect might be heard
Above us, all so soft we stirred.
We saw him now through the high grass,
As on our hands & knees we pass.
Lazily in his wallow lying,
He flapped the flies, nor dreamed of dying.
But the thunder cloud was in the sky,
And the lightning flashed across his eye.
He heard us stealing o'er the ground
And swiftly turned his gase [*sic*] around,
He rose—his motion was his death—
Cautious we held our eager breath,
Click! Bang! One! Two! The Bullets flew
With force and aim both strong & true,
And away the dying Monster sped
With three sure death shots in his head.
He fell—we found him speedily,
And eyed his carcase [*sic*] greedily.
We cut him up, and each mans horse,

Was burdened with the precious corse [*sic*].[16]
And the thunder storm rushed o'er the spot,
And such a wetting as we got!
And young Pilgarlic lost his hat,
But he hit the Bull, nor cared for that.
We reached the camp, and from each crupper
We quickly formed a sumptuous supper.

[*Sunday, July 21*]
A Hazy, chilly, misty morning;
Blessed be day!—But slight and scorning
Do all men yield to such a day
Whatever Saints or Sinners say.
And we get up Just like the weather,
All Surly, Sour, and Sad together.
Pilgarlic nearly had a fight,
Three quarters wrong, and two thirds right.
Rifles were raised and pistols drawn,
All through the chilly, nasty dawn;
But it ended like a false alarm,
They parted friends, and did no harm.
Then travelling was Dick to pay
And teams were doubled all the way
And out of temper, dull & Damp
We journeyed four hours through the swamp
To the great Arkansaw [*sic*], at last,
We came when noon was two hours past;
And here we dined and stopped to tea
At the "Osage Camp"[17] so pleased were we.
An hour before sunset, or so,

[16] A poetic expression for corpse.
[17] During the summer months, the Osages would move west to hunt buffalo on the prairies of Kansas and northern Oklahoma. The Osage village Matt saw was between Ellinwood and Great Bend, Kansas, near Walnut Creek.—Muriel H. Wright, *A Guide to the Indian Tribes of Oklahoma* (Norman, 1951), 189, 193.

Afar we saw a Buffalo,
Away went "Charley" and away
Pilgarlic went—he couldnt stay.
What e'er did of the Strange consist,
Pilgarlic never could resist.
He followed "Charley" till he lost him,
Then sought with loud voice to accost him.
Echo, and Charley's voice were mute,
So was the humpbacked Buffalo brute,
Yet on, still resolutely on,
Through the tall grass all drear and lone,
Pilgarlic went, resolved to find him—
The Camp far out of sight behind him.
Till the sun dropped behind the hill.
Then paused he, desolate & still.
Around one last and lingering look,
Over the lonely plain he took.
Then cheerless turned, to follow back
To camp his solitary track.
Where he arrived in time to take
His Indian pony out to stake
And sup on remnants of the Bull,
So tough they'd serve bad teeth to pull.

[*Monday, July 22*]
Pilgarlic served his debut spell
As night guard and as sentinel,
From half past one, till morning threw
A dim grey light o'er nights dull hue
Pilgarlic watched outside the camp.
In the high grass, chill and damp,
While a staked mule munched grass beside him,
Wondering next day who should ride him.
Pilgarlic watched the dark dull sky,
The few Stars twinkling dim on high;

14

He peered into the darkness deep,
And felt sad feelings o'er him creep—
He thought of her, the lonely one
Who called him last & dearest Son
Now far away, perhaps in prayer
For him who stood so lonely there.
From Sadness now his heart turned soft,
As tearfully he gazed aloft,
And not in words, but through the eye
He sent his humble prayer on high
For her who gave him blessed life.
In the Eastern Sky the day came peeping,
Pilgarlic soon was soundly sleeping,
When Captain Branch gave him a shake,
Insinuating he should wake,
Get up, and come, and Breakfast take.
This done the mules were driven in
Their toilsome journey to begin.
And soon we came to *"Walnut Creek"*[18]
Of which Pilgarlic loves to speak,
For here he spent a *joyful* day—
Something he cannot often say.
The creek was high—the current strong,
The water cool, and far along
The bottom was both hard & sandy,
So bathing was both cheap and handy.
The Waggons cannot cross to-day,
And willingly perforce we stay.
Pilgarlic when lifes cream pot skimming
Among his best joys sets down swimming
And while he reveled in the water,
The sunny hours of noon away,
Musing upon a dear friends Daughter,[19]

[18] See article footnote 33.
[19] His future wife, Cornelia Burke Ludlow.

Of whom he thinks both night & day.
And when the Sunbeams fell aslant,
Throwing long Shades from tree and plant,
He crossed to where the *Pawnee* comes
To fish, and hunt, and gather plums.
And plums were found all ripe & red,
Small bushes round on Sand hills spread:
The boughs that with their burdens teem
Hand o'er the "Great Arkansas" Stream,
So near, the ripe plums drop in *"plumb"*
As ancient tipplers gulp their rum!

[*Tuesday, July 23*]
Our Bacon-box is running low,
And we are out of Buffalo,
And "Walnut Creek" is running high
And the Waggons cant get over dry.
And hints are heard of short allowance
Unless we kill a Bull or Cow hence.
So mounted soon, our way we take,
O'er hill, and hollow, plain & lake,
Lakes, some of them a good mile wide,
Without a ripple or a tide.
And none of them too deep to wade.[20]
They seem as they were only made
To raise Flys [*sic*], long grass, & musquitos,
Those noxious little Ouriditos![21]
Ante meridian now is past,
And we see a Buffalo at last.
A high spot, distant, dim and black,
It might be grass, but we know his back.

---

[20] Rainy summers brought shallow lakes to prairie sinks, but the water holes were not likely to remain in dry weather.

[21] Evidently Matt wishes to call them "surgeons" and uses the closest Spanish word at his command: *quirúrgico*, or surgical.

His hump so high, his head so low,
His lazy motions well we know.
High on a hill he stands agrazing
The Sun so hot the grass seems blazing.
Around the hollow now we ride
Our figures from his view to hide,
And cautiously we mount the hill
Where all unwarned he grazes still.
Alarmed at last, he either sees,
Or sniffs our presence in the breeze.
And now the huge beast starts to run,
And now begins the hunters fun.
Under the blazing, burning sun
On horseback with a loaded gun.
A second now appears in view;
And four of us now chase the two.
And one escapes, the other lies
Tossing and snorting as he died[?].
The first shot entered his right eye,
He turned, and 'twas our turn to fly,
But another sends him stumbling down,
He rises, reels, and rushes on.
And now he gasps upon the ground,
And sees his hunters gather round;
Death from his left eye takes the light,
And now 'tis dark as is the right.
We tear the warm skin from his back,
His flesh we cut, his bones we hack
And once more mounted, home we go
Some fifteen mortal miles or so.
Pilgarlics Pegasus has got,
A most peculiar Indian trot,
And in the dark Pilgarlic met
An admirable summerset[?].

[*Wednesday, July 24*]
We question not the great design,
Or aught that touches things divine.
But still should really like to find
For what musquitos were designed.
This hungry, bloody little creatures [*sic*]—
They've no respect for limbs or features.
And with their pointed needle noses,
They bite us in our evening dozes,
And such a buzzing round us keep
We can as easy fly, as Sleep.
Our blood to them I think is Brandy
They suck it in like sugar candy
And they are quick as they are thick,
You may kill a hundred at a lick.
But who the Devil wants to kill
When 'tis our own blood that we spill!
And then for every one that dies,
A hundred hungry ghosts arise.
To beat them off is all in vain,
Twice doubled they return again
For they are quicker than the light,
And thicker—Yes—*They darken night!*
Poor *Pill* last night was fairly furious,
For the way they tortured him "was curious"
He tried one place, and tried another,
He smoked himself almost to smother,
He rolled thick blankets tight around him,
And still by some strange art they found him,
Face, fingers, feet, toes, and sconce,[22]
He had to guard and scratch at once.
And while his hands were busy scratching,
His enemies more work were hatching,
Till in despair, with one grand jump,

[22] A colloquial expression for head or skull.

He went into the river "plump";
And there, with water all around him
His enemies could no more wound him.
Still "Walnut Creek" is on the rise
And here we are in paradise—
Nothing to do, and plenty to eat,
Makes a paradise of our retreat.
To-day a timber bridge we tried,
But the bridge was weaker than the tide.
And without notice of intent,
Or asking leave, away it went.
Pilgarlic lies upon the ground
Under his *"Para Agua's"* [umbrella's] shade,
He having with a blanket found,
A little tent could well be made.
He burst a pistol, and what's worse,
He fell head foremost from his horse,
And he thanks his God he's not a corse!

[*Thursday, July 25*]
Moonlight upon the great prairie
About this word good speakers vary
Since the vulgar acceptation
And not the true pronunciation
Because it easier makes a chime
And flows most natural into rhyme
Moonlight upon the great prairies!
Ah! would the moon were yet more bright,
Or could I but a candle carry
To paint the beauty of the night!
From under my musquito bar
I gaze upon each lovely Star
And yon great lantern of the Sky
Riding refulgently on high.
And is yon little twinkling light

Burning so far away in ether
The center of a system bright
That binds yet unseen worlds together?
Yon myriads in the milky way,
Planets and peopled worlds are they?
'Tis wondrous—yet as wondrous here
Smaller and meaner things appear.
This little Bug! Why does it breath?
What purpose in its life or death?
Tho' trifling and inferior; still
Certain it hath a power and will,
It flies from danger, and it knows
When storm or calm the evening blows.
And in its shape what system shines!—
Order with harmony combine—& c. & c—

[*Friday, July 26*]
Past noon and Walnut Creek is falling
And we may cross without fear of stalling.
And half the Waggons now are over
And beneath one "Garlic" lies in clover.
Last night again Pilgarlic stood
On guard again—not in the mud
But with the ground right hard & dry,
And a brilliant moonlight in the sky.
And a cool breeze from the Northeast blowing
Grateful through our blankets flowing.
We now leave our abandoned bridge
More than half raised from ridge to ridge.
And through the Shallow—Sandy stream
We drag each *raised*, still loaded team.
Pilgarlic's muse has fallen asleep.
And he scarcely can his Journal keep:
And he feels no more the young delight
That used to cheer his rhymings bright.

20

[*Sunday, July 28*]
"Ash Creek"[23] The Sun a half hour high,
And we are bent for "Pawnee Fork"[24]
To breakfast on a Buffalo pie
At which our cook is hard at work.
Or if he aint, he ought to be
The same to you, but not to me.
We killed a Buffalo yesterday,
And supped on soup in the evening grey,
No Turtle soup was ever finer
At any Aldermanic Diner [*sic*].
We passed quite near to "Pawnee Rock"[25]
From whence we saw a young Elk flock,
Rather Some twenty young Does, led
By an Elk with large horns o'er his head.
I lay last night in the fair moonlight
With a clear sky, shining o'er me
And my thoughts went back o'er our dreary track
And forward to that before me.

Some thirty days in the fierce moon haze
    I have travelled the Desert prairie
And some thirty more are yet in store
    Ere our life so lorn can vary.
A life of Romance, Adventure & Chance
    Hath its charms to bewitch and bedevil,
But nought we admire but sometime may tire
    And our best pleasure change to an evil.
The Night-Guard is a thing not poetic to sing,
    Nor is it delightful to serve on

[23] Ash Creek flows into the Arkansas from the west near Pawnee Rock. It was known also as Crooked Creek and provided a scenic setting surrounding the famous overlook. Ash Creek should not be confused with Ash Hollow on the Platte River section of the Oregon Trail in western Nebraska.
[24] See article footnote 134.
[25] See the article entitled "Pawnee Rock" and article footnote 37 on elk.

Rain, hail, dark or light, to get up in the night
  Requires a mans best coat of nerve on.
The hours of the night were made for delight,
  To sleep, Nature's gentle restorer,
Or blissful to pass with a kind hearted lass
  Till the first rosy beam of Aurora.

At "Pawnee Fork" two hours past noon,
The river low, and we'll pass it soon.
And as we came we took a tramp
Through a deserted Indian Camp.
A hundred lodges—perhaps two,
Were there, each lodge contained a few,
There were the frames of their brush tents
One [?] story, ground floor tenements.
And the hoops across their large lodge fires
As tough and strong as iron wires
On which they used to roast their meat
So needs be they must stand the heat.
Bits of bright cloth, and stray feather
Lay sometimes here or there together.
And round the camp, along the road,
We saw the signs of war & blood.
The Hunters War—The Buffalo
Met here his fatal slaughtering foe.
And the many carcases around
Tell of the Bloody hunting ground.
His ribs and skull fast growing white
Scorching by day, bleaching by night.
And now we're crossing "Pawnee Fork"
The last of our creek-fording work,
We've bridged one bank with sticks & brush,
Our Waggon's over with a rush.
And Pilly sits beneath the shade
Watching "*Los Mulos*" as they wade,

Goaded and whipped and half afraid.
The view from off the "Pawnee Rock"
Where we first saw the young Elk flock,
Was vast, was beautiful and grand,
So large a tract of lovely land.
Spangled and decked with grass & flower
Worthy to grace a fairy bower.
And the silken carpet of soft grass,
O'er which we now begin to pass
Makes a Palace for the Buffalos
Richer than richest King can know.
And the devouring Mastadon [*sic*]!
Where has the towering Monster gone,
Of the lordly race a scattered bone
Dug from the earth exists alone
Yet numerous as Buffaloe [*sic*]
Doubtless he once was wont to go.
And Indians lived upon him then
As now another race of men
Hunt and devour the Buffalo
Where the bright prairie waters flow—
For where his mammoth bones are found,
Flint arrow heads are scattered round.
Ah! Poets pen can add no grace
To the wonders of this Desert place.
The wild Sun flower that turns its breast
Through the glad day from east to west
In rich luxuriance here is seen
Gracing and cheering the prairie green
Smiling by day and hanging its head
At night when its God from earth has fled.

[*Monday, July 29*]
My hands are red and crisp with the flow
Of the blood of a slaughtered Buffalo

And this innocent page of spotless white
Grows soiled and red as the words I write[26]
And alone I sit by the Buchered [*sic*] beast
Watching the meat of our noon day feast.
While a spirit from out the glazed eye
Of the carcase cold seems asking why
I have come to its home in the western wild
Where heaven & earth on its fortune smiled
To hunt for his life over valley & hill
His carcase to eat and his blood to spill.
His food is the carpet beneath his feet
That springs up inviting his bands to eat
And none of Gods creatures, not even a fly
For his range or his hunger was ere doomed to die.
The greedy crows are hovering o'er me.
Watching the carcase that lies before me,
And screaming as tho' they would scare me away
From the bones and the offal, their rightful prey.
And the wolves from the hollow are peeping out
Watching my horse as he grazes about
Tied by a rope to the Buffalo's horn
Which shall whiten here many a midnight & morn.
When the wolves and the crows, and the insects are done
Their gorging and merriment, feasting & fun—
The waggons are crossing a gully in sight,
And will reach me before my description I write,
The hunters all eager, have tasted the fun,
And after yon band of wild creatures are gone,
Some eight or ten hundred, away to the right,
All harmlessly grazing are now in full sight,
And our mule-mounted hunters are after them now
Resolved for our Dinner to butcher a cow.
    The sun set and the rising day,

[26] Time has removed most of the bloodstain from Matt's journal, although imagination may easily restore the mark.

Themes ever told and never tiring,
  The gem of every poet's lay,
And every poet's pen inspiring. &c. &c—

[*Wednesday, July 31*]
Two days ago a keg we filled
With liquor from the heavens distilled,
And lashed it underneath a waggon
To carry as our Desert flaggon [*sic*].
And here we're stopped at main "Coon Creek"[27]
A hollow generally dry,
But yesterday a heavy leak
Let down the water from the sky,
And filled Coon Creek, so fast it dropped,
So here our cavalcade is stopped.
We have seen *ten thousand* Buffalo
Over the Desert moving slow
They opened a passage far and broad
As they saw us coming along the road
And closed again in a darkening mass
When they saw our waggons safely pass.
We cut of [*sic*] a band of some twenty or more
From the numerous herd that was running before,
And over a hillock we chased them away
In the cool clear light of the darkening day
Till another *Branch* of our party sent
Their smell on the breeze o'er the way they went
And then 'twas exciting to see them track
The very same hoof-prints in turning back
Till another scent crossed them, and then far away,
They went o'er the hills in the evening grey.

[27] Coon Creek (Big Coon Creek) drains into the Arkansas through the river's north or left bank near Garfield, Kansas (between Larned and Kinsley, Kansas). The trail crossed the creek close to the mouth and ran southwest between the Arkansas and the upper part of the creek.

And here we are merrily crossing the coon
Very high to be sure, but we'll be over soon
And Pegasus pony is neighing aloud,
Being held by a rope far behind from the crowd.
To Pilgarlic there's nothing so hateful as neighing,
Unless a mules bellow, or Jack-Asses braying.
And he thumps his Pegasus every time
He makes such a noise twixt a grunt and a whine.
And now he is vexed because he cant thump,
Being squat on the ground and too lazy to jump.
We've original here. *Young Hasey*
He does'nt shave, but he's not *lazy*.
He does'nt shave because he fears
Shortening his hair may speed his years.[28]
For he's a Jocky fond of living
And not at all in love with grieving,
But, to be serious, he is
Just half philosopher and Quiz.[29]
A man who has made up his mind
That life's a treasure worth possessing
And that its joys are not confined
Either to eating or to dressing—
So his eating is not over nice
Nor his garments of the highest price.
His motto is—"If *one* will do,
Where then can be the use of *two?*"
And "If a coat keeps out the cold,
What matter whether new or old?"
A man who speaks less than he thinks,
He sometimes Smokes but never drinks.

[28] The general superstition that hair was a sign of strength, fairly common in the nineteenth century, held that cutting it caused weakness. Variations of this belief may be found in the Scottish highlander's warning that "no sister should cut her hair at night if she has a brother at sea" and in the general contention that "hair should only be cut while the moon is on the increase."—E. and M. A. Radford, *Encyclopaedia of Superstitions* (London, 1947), 139.

[29] An eccentric.

He says the finest stimulus
Is that which heaven sends down to us,
The water dropping from the skies
Coming direct from paradise.
His picture, drawn by Hogarth,[30] would
Doubtless have been considered good.
Mounted upon his Indian pony
He is a perfect macaroni.[31]
His saddle, bridle, self & steed—
A charger of the Indian breed—
Gentle, and blind on the near side,
But that's no matter if he'll ride—&c &c

[*Thursday, August 1*]
And now Pilgarlic Jonny Raw[32]
Has reached at last the Arkansas.
Running monotonous along
Like an oft heard and tiresome song.
We saw a herd of Buffalo
Into the river headlong go
And heard their low distant roar
And their loud splashing crossing o'er
Like the murmuring of a coming storm
Or the raging of a furnace warm.
And now we camp in close corral,
The heavens portend a heavy squall,
And even now a herald drop
Arrives to bid my pencil stop.

[30] William Hogarth (1697–1764), the English painter and engraver, is known best for certain of his "tableau works": *The Rake's Progress* and *Marriage à la Mode*. Regarded by his contemporaries as a rebel against society, he died in very poor circumstances.—Samuel Redgrave, *A Dictionary of Artists of the English School* (London, 1878), 216–17.

[31] A dandy.

[32] A "Johnny Raw" was a greenhorn or a new recruit.—James Maitland, *The American Slang Dictionary* (Chicago, 1891), 157.

[*Friday, August 2*]
The driving rain at length is past,
And calm has followed the chill blast.
But such a night and such a rain
May Arkansaw ne'er see again.
The rain came on before the wind,
A flood with a hurricane behind,
And ankle deep the water spread
Around Pilgarlic's lowly bed.
And the blast, as chill as the freezing tones
Of charity, went through his bones.
Houseless and homeless, drenched & cold,
The victim too of slow disease,
Pilgarlic, in wet blankets rolled,
Lay shivering in the midnight breeze.
At length he left his watery bed,
And sought in vain to lay his head
In some dry place around the camp,
But all was comfortless & damp.
Ah! Sadder than this pen can write
Were poor Pilgarlic's thoughts that night.
What is an hour of gloom or pain,
When hope still points to day again!
But ah! When hope deserts the breast,
Where shall the victim turn for rest?
No mind, whose body is at ease
Can judge of one that feels disease
And gentle should our judgement be
When scanning other's misery.
A Dreary day has passed away
And we are camped in the evening gray.

[*Saturday, August 3*]
The "Arkansaw" in the noon-day beam
Is a beautiful and a grassy stream.

With its Buffalo herds on its banks of green,
And its fairy-like Islands that lie between,
Is a sight, in the sun or the moonlight sheen
Lovely and beautiful to be seen.
And we found a Buffalo prisoner here
Tearing the bank with rage and fear.
He had swam the river and left the deep
To climb a gully both narrow & steep
And the banks were worn with his effort to gain
His freedom again on the prairie plain
He tore the bank with his short thick horns
When he saw us gaze at his state forlorn
And he raised his paws for the hundredth time
The steep and slippery bank to climb.
He could not turn, and he would not back,
Such is his disposition strange.
He will forward follow his leaders track
And nothing his stubborn will can change.
We left him impounded a prisoner still,
We could not the helpless unfortunate kill.
Or rather his cell was so deep and narrow
We could not get at him to cut up his marrow
So we left him to die in his close prison walls,
And husbanded wisely our powder & balls.
The prairie now is smooth and as flat
As the well pressed crown of a new beaver hat.
And the heavens bend down to old earth in a line
And a circle drawn by a hand divine.
Beds of wild flowers are sprinkled about
In irregular beauty art lays not out
The yellow Sun-flower is hanging its head
For the sun has gone down to its western bed
And the zephyr that plays in the evening hour
Is wantonly fanning each blade and flower.
The low silken grass as it waves in the breeze

Resembles the ripples of summer seas.
And the golden sun that has just gone down
On a spot more beautiful never has shone.

[*Sunday, August 4*]
We struck our camp in the morning grey,
And Aurora passed as we moved away.
Spectres on stilts our long shadows ride
Silent and solemn along by our side.
We looked from a hill on the Arkansaw
Winding away on its Journey far
Reality never usurped so well
The fairy creations of fancy's spell.
Beautiful Islands all bright and green,
Glass-like water flowing silent between.
Groves of brush-wood and timber tall
And a carpet of silk more lovely than all.
Then the white logs on the banks of sand,
And the blasted trees upon the land
Showed where the lightning and storm had been
Adding wildness to the beautiful scene.

The Butchering

We stole on a herd of Buffalo cows
Cautious their speed and their fears to rouse.
Close by the river they grazed in a hollow
While the lazy Bulls grunted & rolled in each wallow.
Silent as midnight our hunters crawl
With their deadly rifles and speeding ball.
Crack! Crack! and two shots were heard in the air
And the Buffalo band arose from their lair
Away they start with a phrenzied rush
And one on the other recklessly push.
While their gutteral [*sic*] bellowing aptly seems

30

Like the midnight thunder half heard in dreams.
But a wounded cow is observed to stand
A moment behind the departing band;
Again she starts and again stands still
While blood from her nostrils is seen to spill
And three or four Bulls return in fright
To witness the cow in her hapless plight.
They smell the blood and they stamp the ground
And toss their horns in a fury roused.
When one last effort she makes to run
But falls to the earth for her life is done.
The Hunters appear, and again, and again
The Bulls look back as they leave the plain,
And in two hours after the slaughtered beast
Furnished the hunters a glorious feast;
Our Hall was the glorious sunlit skiess[?],
Our Table the prairie smooth & green.
Our plate was tin, and our meal was meat,
And we wished no richer or better to eat.
Oh! There's Joy in the darkest corner of earth
And pain is often the forerunner of mirth,
And life is ever the living worth!

[*Monday, August 5*]
An Indian Fort! and a blasted grove!
In a swampy bottom with cliffs above
Built by the Pawnee, Big Indian & squaw
On the banks of the murmuring "Arkansaw."
A blasted Grove! and the rifted trees,
Hollow and white scarce bore the breeze,
Which hardly needed its gentlest swell
When down the crumbling branches fell.
And the Indian Fort was formed from these
Blasted and broken and barkless trees;
Trunks and limbs and splinters are piled

31

In a rampart strong, tho' rude & wild.
And here 'tis said four Palefaced men
Were slain by an Indian band of ten.
They were desert travellers speeding their course
On their lonely rout [*sic*] with a single horse,
Bearing Buffalo skins and Buffalo meat
And Buffalo chips when they wished to eat.
The unlearned must know a Buffalo Chip
Is the technical term for a prairie *Cow Slip*
And of it the hunters their camp fires make
To bake their bread and their Buffalo steak.
Well, the men were slain, and their horse was shot
And further deponent saith not:
But a spell of terror hangs round the spot
Where white mens bodies were left to rot.
And the old Log Fort is existing still,
For the murdering Pawnees to scalp and kill.
And 'tis known that the Pawnees still resort
To the Blasted Grove & the ruined Fort!

The Blind Bull

An Old Blind Bull Straight before our way
Coursing a circle and running the Way!
A Buffalo Bull, when his eyes are out,
Keeps running a circle round about.
A Singularity others may trace
And set forth the reasons that govern the case.
He smelt us crossing his circular path
And he charged on our band with a dangerous wrath.
Pursued, it was now his turn to pursue,
And the Hunters were now the hunted crew.
He scattered our band, but we shattered his skull
And he fell on the prairie a done over Bull—

Bleeding and blowing and seeking to rise
With many a struggle the Buffalo dies!

Cornelia's Island[33]

[*Tuesday, August 6*]
An Island and a grove of green
Glittering in the mid-day sheen.
When youthful Love's first witching trace
Pilgarlic found within his breast.
He wished for some lone, lovely place
To live, and love, and be at rest;
And such a grove and such a stream
Was pictured in his fancy's dream.
And there it lies without a name,
A paradise unknown to fame.
"Sweets to the sweet!" Pilgarlic knows
Of one far distant blooming rose,
That like this Island lives apart
In the life current of the heart.
Her name shall add another grace
To Arkansaw's most lovely place.
Perhaps Pilgarlic ne'er again
May Journey o'er the desert plain,
Perhaps he ne'er again may see
The spot he shrines in memory.
No other eye may ever read
The page which thus recounts the deed;
His heart shall be the world alone
Where *"Corney's Island"* shall be known.
None but the breeze is listening
And the Sun sees the christening.
Strange! Strange! Does Heaven bless the spell?

[33] Named by Matt after his fiancée, Cornelia.

A summer drop this moment fell
Upon his page—yet bright and fair
The Sun is riding through the air!
Yon little cloud!—A spirit there
Perhaps observes his bosom's care
And sends this essence drop of rain
To bid his spirit not complain.
Ah! Gentle Spirit! Turn thine eye
Around thy palace of the Sky.
Go Piteous Cloud! and drop thy dew
Upon the cheek of Corney too;
And let thy dew drop be a tear,
For him who lonely muses here.
Go visit her, fair cloud in dreams,
And tell her of these beauteous streams,
Picture her own sweet fairy Isl [*sic*],
And o'er her slumbers wreathe a smile.
And while she smiles, Ah! whisper Thou,
His name who sighs "Cornelias" now!

The Storm—The Night Guard

[*Wednesday, August 7*]
The storm is past! and starry light
Is shining on the chill midnight.
The storm is past! At close of day
It burst across our lonely way.
The clouds came gathering fierce & black,
Hiding the azure of the rack.
And, like an angry spirit band,
Bore down upon the prairie land
The thunder loud and lightning stroke
In flash and roar and fury broke.
The sharp loud peal went rattling by
Like a loosed fiend shrieking through the sky

34

And the long flash of lurid red
Showed us the black clouds over head,
Like guilty thoughts, when unconfined
In chaos darkening the mind.
And then came down the heavy rain
Beating like hail-stones on the plain
Driven before the furious swell
Of the swift storm wind as they fell.

The Night Guard

The storm is past! The stars are high.
Whil'st far around the distant sky,
With lightened shade, and ragged form,
Float by the fragments of the storm.
The *Night Guard,* on his lonely post,
Muses in sad reflection lost.
The Arkansas is sweeping by
Up to the green bank smooth & high.
The rivers rush, and insects hum,
Are sounds that through the stillness come,
And the mules, munching their night meal,
And now and then a quick, low squeal,
As the poor mule's approaching stamp
Disturbs the tenants of the swamp.
The Night-Guard by the Mule's side
Stands for his best and safest guide;
For his low snort, and pricked up ear
Tell first of secret danger near.
With cautious look, and footstep slow,
Now seated still, or bending low,
The Night-Guard watches for his foe.
And weary cares his mind harass,
Perchance some tuft of waving grass
Appears in the uncertain light,

35

A creeping Indian to his sight;
And slowly with his rifle's raise
He peers into the midnight haze.
Till the Relief Guard, or the morn
Relief as [?] him from his post forlorn.

Waggoners Song

Ge up! Ge ho! Tho' the sun is burning o'er us.
Mula! Mulo! And the grass is short and dry.
Prick your ears, and go, for Big timber is before us,
And we'll all fill our belly's where the grass grows high.
O' the World is turning round as our waggon wheels are turning
And to get through life we must sometimes meet a swamp,
But we're on the hills now, and our axle trees are burning,
And we'll grease our wheels and belly's when we stop to camp.
          "Ge up! Ge ho!"
Of a Blind Buffalo you can make a *"blind bridle"*
But we scorn Bull Buffalo's and Bridles now,
For while Jerry can crawl, and Valentine can sidle,
We shall never want a Dinner from a young fat cow.
          "Ge up! Ge ho!" &c
There's our waggoner *Bell,* and the gentle spoken *Decker,*
"You Pomp! You Nell! Get up! Get out of that!"
They would drive a team to hell, and never need a checker.
Provided they could grease their wheels with Buffalo fat.
          "Ge up! Ge ho!" &c
And when a comrade goes to the world that lies before us,
And we make his last bed in the Desert prairie,
His memory shall live in the numbers of our chorus,
And "Ge up! Ge ho!" shall his requiem be!
          "Ge up! Ge ho!" &c

The Burial

[*Thursday, August 8*]
A poor man dies! What matter then?—

To die is still the doom of men.
A man is gone, A lump of clay
Has breathed its sense of life away.
Still the sun shines, and the world rolls round,
And the man lies slumbering in the ground.
Our party is one man less,
A Spaniard—Cook of Besay's mess.
He sickened, pined, and passed away.
Without an english word to say.
In the wild desert—None were nigh
Who cared to hear his parting sigh.
The hands that closed his eyes in sleep
Belonged to eyes that could not weep,
And those who laid him in the earth
Forgot him in the next hour's mirth.
Oh! Poor Bernardo! Thy lone grave
Is by the swift "Arkansas" wave.
No friendly tear can bless the spot
Where thou are slumbering forgot,
None but the wolves shall visit thee,
Their howl thy requiem shall be.
And not unlike, some ripped up bone
Shall be thy brief recording stone.
Yet shall thou have a glorious rest
In the great prairie of the west.
No crowded sepulchre of bones;
No heavy monuments of stones;
But the wild flowers round thy tomb,
In summer time shall bud and bloom.
And no stranger's foot shall rudely tread
Upon thy last and lonely bed.
Farewell Bernardo! Rest in Peace.
One lip has breathed a prayer for thee,
Death often is a kind release,
Tho' coming dark and fearfully.

The dew drop from the midnight sky,
Shall come as from a pitying eye,
And the swift rain-drop from the cloud,
Shall bath [*sic*] in balm thy lowly shroud.
Over thy grave the grass shall grow,
And birds shall sing, and flowers shall blow.
The "Arkansas" eternal swell
Shall ring for the [*sic*] a murmuring knell,
And still thy memory shall live
With what poor grace this rhyme may give!

Nooning

[*Friday, August 9*]
Noontide is sleeping on the hill.
Midnight is not more calm & still.
Stillness, with lorn and solumn reign,
Sits, like tired glory o'er the plain.
Yon lazy band of Buffaloes,
Deep in the valley green repose.
The Bulls within their wallows lie
While the musquito and the fly
Pierce their tough coats until they roll,
Boring more deep their wallow hole.
Together in a compact band,
The Cows and Calves more peacful [*sic*] stand.
While the young calves their noses ram
Against the udders of their Dam.
But Hark! What sounds are those which fill
The stilly air from yonder hill?
Mark how the timid Buffalo
In terror snuffs his deadly foe.
Behold a Waggon top of white
Now slowly rising on his sight,
Like to a distant sail at Sea

Appearing spotlike o'er the lea.
Another comes, and now a third,
While nearer still the sounds are heard.
The Drivers oath and sharp whips crack
Lashing the weary mulo's back.
In bold relief against the sky,
Slow crossing o'er the hill-top high,
In a long line the Waggons now
Their way into the hollow plough.
The Bulls up from their wallows spring,
With their peculiar bellowing
And turning oft to gaze again
They stretch their stout limbs o'er the plain,
While Cows and Calves with limbs more fleet
Beat hastily a swift retreat,
Near a small lake the Waggons stop,
And quick the Mulo's harness drop.
Which, with their ten foot halters round
Their necks, graze o'er the grassy ground.
Or plunge into the shallow lake[34]
Their long and burning thirst to slake.
Dry branches of the Cotton Wood
Burn quickly in the camp fires good.
And steaks and chops of Buffalo
Before each fire is roasting slow.
Coffee for breakfast now is burning
Hot bread and roasting meat is turning.
And soon each mess is seated round
Their breakfast spread upon the ground.
"Breakfast at noon!" some readers say,
"And why not earlier in the day?"
The mystery we'll quickly ravel.

[34] After hours of travel on any dry trail, stock and men would plunge head-long into the first water hole. Caution had to be taken to control the stock enough to keep the water fit for the men.

'Tis thus arranged to suit the travel,
We start at day, and five hours ride,
Then slumber three in the noontide;
And when our three hours rest has flown
We travel till the Sun goes down.
Breakfast or Dinner, which you please,
Is past, and now we rest at ease
Beneath the Waggons cooling shade
Where the breeze waves the tall grass blade.
In sleep, or sociable converse,
Wherein great deeds we oft rehearse,
We while away the warm noontime
Travelling through the prairie clime.

The Night Camp

[*Saturday, August 10*]
There is no scene on earth more grand
Than the long rolls of prairie land,
Meeting the far horizon's verge
Like swellings of the ocean surge.
And when the evening closes o'er
The lone "Arkansas'" winding shore,
And weary "Sol" goes down to rest
In his far palace of the West,
Silence falls o'er the rhymesters pen
As stillness o'er the evening then,
For silence only may express
Its grandeour [*sic*] and its loveliness.
Silence may be the only word
For glory seen, but never heard.
The camp is formed. The tired mules feed
In freedom o'er the grassy mead.
Coffee, New bread, and buffalo
On the camp fires are cooking slow.

And loudly jest and laughter sound
From the gay messes gathered round
Their camp fires, roasting their choice bits
Of Buffalo on green wood spits.
While now and then some glancing eye
Shows conciousness [*sic*] of danger nigh
By turning from the merry blaze
To wander round the deepening haze.
Night comes. The evening meal is o'er,
Blankets and Buffalo skins are spread
Thickly about the grassy floor
To form the prairie travellers bed.
Musquito Bars are streched [*sic*] on stakes,
Near rivers, creeks, or swampy lakes,
To guard the sleeper from the sting
Of tiny foe with buzzing wing.
The Camp is still. Now stalks the guard
Around the mules on duty hard.
And as he slowly moves about
He sees the fires go glimering [*sic*] out;
While o'er the grass the chill night dew
Falls till his boots are well soaked through.
Small stakes are driven in the ground
For the tied mules to graze around
Lest they should wander out of sight,
And Indians steal them in the night.
At dawn the sleepy travellers rise
Before the stars have left the skies,
Before the sun sends forth a ray
The Camp is struck, the teams away.

The Spring

[*Sunday, August 11*]
The "Arkansas" is a murky flood

With a constant ripple of eddying mud;
And yet from the land 'tis a lovely sight
To look on the winding waters bright.
Bright in the sun beam under the blue
Tho' its waters are of a milky hue.
To the thirsty traveller pausing here
No Chrystal [*sic*] can shine more bright & clear—
The traveller who has often drank
From the stagnant pool in verdure rank—
Or from the liquid in the hollow
Where the Buffalo doth roll & wallow—
A draught he sips, but does not swallow.
In long hunts after Buffalo,
When miles from camp the hunters go,
They'll sip the slop from a Bull's foot print,
Made in the mud with thin mud in't.
The rain drop in the waggon rut
Doth often soothe a thirting [*sic*] gut.
On hands and knees are often seen
The travellers on the burning green,
Sucking up moisture through a reed
From holes where Snakes & Lizards breed.
Or plunging parched and puckered lips,
In waggon ruts with eager dips,
Toads squealing at him while he sips,
Squealing to see their little store
Robbed without hope or chance of more.
A Spring! A clear, cool, gushing Spring
O'er rock or sand bed rippling,
Is a beautiful and blessed thing.
A Spring, deep in the desert drear,
Gushed from the low bank, cool & clear,
Clear as the ray from beauty's eye,
Cool as the Snow on mountain high.
And into the "Arkansas" proud

It broke like sunbeam thro' a cloud.
Driving the muddy current back
E'en to the center of its track,
But the mud, mingling as it crossed
It's diamond brilliancy was lost—
Like virtue, gushing from the heart
And shrinking as its hues depart.
Blessed be the bright "big timber" spring
In the far Desert rippling.

The Flowers

[*Monday, August 12*]
Beds of Wild Sunflower brighten the scene
Far as the eye can rove over the green.
Beautiful ever, but beautiful most
When the Sun first shines on the flowering host,
And they turn their heads to the glade'ning [*sic*] ray.
Like eastern pilgrims bending to pray.
Towering above the traveller's head
As he guides his horse thro' each clustering bed—
With their seedy centers, and radiant leaves,
Lovely as any that Flora weaves.
And the many wild flowers that intervene,
Checkering brighter the beautiful scene.
Nameless they flourish, unknown & unsung
To admire not an eye, To record not a tongue.
And the lumbering waggons drive o'er their beds.
Blighting their beauty and crushing their heads.
Many a flower is born to blush
And wither beneath the Buffalo's crush.
Many a blossom, & many a bud
Falls in the night storm and dies in the mud.
And valley and hollow breathe beauty away
To the sun beam that lends them its generous ray.

43

No flower of the prairie is plucked for the hair
Or to die in the breast of the beautiful fair.
Nor can the flower droop at its lonely lot,
For, if never *seen*, it is never *forgot*.
And who shall say which is the happiest fate,
To fade in the valley, or wither in state?
Doth the rose ever languish to leave its stem
And fade in the folds of a Diadem?
Doth it pride in the fate of its tinted leaves,
When beauty to beauty it gives and recieves [*sic*]?
Or would it not joy to be never seen,
To flourish and fade on its branch of green?
To laugh in the sunbeams, to bath [*sic*] in the dews,
And breathe to the Zephyr, its sweets & its hues?
'Tis hard to see things that are dear to the heart
While we joy in their beauty, decline & depart.
And the bosom then touched with the arrow of grief
May be like the rose when it loses a leaf.
Its perfection is broken, and like the poor flower,
Its tints and its leaves fade away by the hour,
Till its last seed of happiness withers away
It droops, dies, and drops to the dust in decay!

"Fort William"[35]

[*Sunday, August 18*]
Bricks moulded from the prairie clay
And roasted in the noontide ray.
Large as the stones of city halls
Form good "Fort William's" strong built walls.
And trunks and boughs of "Cotton Wood"
Form gates and beams and rafters good.
While grass and mud piled closely o'er,
Forms sheltering roof and sanded floor.

[35] See the article entitled "Robbery of Fort William."

A strong-barred gate, a rampart wall,
And Bastions, guard the stock corral,
And here some fifty inmates dwell[36]
From year to year content and well.
Buffalo being brave [?] support
To the gay dwellers of the fort.
Buffalo fresh, Buffalo dried,
Roasted, boiled, or stewed or fried,
Buffalo serves in every stead
For poultry and pastry, for meat & for bread;
And a Buffalo skin neatly spread,
Is bolster, and blanket, and bedstead and bed.
In summer time, or in the snow,
Wrapped in a skin of Buffalo,
In fair moonlight, or in the storm,
The Desert Dwellers slumber warm.
They make their boats of Buffalo hide
And swim them over the headlong tide.
Of five good skins a boat can be made[37]
To serve [?] each end of the prairie trade.
Boats, coats, ropes, candles, all things flow
Out of the useful Buffalo.

[36] Thomas Jefferson Farnham, on his way west with the "Peoria Party," estimated that sixty men were associated with the fort. At least 25 per cent of them were busy transporting robes to market and bringing in eastern produce. Other smaller parties hunted, guarded stock, visited Indian camps, and remained within the fort to defend the walls and perform clerks' duties.—Thomas J. Farnham, *Travels in the Great Western Prairies* (Part I) (volume XXVIII of Thwaites, *Western Travels*), 163.

[37] A good bullboat was made by sewing together buffalo skins (frequently two to five) over a willow-cottonwood frame. This "small half-orange" could carry two and one-half tons of cargo in a twelve- by thirty-foot space, yet draw only four inches of water. The craft had to be carried ashore regularly and dried to prevent saturation and rot. It was excellent for shallow, rapid streams but seldom survived more than one long trip.—Hiram M. Chittenden, *The American Fur Trade of the Far West* (3 vols., New York, 1902), I, 35; Bernard DeVoto, *Across the Wide Missouri* (Boston, 1947), 116–17; Cleland, *This Reckless Breed of Men*, 26–27.

45

They pack his flesh in his own hide
When back to camp the hunters ride.
They make a hammer of his hoof
To knock his fatted hump-ribs off.
And white as monumental stones,
The prairie glitters with his bones.
And thus "Fort William" is forgot
Scetching [?] the hunted Buffalo's lot.

"*Pueblo De Leche*"[38]

Ne'er could romantic wanderer chance
On a scene more likened to romance.
And fiction never found a place
More fit the rhymesters pen to grace.
"*Pueblo de Leche*," or "*Milk Fort*"
Of all strange things the strangest sort.
The place, the men, the women seem
Shaped in some disproportioned dream
Or in that dull and dreamy trance
That follows reading old Romance.
Long bearded men, and squallid [*sic*] brats
Horses, and mules, and goats and rats.
Live, laugh, and rub against each other
Where any Christian thing would smother.
A race disclaimed & nondescript
From out some hole in terra slipt.
Where Nature threw her remnants when
She formed and animated men.
But Woman! Ah! 'Tis sweet to turn
From clouds, to things that beam and burn—
Dear, gentle Woman, even here
Sheds brightness round the atmosphere.
And the bright eye, and dark Brunette,

---

[38] See the article entitled "Pueblo De Leche."

46

Saves "Milk Fort" from Damnation yet.
A mongrel Spanish, Indian race
Make *"Leche"* Fort their biding place.
Long beards, dark faces, Deer skin clothes,
Armed always for the chase, or foes,
Make them appear a fierce Banditti
Told of in novels in the city.
Yet Rhymester Pilly means no lible [*sic*],
And would not swear it on the Bible,
They are, and he believes it too,
An honest, trading, thriving crew,
Who took nought from him, but were more
Inclined to lend their own good store,
For ere Pilgarlic got to *Touse* [*sic*]
He thanked them for a good fat Louse;
With fifty little scions sent
To found a foreign settlement;
But Pilly claimed preemption there,
And drowned them in the *"Picket Ware."*[39]
A House of mud! A Fort of brick!
With battlements of grass and stick!
Comanchies [*sic*] steal their grasing [*sic*] stock,
But Mud-built walls the Indians mock
As potently as gates of rock.

The Mountains

Like low and distant clouds they stand
Upon the verge of sky and land.
The Mountains! Rising on the view
Deeper, not darker than the blue.
Thus from afar, but near seen,
They show their garniture of green
Their shadowy vales, and rocky peaks,

[39] The Purgatory. See article footnote 61.

Their barren sides, and snowy streaks,
Now traversing the hills around,
Their piney tops the prospect bound.
Till soaring on the grassy plain
The Rocky Mountains rise again,
And closer still, and nearer now
The sun sinks o'er the mountain brow.
Behold! Is there no God of bliss
To praise for such a scene as this?
Why does the bosom's finest string
Thrill with this silent whispering?
The blazing disc has sunk below
The far off mountain's peak of snow.
The ray that doth no longer blind
Still tips the hills we've left behind.
Those fleecy clouds, in glory rolled,
Seem falling heaps of molten gold.
The live rays shooting from the mount
Make it appear a fiery fount;
Or like a raging volcano
Flaming the skies with furious throe.
And mark; how fast the dazzling blase [*sic*]
Fades into soft and milder rays;
Sublimity lays down to rest,
Losing itself on Beauty's breast!
Whose blushes tint the evening sky
Till peaceful Cynthia[40] beams on high,
Like calm content that never cloys,
Smiling at soon-departing joys.
Nearer; and changing still the scene.
Storm darkens round the azure sheen.
In shadows now the mountains stand
While sunbeams gild the prairie land.
Thus often through the live long day

40 The moon.

The clouds around the mountain play,
Till night sets loose the tempest fiend
With rage, and roar, and howling wind,
Vexing every [?] Rock [?] and gentle fairy
Queen of sweet flowers and sunny prairie.

The Ratone[41]

From the mountain high, through the valley lone,
Springs and ripples the bright Ratone
Wandering like a laughing child
And gaily singing in gladness wild
Through beething [?] rocks, and shadowy groves,
Winding and sporting, away it roves.
A shallow, pebbly, purling stream,
Beautiful as an infants dream.
And like a dream it glides among
Things wilder than e'er rhymester strung,
Or fancy weaved, or poet sung.
It's green bank grows the prickly pear,
It's bushes feed the grisly [*sic*] Bear;
The fleet Deer, and the bounding Doe
Drink from its limpid chrystal flow
And the wild bird with sudden scream
Off darts across the lonely stream.
Loveliness shrined in wildness lone,
Art thou, most beautiful Ratone!
And yet, how strangely things most vile
Taint gentle Nature's fairest smile!—
The high hills silver echo here,
That rings so sweetly on the ear,
Doth often from it's slumber wake
With sounds which curse the lips that spake;
The teamster's high blaspheming oath,

[41] See the article entitled "The Ratone."

Blindly conceived, and breathed in wroth;
Rises above the ripple's song
To urge the jaded mule's [*sic*] along.
The lovely turns, so sweet to view,
Are torments to the trading crew.
For, tho' so beautiful, Alas!
O'er every wind that road doth pass
And what may gladden fancy's eye,
Wont keep the good "Domestic" dry.[42]
When sideways down the lumbering team
Turns over in the silver stream.
And on the musing poet's dream
The whip-crack and the Driver's shout
Breaks, and puts all his rhymes to rout.
Glade, glen, streamlet, and winding dells,
Where Beauty, lorn and silent dwells,
Were made for Muse and fairy spells,
And not for angry driver's yells.

Saturday 21st. of Sep. left *Santa Fe.* Dr. Waldo[43] packed my trunk on a mule and accompanied me. Our supper was goats milk and ground corn boiled into mush, which we took in an old ruined

[42] Textiles formed a large part of American merchandise carried to Santa Fe.

[43] Dr. David Waldo, born at Clarksburg, Virginia (now West Virginia), in 1802, spent most of his adult life in the Southwest. As a young man, he logged on the Ohio River; then wandered to Missouri. His eye was on a medical career rather than a Missouri farmer's life, however, and he enrolled at Transylvania University in Kentucky. Completing his medical study, he returned to Missouri and made his home on the Gasconade River and at Osceola, in St. Clair County. Later he moved to Independence, entered the Santa Fe trade, and built up a sizable fortune. During the Mexican War he served as an officer in the First Regiment of Missouri Mounted Volunteers and after the conflict married Eliza Jane Norris. Before his death at Independence in 1878, he tried his hand at banking and for a period of time freighted goods to Utah and the Platte Valley.— Josiah Gregg, *Commerce of the Prairies* (Part I) (volume XIX of Thwaites, *Early Western Travels*), 133–34, 164; Stella M. Drumm, "Waldo, David," in the *Dictionary of American Biography* (22 vols., New York, 1928–44), XIX, 332.

mud church in an abandoned Indian town 45 miles from Santa Fe, where we also slept.[44] At midnight we rose, packed our mule, and travelled tile [*sic*] nine next day, when we reached San Miguel.[45] Here I got a Dinner of meat and bread for two *Reals*[46] and then slept in the house of Thos. Rowland.[47] Went to High Mass in the Cathedral—*A Dios!*

Started next day at 9—found the Spaniards with whom I am to travel, familiar [?] and gentlemanly. Nooned 10 miles from San Miguel. Got out my grammar and taught old Don Jarvis his letters in English—

Guyines Creek [Gallinas River]—*Begus Town* [Las Vegas] —*Martes 24th* inst 20 millyas [miles] from San Miguel—road pretty good, except one bad miry place 2 days from St. Miguel. A creek half way, *shallow*, and rocky.[48]

Miercoles 25th Travelled from 7 A.M. till 5 P.M. Camped at a beautiful creek which we had to cross twice—gave a sick Soldier pills—Count it 70 miles to Santa Fe.

Jueves 26 Started with the Sun and travelled till 5 P.M. without Nooning—Camped at *Santa Clara*.[49] *Capitan Jose Hernandez* invited me to *Cinar* [supper] with him—Bread and cheese, and mush.

Viernes 27 The whole Spanish camp was up at 3 P.M. [*sic*] Sun rose at cinco y Media [five-thirty]. Cold. *muchos frio* [very cold]—Started for *Rio Colorado* [the Canadian]. Indians appeared—we made ready for battle. They were *Eutaws*, and pro-

[44] See the article entitled "The Sacred Fire."

[45] See the article entitled "A Sunday in San Miguel."

[46] The Spanish *real* was worth about 12½ cents.

[47] See article footnote 109.

[48] Probably Tecolote Creek. Las Vegas on the Gallinas (Vegas) River, founded about 1835, was little more than an adobe village. Nonetheless, to traders approaching Santa Fe, Las Vegas was the first welcome evidence of civilization.

[49] Santa Clara Spring was near Wagon Mound, New Mexico, to the right of Matt's route as he returned to Missouri. He had just crossed Vermejo Creek (a branch of the Canadian).

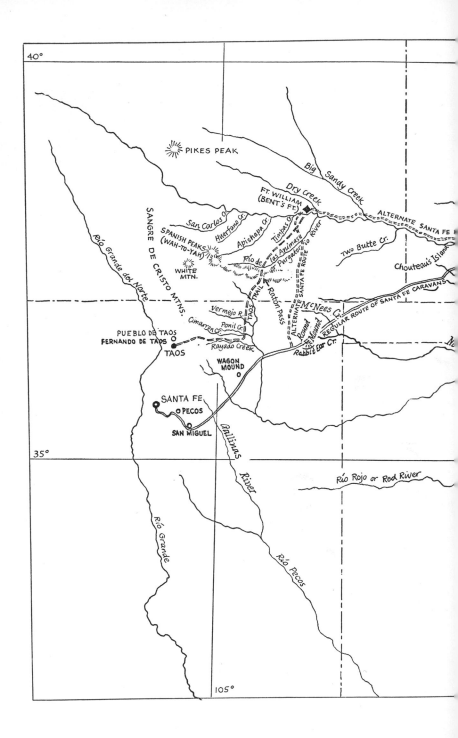

40°

PIKES PEAK

Big Sandy Creek

Dry Creek

FT. WILLIAM
(BENT'S FT.)

ALTERNATE SANTA FE

SANGRE DE CRISTO MTNS.

San Carlos Cr.

Huerfano Cr.

SPANISH PEAKS
(WAH-TO-YAH)

Apishapa Cr.

Timpas Cr.

Two Butte Cr.

Río de las Animas
or Purgatoire

Río Grande del Norte

WHITE
MTN.

Río to River

Chouteau's Island

McNees Cr.

REGULAR ROUTE OF SANTA FE CARAVANS

Vermejo R.

Cimarron Cr.

TAOS TRAIL

Ponil Cr.

Ratón Pass

ALTERNATE SANTA FE ROUTE to River

PUEBLO DE TAOS
FERNANDO DE TAOS

Rayado Creek

Round
Mound

TAOS

Rabbit Ear Cr.

N

WAGON
MOUND

SANTA FE
PECOS

Gallinas River

SAN MIGUEL

35°

Río Rojo or Red River

Río Grande

Río Pecos

105°

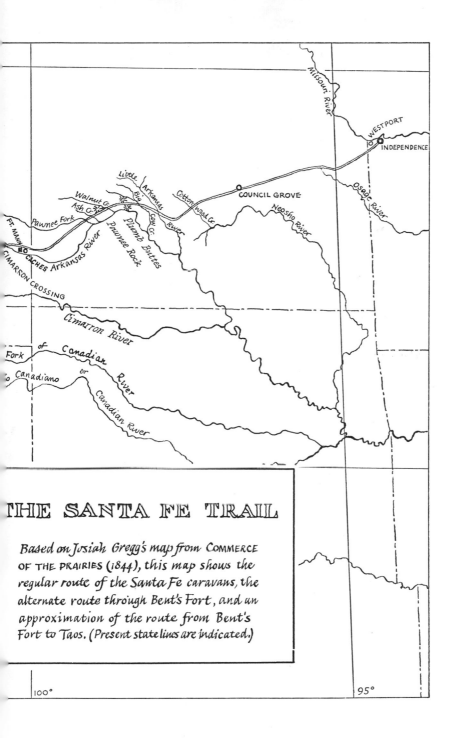

Missouri River

WESTPORT
INDEPENDENCE

Osage River

Little
Arkansas

Walnut Cr.
Ash Cr.
Pawnee Fork
Big
Cow Cr.
Arkansas
River
Cottonwood Cr.
COUNCIL GROVE
Neosho River

Ft. Mann
Caches
Arkansas River
Plumb Buttes
Pawnee Rock
Pawnee River

CIMARRON CROSSING

Cimarron River

Fork
of
Canadian
River
o Canadiano
or
Canadian River

THE SANTA FE TRAIL

Based on Josiah Gregg's map from COMMERCE
OF THE PRAIRIES (1844), this map shows the
regular route of the Santa Fe caravans, the
alternate route through Bent's Fort, and an
approximation of the route from Bent's
Fort to Taos. (Present state lines are indicated.)

100°   95°

fessed friendship.⁵⁰ They were in search of Buffalo, and they looked like very Devils scouring about the plains in all directions. Camped at the *Colorado* [the Canadian] at 1/4 before 5. Rain.

Sabado 28 Slept well and pleasantly in *el Carro* [the cart]. Started *pronto*—pleasant *dia.* Saw Sigualla [?] at noon—was nearly run over by one—chased, killed and brought in *carne* [meat] to camp at *Al Rollo Del Palo Blanco* [Palo Blanco Creek or Arroyo].⁵¹ *4 o'clk.*

Domingo 29 Met *Senór Cordero's* Companero⁵² [company or group] at 10 A.M. Dined with the American Drivers. Camped at good water at 1 1/2 P.M.

Lunes 30th Rainy night—Rainy morning—Started at 9 o'clk, and travelled till 4 1/2—about 15 miles—Camped at *Al Rollo de Oryas* [Rabbit Ear Creek]—or *The Asses-ears*⁵³—good water, wood, and grass. Plenty of Buffalo.

Martes Oct. 1st Got under way at 7 A.M.—Met 36 waggons at 12. Commanded by *Hicks & Barney.*⁵⁴ Killed a cow—Buffalo

⁵⁰ Most writers agree that although the Utes (Yutas or Eutaws) were "nominally at peace" with Santa Fe traders and the New Mexican government, they had to be watched closely. Individual traders or small parties were at times attacked or laid under tribute. The Utes, in other instances, used their horsemanship to advantage by raiding New Mexican towns and carrying off stock and hostages.—Sister Mary Loyola, "The American Occupation of New Mexico, 1821–1852," *Historical Society of New Mexico Publications in History*, Vol. VIII (September, 1939), 76–77; Josiah Gregg, *Commerce of the Prairies* (ed. by Max L. Moorhead) (Norman, 1954), 208, (Subsequent references will be to this edition); Frederick W. Hodge (ed.), *Handbook of American Indians North of Mexico* (2 vols., Washington, 1907–10), II, 875.

⁵¹ An upper branch of Ute Creek, Palo Blanco flows south a bit northnortheast of Farley, New Mexico.

⁵² See article footnote 120.

⁵³ About four to five miles northeast of Mount Clayton, New Mexico.

⁵⁴ This may be a reference to the trading partnership of "Hoffman & Barney."—30 Cong., 1 sess., *House Report No. 458.* Also, this may be a reference to James Prewitt Hickman, a Kentuckian who moved to Copper County, Missouri, and became a leading merchant at Boonville. He opened stores at Independence and Fayette and took goods to both El Paso and Chihuahua. For a time he lived in Chihuahua; then settled in San Antonio, where he raised a family and resided until his death in 1893.—Susan Magoffin, *Down the Santa*

not so plentiful as yesterday. Found bad water in a Sand Creek, and camped at 3. Quisas quince milljas [perhaps fifteen miles].

Miercoles 2nd Started with the Sun, fine Day—Killed a fat cow, and camped at 1/2 past 12. Slight shower.

Hueves [?] *3rd* Travelled till noon & camped for the night at good water & wood. Saw a fat Buffalo Cow flayed alive by the Spaniards.

Viernes 4th Touched the Semirone [Cimarron] at *Medio Dia* [noon], and travelled till *á las Trece de la tarde Siguala Line* [three in the afternoon on the route?] for fuel. The water the Spaniards called *Al Rollo de Orejas* [Arroyo of the Ears?] must have been *Agua Frio* [Cold Spring], as otherwise we have not seen it.

Sabado 5th Travelled along the Semirone from 6 A.M. till *Trece y Media* [three-thirty]. Saw a Stray Dog.

Domingo 6th Travelled from 6 till 3 *de la tardy* [in the afternoon]. Long, flat, tedious prairies, grass croped [*sic*] short, ground hard, strong wind. Found fresh horse tracks—Stray Dog still following us.

Lunes 7th Made the *Rio Arena* [Sand Creek] at 2 o'clk the wind blowing a hurricane and the mules trotting in their harness all the day. *Muchos polveriento* [very dusty].

Martes 8th Camped at noon at a little lake of good water in the middle of a flat prairie.[55] Started at 2 and travelled all night, the wind blowing furiously, and cold. At noon we fired the cannon at a band of Buffalo. No water.

Miercoles 9th Travelled till late in the dark in hopes of reaching the Nepestry [Arkansas]. Ten mules gave out, and we camped without food or water. blowing whirlwinds and raining slugs.

Jueves 10th Made the Nepeste [*sic*] and camped at 7 A.M. remained for the rest of the day on the Mexican side of the river.

Fé Trail and into Mexico (ed. by Stella M. Drumm) (New Haven, 1926), 58–59.

[55] Wagon Bed Springs (Lower Spring)?

Wrote a letter in Spanish to my friend *Branch* in Santa Fe.

Viernes 11th Crossed the river without a single stop at 1/2 past 8 A.M.[56] Fired the *cannon* at a band of Buffalo drinking. Travelled twenty miles, and Camped at sundown. 1/2 past 4 on the Arkansas. clear day. killed an old Toro flaca [lean buffalo bull] for its skin. Caught it with mules.

Sabado 12th Continued on the Arkansas till noon—passed the *"Caches"*[57]—left the river, and at 4 P.M. camped at a shallow pond on a high prairie. Saw wild Horses running with the Buffalo.

Domingo 13th Travelled till 10 A.M. mules tired—pasture bad last night—Started again at 3 P.M. and travelled an hour by moonlight—Camped without wood or water. A wild horse ran among the mules in the night.

Lunes 14 Travelled from *5 de la mañána* [in the morning] till *4 a la Tarde* [in the afternoon], and camped at *Rio de Pananas* [Pawnee Fork].[58] Rode 15 miles ahead of the waggons, and made up my mind to *camp out*, but they came up before night.

Martes 15th [The original text of one of Matt's poems, entitled "The Pebble's Song," appears here, dated *Red River. New Mexico. Aug. 28th, 1839*]

Martes 15 Crossed "pawnee fork" at 8 A.M., "Ash Creek" at 10 A.M. Scratched my name on "Pawnee Rock" at 12.[59] and travelled on till *cinco y media*—half an hour by the moon—camped at a stagnant pond. Saw the prairie in flames *adelante* [ahead]. A false alarm in the night.

Miercoles 16th Crossed *el Rio de Nuezes* [Walnut Creek][60] without any trouble at *Siete y midia a la manana* [seven-thirty

[56] This crossing was made, probably, at Cimarron, Kansas (the middle crossing of the Arkansas); yet Matt's mileage notes suggest his group may have crossed upriver at the lesser-used crossing at Ingalls, Kansas.

[57] See article footnote 45.

[58] See article footnote 134.

[59] See journal footnote 23 and article entitled "Legend of Pawnee Rock."

[60] See article footnote 33.

in the morning]—*aqua bajo* [low water]. Camped, and started again at 1, when we travelled until 4, and camped for the night on the Arkansas. We fired the prairie behind us, and the prairie is burning before us; so we are between two fires! Weather delightful—bathed in *Walnut Creek.*

Jueves 17th Left the Arkansas at 6 A.M. Passed a bad mud creek at 7—*Punta la Ciruila* [Plum Point] at 9, and *"Cow Creek"* at 10 P.M. where we camped for the night. Met the burning prairie at *Round Mound,* from there to *Cow Creek* looked like an immense bed of charcoal—saw many Buffalo and passed several ponds of water, though the Creeks are nearly dry. Some of the ponds, good water; others, very salty.

Viernes 18th Confound the lazy Spaniards! Because the day is a little cold they wont travel, and here they sit round a pile of ashes all day with just enough fire to blind them with the smoke.

Sabado 19th Started at 9 A.M. Passed a creek of wood & water at 10—another at 11—and camped at a third at 12 1/2—Bitter cold wind. Some snow. "Mem. *Fumo es fuerta*" [dense, or strong, smoke]

Domingo 20th Underway at 5 A.M. Crossed *al Rio de Nepestita* [the Little Arkansas] at 11, and then travelled till 4 P.M. over burnt prairies. Camped with water and grass, but no wood.

Lunis [*sic*] *21st* Travelled from 5 A.M. till 4 P.M. over burnt prairie, and camped at *"Line Algodan Arbolida"* [Cotton Wood Grove], or *Rio de Alamos* [Poplar River]—a strong wind but not cold. Plenty of grass remaining unburned. Saw two mounted Indians at a great distance.

Martes 22nd Cashed [*sic*] our Brass Cannon at Cotton Wood Grove, and started at 7 A.M. Passed a pond of good water at 10. and camped at a swamp where we had shallow water and grass unburnt at 2 P.M.

Miercoles 23rd Travelled from 5 A.M. till 2 P.M. Passed 3 creeks of wood & water, and camped at a 4th, without reaching *Council Grove.* Weather mild—*muchos ayre* [very windy]— *No frio* [not cold].

Jueves 24th Started at 6, and reached *Council Grove* at 9. We had a thunder shower last night and the travelling is very bad. Camped at *Concilio Arboleda* [Council Grove] for the day. The sun shone out, the wind died away, and I had a delightful sleep under the trees, and a delightful swim in the Rio. 150 miles from Independence and Hurrah for home! and confound the *Heart burn!*

Viernes 25th Left *Council Grove* at 6 1/2 A.M. and camped at the next Grove, about 8 miles,[61] at 9 1/2—a heavy thunder shower pouring on us. Met *Jim Rogers*,[62] a half-breed with two horses, and trapping aparatus [*sic*]. Two vagabond *Kaws* came into camp *a pie* [on foot]. It rained heavy as lead right through the waggon tops.

Sabado 26th Travelled from 5 *hasta* [until] 11 A.M. probably 4 Leagues. Met another *Caw* [*sic*] Indian, could'nt speak english. Water and Wood in plenty every 4 or 5 miles.

Domingo 27th After a cold rainy night, we got moved at 7. The sun shone out, but the road was very bad from the rain. Crossed a good creek of wood and water at 12 and camped 5 hours—probably not more than 12 miles.

Lunes 28th Started with 3 companions and 3 Spanish domestics at 2 o'clk, A.M. A bright moon, and not very cold. Passed a creek of Brush and water. The road wound round a swamp for more than an hour. Passed a creek at 1/2 past 7—terrible bad crossing—high steep banks, and muddy bottom. At 1/2 past 8 crossed another Creek very thickly wooded. here we found 1/2 a Doz. Indian families encamped. One man only appeared—a fine warlike looking fellow, who either could'nt or would'nt speak any english but "Go way!" and we did "go way." had there been more of them perhaps we might have met a still more disagreble [*sic*] greeting. From this creek we rode till 11 o'clk,

[61] Rock Creek, approximately seven to eight miles east of Council Grove on the trail, may be the camping spot Matt refers to.—Eskridge, Kansas, Quadrangle (1918).

[62] See article entitled "Jim Rogers."

without touching another, and then turned off about 100 yards from the road, where we found wood, water, and grass in a gully.

Mounted again at 2 P.M. and rode till 7—3 hours in the dark —no moon. prairie burning here and there. Turned off from the road, and found just enough brush to warm us and boil our coffee. 3 of us slept in a bed of 9 blankets and a Buffalo robe.

Martes 29th "*A Caballo*" [on horseback] at 4 1/2 A.M. rode till 8—saw 4 Oxen and 2 Horses. Camped at a bend in the road where there was water, Brush, and 2 solitary trees. Sky cloudy and some rain.—Started again at 11 A.M. and reached a Farm house at dark where we got a Christian supper of Bacon, Corn bread, Coffee & Milk, slept in a log outhouse, and said no prayers.

Miercoles 30th Sixteen miles to go—rode 8, and took lunch of corn bread and milk at Farmer Rice's[63]—a beautiful day—had my own fun with the Spaniards, and camped at *Pollard's Hotel* in *Independence* at 2 in the afternoon.

[A brief financial record, selections from two poems, topics for newspaper articles, and a list of the men who accompanied Matt to Santa Fe occupy the remaining pages of his journal, not reproduced here.]

[63] See article footnote 12.

II

Matt Field's New Orleans *Picayune* Articles
Published December, 1839–October, 1841

A Western Oddity

There was on board the steamboat on which we left St. Louis, an oddity of the first water. This was a man who had, for seventeen years, been domesticated among the Indians. The lines in his face were so strongly marked, that, when brought into play, their shadows resembled the painted marks which constitute the Indian's beauty. He had that free and lordly tread so characteristic of the Indians, but it was most strangely amalgamated with a dancing-master trip, which he was in the habit of assuming, and he would cock his hat over the right eye, and run his fingers through his hair in the most approved and accepted fashion of a modern beau. He had been a Frenchman—I say *had been,* for really I feel a hesitation in saying that he is one—and these symptoms plainly told that he has been a youth of some fashion— noticed by the fair—a wild boy, and a rake. His language he had forgotten. English he spoke about as well as a border Indian, who catches enough to trade his skins, & c. True, he may never have spoken it, but his French was about as bad as his English, and he evidently had no relish for either. I drew him into conversation, and questioned him freely about his life. After many years residence among a tribe where he had his family, his dignity, his wigwam, and his home, he had visited St. Louis with $3,000 dollars, and was now returning to his forsaken squaw without a dollar. He seemed delighted when I asked him to *"talk Indian"* for me, and he gave me specimens of the language of three different tribes, which, of course, may all have belonged to *one* tribe for ought my erudition could determine. I soon had reason to regret, however, the acquaintance I had made, for in the evening he became excited with liquor, and abandoned himself to his savage manner.

There was a passenger with a violin practising in the Social Hall, and he commenced the strange manoeuvring and wild contortions of the Indian—the unthinking passengers still encouraging him, until he worked himself into what seemed to me madness, or a fit. In this state he pounced upon me, his acquaintance of the morning, and it required my utmost address to shake him off and take refuge in my state room, from whence I heard him half the night yelling and whooping, and now and then mingling a French or English oath with his Indian lingo.

What a most novel, yet most melancholy subject for reflection was this man! There can be no doubt but in the excited state in which I saw him he actually fancied himself an Indian. His habits, even his tastes, his very nature had become *savage*, and I saw before me the degrading spectacle of a Christian being wandering forever like a thing accursed, an outcast from his kin, his people and his God.

Independence

The town of Independence in Jackson County, Missouri, is the principal meeting and starting place from whence traders set off for Santa Fe.[1] It numbers about five thousand inhabitants, or did eighteen months ago, at the time of this writer's experience. The location is well chosen, salubrious, and has many natural advantages, though one drawback upon its prosperity has been its

[1] Independence was settled in the years 1827–31. Three men, with the approval of the Missouri General Assembly, pre-empted 160 choice acres in Jackson County, had the plot surveyed and accepted, and carved the survey into lots which were sold for cash and credit to an initial group of sixty buyers. The Assembly contributed eighty additional acres, and by 1831 the new county seat of Independence was ready to serve the Santa Fe trade.—Howard L. Conard (ed.) *Encyclopedia of the History of Missouri* (6 vols., New York, Louisville, and St. Louis, 1901), III, 349.

removal some three miles or more from the river bank,[2] the precipitous and irregular nature of the land nearer the water forbidding the formation of any settlement likely to spread and arrive at importance. The Mexican trade, together with the vast farming business of the neighborhood, the military posts about the outskirts and bordering the prairies,[3] and the trade with Indian tribes dwelling near, all combine to promise prosperity to Independence, and the advance made by the town in a very few years is sufficient to confirm the most sanguine anticipations. Added to this, the vast mineral deposits yet undeveloped in Missouri, must extend a prosperous influence wherever the steps of trade have advanced.[4] There are two landing places for boats,

[2] Missouri river boats landed four to six miles north of Independence and unloaded merchandise, which had to be carted inland over a poor road. The river tore at the steamboat landing, created a commercial hazard, and forced pilots to seek new piers. By the late thirties river trade had pushed upstream a few miles to Westport Landing, and Independence lost control of the Santa Fe trade. The Westport area supplanted Independence, just as Independence had superseded Old Franklin, Lexington, and Boonville.—R. L. Duffus, *The Santa Fe Trail* (New York, 1930), 104–105.

[3] Fort Osage, located on the south bank of the Missouri River nineteen miles due east of Kansas City, was established in 1808. During the War of 1812, the installation was evacuated temporarily but was reoccupied in 1816 and maintained—in the twenties as a government warehouse—until abandoned in 1827. —Kate L. Gregg, "Osage, Fort," *Dictionary of American History* (5 vols., New York, 1940), IV, 189. At a point on the west bank of the Missouri, twenty-five miles northwest of the Kansas City area, the army constructed Cantonment (Fort) Leavenworth in the year Fort Osage was abandoned. A malaria epidemic in 1829 drove away most of the garrison, but the army returned and developed the fort into a supply depot, Indian council site, and reservoir of military protection for westbound emigrants and traders.—Ralph P. Bieber, "Leavenworth, Fort," *Dictionary of American History*, III, 258; Elvid Hunt, *History of Fort Leavenworth, 1827–1927* (Fort Leavenworth, 1926), chaps. II and III.

[4] An alphabetical list of Missouri minerals was compiled by Alphonso Wetmore in his *Gazetteer of the State of Missouri* (St. Louis, 1837), 261–65. To lure developers, he added (p. 28): "Beneath the clay and soil of Missouri, marble, firestone, and buhrstone may be quarried. Iron, lead, copper, and tin may be placed on the list of minerals, more abundant, useful, and valuable than anything the earth can be made to yield up here, and are the leading heavy articles of export that Missouri can furnish. . . . The coal-beds and salines . . . are places of deposite [*sic*], where honest enterprise can have credit."

where ferries are also stationed to cross the river. These ferries are open flat boats, worked by two negroes with long paddles, but Col. Owen,[5] proprietor of the lower landing, is about having a steamboat built for his ferry, the increasing business giving warrant already for such a proceeding. Upon the opposite side of the Missouri, about six miles from the river bank, is located the beautiful town of Liberty,[6] on a romantic eminence. Fort Leavenworth is further up the river about thirty or forty miles.[7]

Precipitous bluffs shut off Independence from the river, but the spirit of western enterprise is at work, and former difficulties of access to the town are fast disappearing. From each landing place the roads to the town are now in a state of prosperous improvement, and the rush of emigration and business to this quarter must speedily secure still further facility in means of conveyance.

As is customary among new western settlements, a spacious square forms the centre of the town and from it the different streets branch in all directions. In the centre of this square there is now a handsome brick court-house two stories high, where legal

[5] Colonel Samuel C. Owens, wholesale dealer in the Santa Fe and mountain trades, operated a flourishing business on the southwest corner of the Independence town square. He served Jackson County in several political capacities, was briefly a state representative, and later was involved in the swirl of the Mexican War. In 1846 the army placed under his command a special battalion of traders who were on their way to Santa Fe. He fell in the Battle of Sacramento (February 28, 1847) and was buried near the battlefield.—Statement of Edward R. Schauffler, in *Kansas City Times*, November 22, 1947; statement of Stella M. Drumm (1926), in "Missouri History Not Found in Textbooks," *Missouri Historical Review*, Vol. XLIII, No. 2 (January, 1940), 192–93; Union Historical Company, *The History of Jackson County* (Kansas City, 1881), 172.

[6] Liberty, county seat of Clay County, Missouri, lies above Independence, approximately four miles north of the Missouri River. In 1839, Liberty was thriving, new construction was underway, and mechanics were in demand. The town boasted two dozen skilled tradesmen (saddlers, tailors, carpenters, and cabinetmakers), seventeen business firms (dry goods, drugs, and groceries), and one dozen professional men.—*Missouri Republican* (St. Louis), April 30, 1839, quoting from the *Far West* (Liberty).

[7] See article footnote 3.

business is transacted, and public meetings, balls, &c. are held.[8]
But to assimilate this into character with out former sketches, we
must lay aside statistical detail and take up the painter's brush.
Suppose the starting of a caravan for Santa Fé. In the square you
observe a number of enormous wagons into which men are pack-
ing bales and boxes.[9] Presently the mules are driven in from pasture, and a busy time commences in the square, catching the
fractious animals with halters and introducing them to harness
for their long journey. Full half a day is thus employed before
the expedition finally gets into motion and winds slowly out of
town. This is an exciting moment. Every window sash is raised,
and anxious faces appear watching with interest the departure.
The drivers snap their long whips and swear at their unruly
mules, bidding goodby in parentheses between the oaths, to old
friends on each side of the street as they move along. Accidents
are very apt to occur on the occasion of a setting out. Sometimes
the unmanageable mules will not stir at all, and then they are
just as likely to take the opposite notion and run off with the
enormous weight of merchandise behind them. This occurred on
the day of our departure. A drunken driver lashed his mules into

[8] A two-room cabin-courthouse, built in 1828, was replaced eight years later
with a two-story brick structure, costing $1,500. According to local legend,
"sheep were allowed in the building before each court session to carry out fleas
brought in by hogs and chickens that roamed at will through the halls." The
building was remodeled and increased in size in 1846, 1872, 1887, 1907, and
1932.—Vernon E. Moore, "This Courthouse Was Remodeled Five Times,"
American Architect, Vol. CXLIV, No. 2621 (January, 1934), 33–36.

[9] American traders traveling to Santa Fe used several types of wagons, particularly the historic Conestoga. Early Conestogas were made in Pennsylvania;
later ones were manufactured by Joseph Murphy in St. Louis and by wagon
makers in western Missouri. An average loaded wagon, weighing 5,000 pounds,
required the pull of ten to twelve mules or six yoke of oxen. Sagging wooden
beds, "outward leaning sideboards," and canvas-covered arches marked the
wagons as sturdy, yet lumbering, prairie clipper ships. With teams in reserve,
cargo wrapped in blankets and burlap, and spare parts stowed away, the
Conestoga was ready for Santa Fe.—Duffus, *Santa Fe Trail*, 133–34; Max L.
Moorhead, "Spanish Transportation in the Southwest, 1540–1846," *New Mexico Historical Review*, Vol. XXXII, No. 2 (April, 1957), 118.

a fright and then tumbled into the road, while the team dashed aside, and dragged the loaded vehicle down a steep lane over stumps and stones and other inequalities with most dangerous velocity, until they were brought up against a log house in the middle of the way. Nothing could have appeared more alarming than the huge wagon loaded heavily with new goods, jumping over the tree stumps and seeming every moment on the point of being dashed to atoms. Another accident happened before the wagons got well out of town. The fact was the drivers had all made the most of their last day in *Independence,* and were in condition better adapted to anything else than the performance of their duty. The whole road from the town, four miles, to where the prairie opened was at that time in very bad order, and at one place a wagon tipped over in a gully, the body of the vehicle with all the merchandise being cast entirely clear of the wheels, which fell back into their proper position. On account of these disasters it was midnight when we reached and camped for the first time upon the prairie.[10] The vast wilderness was sleeping in a silver flood of moonbeams. Perhaps the singular solemnity and beauty of this scene may be imagined. Like the ocean, ever like the ocean, and only like the ocean is the far stretching wilderness of grass. And midnight with such a scene around awakens thoughts that startle us, thoughts we never dreamed before were in our hearts. The interminable solitude, not a house or a fence or a creature, not even a tree or any object to which our eyes are accustomed. A sense of loneliness falls over us more impressive even than the new traveller may know upon the wave.

Here we took

Great nature's second course

upon the grass with as full and pure satisfaction as was ever known upon the softest pillow of luxury.

---

[10] The most likely location for the camp was two to three miles west of Little Blue Creek (eight to ten miles due east of the Missouri-Kansas border).

About an Old Woman and a Pipe

Upon the second day after commencing our journey from Indepence, about noon we came in view of a neat and substantial looking farm house. Having already had a taste of camping and dining on the grass, with a long continuation of the same sort of fare in prospect, we of course were not disposed to miss this opportunity of enjoying once more the luxury of table and chair. The farmer, a fine old fellow, with the head and features of a Cincinnatus, received us at once with the frankness of a backwoodsman and that natural politeness, which, from bearing the impress of sincerity, is often far more grateful to the heart than the highest refinement of a studied courtesy. His wife, with like open and unceremonious manner, rose to welcome us, saw us seated, and then returned to her knitting, wasting no moment from her domestic employment, yet extending to us every attention we could have expected or desired.

In a low rocking chair near the door sat an old woman, a white haired, withered, toothless, deaf, and almost unconscious remnant of breathing life. With slow and regular motion, like the pendulum of a clock, she moved backward and forward in the chair, with her glazed eyes fixed upon the vacancy without. Our appearance drew from her no attention, and whatever her musings may have been, she suffered no interruption by our entrance; but to us she instantly became an object of absorbing interest. Like a yellow leaf still fluttering on the bough so tenderly you wonder why it does not fall, was the spectacle we looked upon. She was the mother of the farmer's wife, and eighty-seven years of age. There it was her custom to sit through the long summer day, and all the recreation she ever sought was in a pipe, which the daughter told us had now been two days broken, and the poor old woman was silently and uncomplainingly inconsolable.—The farmer was so employed as to be unable to go to Independence until the following week, and until then it was impossible to replace the broken tobacco consumer.

Our companion, Jerry, had a rich and elaborately ornamented Indian pipe, which came to pieces, and was thus exceedingly convenient for carrying in his pouch. He was a confirmed and inveterate slave to smoking, and some admiring friend had made him this useful beautiful present upon his leaving St. Louis for his long and dreary journey. In addition to the pipe, Jerry had a heart constantly overflowing with the rich cream of human kindness, and we no sooner heard the story of the broken pipe than our eyes were all turned upon him, knowing his beautiful pipe was bound to go, and compassionating him sincerely, for there was now no possibility of his obtaining another. Jerry's hand, as we anticipated, was thrust immediately in the tobacco pouch which he always carried slung around his neck, and the pipe was half drawn forth, when one who saw through the action and wished him to consider, took him by the arm and led him aside under the pretext of calling his attention to some peculiar object about the farm.

We were called to dinner, and sat down with sharp appetites to young boiled pork and cabbage, hot corn cakes, buttermilk, fresh milk, ham, eggs, and the sweetest fresh butter that ever was churned. We were all in the gayest humor, but Jerry wore a troubled expression of countenance. He was ill at ease, and could by no means enjoy his dinner. We all saw what was troubling him, and could not help enjoying his perplexity, though it was clear the pipe would have to go, and poor Jerry would rob himself rather than leave the old woman without the indulgence she was pining for. She sat still on the low chair, and having disposed of a plate of soft victuals, she again silently resumed her measured rocking, seemingly wrapped in some absorbing and sorrowful abstraction.

"She can't endure the loss of her pipe," said the farmer; "she has not been deprived of it before in many years, and now she seems as if nothing in the world could console her for the want of it."

Jerry laid down his knife and fork and rose from the table. His countenance cleared instantly, for his mind was made up, and, pulling out his Indian pipe, he filled the bowl, lighted the weed, and handed his treasure to the poor old woman.

Jerry was a fine looking fellow, but he never looked handsomer than he did when, turning to the farmer, he said "I don't know how to talk to the old lady, and as you say she can't hear, maybe it aint worth while, but I just want you to say to her that that pipe is a present from a boy that's gone to Santa Fé, and she'll oblige me very much by smoking it just as much as suits her fancy. If I ever come back again, I'll stop in here and take a whiff with the good old soul, and if you should hear of some professional Camanche barber having walked off with my scalp, why the kind old girl I dare say will shed a tear for me, and who wouldn't give an old pipe for a woman's tear?"

Jerry sat down again, and now he was the merriest fellow at table. He tossed off bumpers of buttermilk with a bacchanalian grace of action that showed his familiarity with the wine board, and doubtless his generous deed had kindled in his veins as pleasant an exhilaration as he ever imbibed from sparking [*sic*] brimmers of the grape's delicious juice.

When Jerry was going the old woman's glassy eye followed him to the door, and then she stretched out her withered hand offering to return him the pipe.

"If I take it may I be shot!" exclaimed Jerry. "Look here, old lady—O, I forgot you can't hear—but I want you to keep that pipe till I come back, any how, and I'll make out to find another. God bless you, mother, good by." And Jerry shook the thin hand that was extended to him, and departed. There was moisture in his eye as we rode away from the gate, but whether it was caused by his tender parting with the pipe, or the old woman, we did not ask, and if we had it would probably have been a difficult question for him to answer.

Six months after one of the fine companions returned home by the same road, and stopped at this farm house. There hung Jerry's pipe over the mantlepiece, but the old woman was dead.

The Route to Santa Fe

On the 5th of the present month an extensive caravan under the protection of the Texas Government, and numbering in all about three hundred strong, left Austin for Santa Fe.[11] It is now about the season that trading companies move off for the same destination across the plains of Missouri, and many of the traders for both routes may be found now in this city making purchases for the Mexican market. A brief sketch, therefore, of the Missouri route, enumerating the creeks, wooded places, buffalo regions, distances, &c., we deem must be found at this time useful as well as interesting.

From the town of Independence the road runs for about four miles through a dense forest, very thinly scattered with farm houses, until it opens suddenly upon the broad, oceanlike, far-famed Western prairies. Here it is that the young traveller becomes absorbed in the dreamy delight of long cherished and now first gratified curiosity. The sight is not surpassed, not even by the snow-capp'd rocks of Oregon, while the far plains are black with buffalo, and then a new excitement springs up in the youthful hunter's breast, which the writer need not waste time in describing, as it can only be appreciated by personal enjoyment.

About half a day's travel brings the Santa Fe bound traders

[11] The disastrous Texan Santa Fe Expedition of 1841 included at least 320 and perhaps as many as 483 members. The party moved north from Austin, Texas, and then west over hot prairie-canyon country towards Santa Fe. The Mexicans took them into custody and marched them from San Miguel, New Mexico, to Mexico City. On the way at least forty perished, thirty others having been lost before the Mexicans made them prisoners. Although the Mexican government regarded it as a military movement and treated it accordingly, the rank-and-file expedition members maintained they wished only to trade, to visit Santa Fe, to see Indians, to better their health, and to sample southwestern adventure. George Wilkins Kendall, co-owner of the New Orleans *Picayune*, was with the expedition, was taken prisoner, and lived to tell the story in his *Narrative of the Texan Santa Fé Expedition* (2 vols., New York, 1844). The best recent account may be found in N. M. Loomis, *The Texan–Santa Fé Pioneers* (Norman, 1958). For Kendall's remarks on East Texas see *The Daily Picayune* (New Orleans), June 17, 1841.

past the flourishing plantation of Farmer Rice,[12] where leisure travellers often linger to enjoy his sweet bacon, fresh eggs, new milk, and the other nutritious and unsophisticated luxuries that always appease appetite without encumbering digestion. Eight miles further, after crossing a stream called the Little Blue,[13] another and the last farm house is reached, after leaving which the wayfarer turns and turns again to see the solitary christian roof fade rapidly down to the horizon's verge, as the desert opens still vaster and wilder in advance.

Without making too minute a detail, it is enough to say that between this and Council Grove, the grand rendezvous of adventurous expeditions, there are about half a dozen creeks, some dry, some deep and difficult to cross.—One of these is a precipitous hollow, that excites the utmost astonishment in a raw traveller, as to how a heavily laden wagon can possibly be transported to the bottom and up again, without being dashed to pieces and killing every mule attached to it. Yet the thing is accomplished, generally, with a little delay, and in the utmost safety.[14] A brief and

[12] Archibald Rice was born December 18, 1782, in North Carolina, and moved to Jackson County, Missouri, in 1832, remaining there until his death seventeen years later. His wife, Sallie, bore him at least six children and survived him three years. Rice's farm was approximately seven to seven and one-half miles south-southwest of Independence, slightly to the left of the outgoing Santa Fe Trail.—Sixth Census of the United States (1840), Missouri Population Schedules; *Vital Historical Records of Jackson County, Missouri, 1826–1876* (comp. by the Daughters of the American Revolution) (Kansas City, 1933–34), 428.

[13] Matt was mistaken. This is Big Blue Creek which the Santa Fe Trail crossed fourteen to fifteen miles southwest of Independence, within two miles east of the Missouri-Kansas line. The Little Blue runs almost parallel to the Big, but several miles east of it and the trail.—D. E. Wood, *The Old Santa Fe Trail from the Missouri River* (Kansas City, 1951), maps.

[14] The procedure was not as safe as Matt intimated, since men were killed or injured at times in the process. Washington Irving, referring to an expedition of 1832 under Captain B. L. E. Bonneville, noted that "rugged steeps and deep ravines incessantly obstructed their progress, so that a great part of the day was spent in the painful toil of digging through banks, filling up ravines, forcing the wagons up the most forbidding ascents, or swinging them with ropes down

pleasant travel from Council Grove, leads the traders to Cotton Wood Grove, another delightful resting place for the prairie pilgrims, and from here the lone and dreary aspect of the travel begins, daily and heavily, to bear upon the spirits.

The next important creek that crosses the road is the Rio de Nepestita or Little Arkansas, which, when low, seldom delays the traders with any serious inconvenience. There are two or three nameless water courses between this and Cow Creek,[15] which is the point where buffalos are first looked for by the traders.— This is about fifteen days smart travel from Independence, and variously estimated to be some 250 or 300 miles from said starting place. Here the night-guard is appointed and set, to be continued in close duty for the remainder of the journey.

The next point is Round Mound, a beautiful hillock, covered with plum trees, in the middle of a flat prairie. From here the travellers strike the Arkansas, and for many days continue along its banks, vast legions of buffalo now appearing almost daily, approaching the wide stream to drink, and leaving it again in search of new pasture.

There is a well-known fording place here, conducting to the Semirone Road,[16] which cuts off a wide extent of the travel, but only the more daring and adventurous pursue it, as depredations from the Camanches have been frequently suffered in that region. Timorous traders, and parties inferior in number, therefore, con-

the face of dangerous precipices."—*The Adventures of Captain Bonneville* (New York, n.d.), 39.

[15] The "nameless water courses" now have names (from east to west): Dry Creek, Jarvis Creek, Long Branch, and Little Cow Creek. All of them flow from north to south and have waterless upper reaches in dry weather.—Lyons, Kansas, Quadrangle (1906).

[16] This is one of several crossings of the Arkansas leading to the Cimarron Road or Cutoff. The "Lower Crossing" was near Ford, Kansas. "Middle Crossing" was at Cimarron, Kansas, twenty miles west of Dodge City. A little-used crossing was at Ingalls, and the "Upper Crossing" was at Chouteau's Island (Hartland, Kansas). The crossings are located carefully in *The Santa Fe Trail* (volume V of series IV of *The Crown Collection of American Maps. The American Transcontinental Trails*, ed. by A. B. Hulbert [Colorado Springs, 1926?]).

tinue forward upon the safer track, and ford the Arkansas at Bent's Ford,[17] about 100 or 150 miles nearer its source.

Following this route, there is a deep water course to be crossed, called Rio de Nuezes, or Walnut Creek. This is one of the most difficult crossings in the whole journey, and travellers are often compelled to encamp, waterbound, upon the bank for many days, unless they determine to cut down trees and build a bridge for the wagons to cross.

It is just one days smart travel from here to Ash Creek, and a brief space then brings up the caravan at an old and favorite Indian camping ground, now in use by the traders, called Pawnee Fork, being a delightful wood and watering place at an abrupt turning of Pawnee River.

Various clefts and channels across the prairie, mostly dry, and known as Coon and Turkey Creeks, now appear at intervals of two, three, and five miles. If necessitated to encamp here, by storm, hunger, or the approach of night, water *may* be found in these hollows, but wood is not to be expected. Should rain water-soak the "buffalo chips," such a thing as camp-fire is impossible.

At this section of the travel, the sand hills upon the Mexican side of the Arkansas form a spectacle of singular and picturesque interest, resembling so vividly spires and domes and castellated clusters, as to fire the fancy with a most pleasant hallucination. In the desert you dream of cities and familiar scenes, and home seems near to you.

Big Timber is the next resting place of peculiar attraction,[18]

[17] Also known as Fort William, the post was founded by William Bent and his associates about 1832 (recent evidence suggests perhaps 1833 or 1834), on the north bank of the Arkansas about seven miles east of La Junta, Colorado. The fort, now under restoration, served both the Santa Fe and mountain fur trades. In 1849, William Bent moved two-score miles down the Arkansas and built Bent's New Fort, leaving the old one partially destroyed.—LeRoy R. Hafen, "Bent's Fort," *Dictionary of American History*, I, 178–79; W. J. Ghent, "Bent, William," in the *Dictionary of American Biography*, II, 206–207; Herbert W. Dick, "The Excavation of Bent's Fort, Otero County, Colorado," *The Colorado Magazine*, Vol. XXXIII, No. 3 (July, 1956), 181–96.

[18] Big Timber was a favorite Indian winter encampment and treaty-making

and after leaving it, a short travel sets down the pilgrims at the gates of Fort William, where the hospitality of the Messrs. Bent is found to be the dearest thing in the recollections of all old travellers through this region of the West.

Near Fort William (named after William Bent, the founder) is *Pueblo de Leche,* or Milk Fort, a mud-built fortification occupied solely by Mexicans.

From the upper turrets of Fort William the first view is caught of the Rocky Mountains, two prominent peaks, on a clear day, appearing, like dim vapors, in the south-western horizon. Here is the favorite fording of the Arkansas, and after crossing, the traders go on, passing various points of inferior interest, the most striking of which is the Ratone, one of the most romantic lines of crystal fluid that ever meandered over the face of nature. Were not the limit of our space already over-stepped, we should dwell here a moment in picturing the beautiful Ratone, although, in the course of our sketchings, it has received attention, for after it there is not another spot of attraction to be named, until the exceedingly novel mud-built walls of Santa Fé cloys curiosity at last with one of the strangest spectacles to be found from end to end of our continent.

We give this brief sketch of the Missouri route, to chime with Geo. Wilkins Kendall's letter, which also appears this morning. He, it will be seen, is now out upon the travel from a new and still more interesting starting point, and, doubtless, he is to traverse scenes intimately in character with those we have been some time describing. This Texan route, however, is new and far

site on the north bank of the Arkansas. The easternmost limit of the timbered area was just above the mouth of Sand or Big Sandy Creek; the westernmost limit was about thirteen miles below the mouth of the Purgatory, or opposite the mouth of Caddo Creek, Colorado. According to a visitor in 1846, "the big timber is a thinly scattered growth of large cottonwoods not more than three-quarters of a mile wide, and three or four miles long [an underestimate]."— Kenyon Riddle, *Records and Maps of the Old Santa Fe Trail* (Raton, New Mexico, 1949), 43, 46.

more dangerous, and must develop incidents of a more startling nature than any yet recorded.[19]

Valentine's Defeat

We were a party of five young fellows, old companions, who started from St. Louis with no serious object, bent only on adventure. At Independence we bought a carryall and its complement of mules,[20] in which to transport our baggage; and fancying it would be a pleasant variety to drive now and then, we agreed to perform the duty in turns and not burden ourselves with another attendant. The consequence will be foreseen—driving instead of being found pleasant was irksome in the extreme. The name that heads this sketch will be recognized by our readers in New York and in St. Louis—a merry, light hearted, kind dispositioned, courteous, and universally admired young man, one of those fascinating characters sometimes, but not often met with, who unite the accomplishments of the drawing room with all the best qualities of a social companion. Jim V. hated the duty of driving worse than any of us; he discovered that there was a slight distinction between driving tandem through Broadway and guiding four stubborn mules across muddy creeks, rocky ravines, and swampy prairies.

We bore the inconvenience grumblingly until we reached the buffalo country, and there the necessity of driving became "most intolerable and not to be endured." V. determined to get rid of the disagreeable duty in some way, and he soon hit upon a method. It was suddenly discovered that he was a very awkward driver, a wheel was broken on one of his days of duty—the next day he officiated there was an upset. These hints did not procure a dismissal from office, and V.'s gathering vengeance at last brought on the catastrophe which forms the subject of this impor-

[19] See article footnote 11.

[20] A "carryall" was a lightweight, four-wheeled carriage drawn by a single animal and built to hold four passengers. Matt, evidently, uses the term in a more general sense to apply to a baggage and supply vehicle.

tant sketch. There are a number of difficult places, called by the traders "Turkey Creeks,"[21] which are to be crossed before reaching the Arkansas. One of these crossed our path on the eventful day on which our carryall made its final crash and suspended operations forever. V., it seems, had made up his mind to end the driving system by breaking the carryall, even if he broke his neck in the bargain; and to speak seriously he came very near doing the latter in accomplishing the former. In truth the quadruple quadrupeds that drew our baggage wagon were a set of most unamiable mules, and doubtless they could have easily managed to destroy the vehicle without any mismanagement on the part of their guide; so that as such unanimity of design existed between the driver and themselves it is no great wonder that the deed was done. There was a steep and ugly descent to make into the hollow, and we rode across to the high ground opposite to have a full front view of V.'s achievement. The carryall reached the edge of the descent, and the mules were instantly seized with a strong desire to get out of the traces and travel off in different directions. "Gee! gee! Where are you going Switchtail? Haw! haw! Take hold of that mule somebody! Ho! Gee! Haw! Wo! Hold on there! Look out!" Crash! One wheel mounted a high rock, and out went V. head foremost, followed by an avalanche of trunks, carpet bags, cigar boxes, pistols, fishing rods, blankets, and all the usual conveniences of the travel.

V. got to his feet and held on to the reins manfully, contriving to increase the fright of the unruly animals until both axletrees were broken, the carryall fairly "dumped" into the creek, and the mules were scampering about, kicking at the broken tongue of the vehicle which was banging at their heels. We wore broad brimmed hats bought in St. Louis to protect us from the sun.[22]

---

[21] "Running Turkey" and "Dry Turkey" creeks, approximately 210 miles west of Independence, flow south and enter a branch of the Little Arkansas between Canton and McPherson, Kansas. In wet weather—and the summer of 1839 was damp—they could be difficult crossing.

[22] Greenhorns bought much of their outfit in St. Louis and usually purchased

V.'s hat was not exactly knocked into a cocked hat, but resembled more a sailor's "sou'wester."

It is customary among the traders when a party is attacked and robbed by Indians, or when any serious mishap occurs, to christen the spot with the name of the individual injured, and call it his *"defeat."* Accordingly, before we left the place we held a solemn convocation and conferred V.'s name upon the precipitous declivity where our carryall was destroyed. A rain came on very *"apropos,"* and we stood bare headed and with grave faces while the wheels and remnants of the carryall were thrown into the creek, and the following poetical effusion, "prepared for the occasion," was recited—

Upsets! breakdowns! stops and disaster!
Broken shins and no shinplasters.
Jim lost a hat and gained a fall,
And sent to pot our carryall.
And now to all our hearts content
The carryall to doom is sent.
Crack went the wheel and out went Jim,
And the trunks went tumbling after him.
The prairie winds at once are listening
Unto a burial and a christening.
Now as Jim V. must bear this blame,
'Tis meet this spot should bear his name;
So where Jim tumbled from his seat,
We christen "Valentine's Defeat."

The traders took charge of our luggage, and we journeyed on, subject to a little more inconvenience, but still heartily glad at having got rid of the obnoxious duty of driving.

"broad-brimmed low felt" hats, which afforded good protection from the elements.—Stanley Vestal, *The Old Santa Fe Trail* (Boston, 1939), 16.

Council Grove

This is a beautiful spot, one hundred and fifty miles from the town of Independence, Missouri.[23] Here the Santa Fe traders generally pause a day or two for rest—to enjoy the shade of the tall trees, and drink the clear cool water that runs bubbling, through the grove—as dear a sight to the prairie wanderer as the glance of love from the eye of beauty. Here the different adventurers meet to elect their leader, arrange their plan to travel, put their fire arms in order, and hold council on other matters connected with their enterprise. From this the place derives its name of "Council Grove."

We were ten days travelling from Independence to this spot; we remained two days, and never in hall or drawing room, did we spend a more delightful time. Reading or sleeping, beneath the trees on the banks of the chrystal water in the hot noon—or fishing, where we could see the little finny creatures playing with our bait. Or, in the evening, singing in the moonlight the songs we had been used to sing at home, those

Native strains that melt us while we sing them.

We sang duets, one on one side, and one on the other of the beautiful stream. We sang loud chorusses [*sic*], and the lonely woods gave us back a running accompaniment of echos [*sic*]. And when the night-birds screamed, after we had laid our heads upon our saddles to sleep, we laughed at the poor be nighted creatures, and raised our voices in merry imitations of the doleful sounds, till the hungry wolves caught up our cry, and awed us into silence with their dismal howlings.

[23] George C. Sibley, who participated in the American-sponsored Santa Fe Trail survey of 1825, suggested the name "Council Grove" for this attractive camping place at a ford in the well-timbered valley of the Neosho River. Josiah Gregg, pre-eminent chronicler of the Santa Fe trade, placed Council Grove "nearly a hundred and fifty miles from Independence." Sibley located it at 160 miles from Fort Osage, Missouri.—Gregg, *Commerce of the Prairies*, 29; Kate L. Gregg (ed.), *The Road to Santa Fe* (Albuquerque, 1952), 57.

It was early in July, about ten o'clock in the morning, that we reached this delightful place. We distinguished the trees about five miles distant, and three of us started forward to reconnoitre the ground. We were raw travellers, full of boyish romance; had never been in the woods; every thing was new to us, and every new thing delightful. We had been told of the beauties of "Council Grove"—had talked of it all the way, and now it was in sight. We watched the long line of trees stretching across the vast prairie, and marking the course of the creek where the cool water was running, and experienced a delicious excitement in seeing them rise rapidly before us as we hastened forward. Short as the distance was, and fast as we rode, our impatience was still the swiftest traveller, and minutes seemed almost hours until we stood at last beneath the sombre shadow of the old trees.[24] We rode on through the thick wood, enjoying the grateful sensations occasioned by the transition from the burning heat of the prairie to the cooling shade of the grove. We reached the water—the crystal stream rushing over its white bed of pebbles. Ah! ye who in cities torture invention for new varieties of drink, to gratify your pampered palates, little can you conceive the luxury of a draught dipped with a shell, and drank upon the border of the lonely desert brook!

'Twas a lonely place, where the trees overhung the stream, covering it with a deep shadow; the water seemed to murmur till it danced and brightened again in the beams of the golden sun. To drink was not sufficient; we doffed our travel-worn garments, and threw ourselves into the liquid element: while, like boys loosed from school, involuntary shouts of pleasure burst from our lips. We could feel,

> *The little trout and salmon,*
> *That were playing at backgammon,*

[24] The river valley supported a heavy growth of oak, maple, elm, walnut, ash, and hickory. Many of the trees were large; their timber well suited for spare wagon parts.

bobbing about our feet in the water, and were considerably startled at seeing a large snake slide swiftly past us, and hide itself among the shrubbury [*sic*] that projected over the bank.

We left Council Grove with sad hearts and many a time after wards when camping without shelter, while the sun was blazing on the prairie, we gave a thought and a sigh to the merry days we had spent in *"Council Grove."*

Disheartened Travellers Returning

We are camped at Council Grove, one hundred and eighty miles from Independence,[25] having travelled thirteen days since the last log house sunk slowly from view, as we turned again and again to see it disappear by inches. In Council Grove (a most beautiful and fairy like place, an *oasis* in reality) we had rested two days, fishing, fowling, and hunting, while the traders were securing strong sticks of timber to repair their wagons in case of accident. Here also council was held, a commander appointed, the plan and all the necessary arrangements of the travel adopted, balls were cast, rifles and pistols cleaned, and every preparation made for the long journey that lay before us.

The warmest description will scarcely convey to untravelled readers even a faint picture of this very beautiful grove. A creek bordered by a tall growth of timber winds across the interminable prairie, and at this place forms a circular bend enclosing a beautiful, green carpeted rotunda, a sort of natural amphitheatre, surrounded by a thick forest of ancient trees. Beneath the twining branches of these old trees, the crystal stream meanders over its pebbly bottom, and here in the breezy shade, while the sun blazes upon the surrounding desert, we sat and watched the little finny people nibble at our bait. We fished, bathed, read, sang, talked of home, of the strange country we were about to visit, of the wild travel we had yet to encounter, and with burning curiosity we discoursed about the buffalo, the lordly brute now sole master of

[25] See article footnote 23 for the accurate distance.

the vast wilderness we were to cross. Through unnumbered myriads of a creature of which we had never seen one, even exhibited as a curiosity, we were to pass, and strange as wanderers in the moon were we to feel while treading the yet unexplored territory inherited by the buffalo.

Upon the third morning, when our arrangements were completed for leaving the grove, the sky became clouded and a heavy rain prevented our departure; so we spent the day in a cheerless, uncomfortable state, cut off from all recreation as well as the excitement of travel. The rain fell heavily during most of the day, but as night closed around us a continuous drizzle succeeded the pelting shower, and we succeeded in keeping our camp-fires cheerfully blazing. Just as the pall of night was chasing away the last dull remnant of twilight, while we were gathered about the fires swallowing, without much tea-table etiquette, our evening meal, we were suddenly startled by a gun shot, and an instant after one of the drivers, who had been strolling outside the camp, rushed in, declaring that he had caught a glimpse of several figures approaching in the direction from whence we had heard the shot. No sentinels were out, as the guard had not yet been organized, having still nearly a hundred miles to travel before danger was anticipated, and as none of our hunters had been out during the day, it was very certain that strangers if not enemies had discovered the encampment.

All the new travellers instantly seized their arms, but those more used to the road, although somewhat puzzled, seemed to apprehend no danger. Presently we heard from the same direction voices calling to us, and soon distinguished the words "Don't fire! We are friends!" This was sufficient, and a crowd of us went forward to meet the strangers. We found an old man not less than fifty years of age, and a younger one of some twenty-five or thirty, both seemingly worn with fatigue to the last stretch of endurance, and leading forward an old horse that seemed like themselves ready to drop with exhaustion. The driver in his alarm had imagined there was a great crowd advancing upon us, but we learned now there were but two poor, half starved wanderers, and an old pack horse nearly in the same condition. We led the men to the fire, set our hot coffee, bread and meat before them, and sent the old horse to make acquaintance with our own animals, grazing near the camp. Delighted as we were to afford relief to these worn out travellers, we could not restrain our curiosity until they had finished their meal, but a perpetual volley of questions from all quarters poured upon them, and while struggling to eat and answer they were nearly choked at every mouthful.

A trader by the name of Kelly had left Independence two months before us,[26] and these were two of his drivers. Kelly had encountered a long continued and distressing spell of rainy weather, which made his travel extremely laborious and slow, and occasioned great discontent among his men. This old man had taken sick, and when nearly half the journey was performed he was seized with an unflinching determination to return home, fearing otherwise that he would never again see his relatives and friends. Nothing could alter his resolution, and the young man, finding him actually going off alone, volunteered to accompany him and share his danger. Their assistant, the horse, had broken down on the third day of their journey homeward, and being thus delayed, their provisions had given out, and for the last two days their whole sustenance had been a small prairie dog, which the young man was fortunate enough to knock out of its hole with a rifle ball.

Tears stood in the old man's eyes when he told us his delight

---

[26] Thomas J. Farnham, traveling west, met Captain Kelly's company of twenty-nine men about sundown on June 12, near Cotton Wood Grove. Kelly, on his way to Santa Fe, "was quite alarmed at the sight of travellers, but soon became satisfied" that his interests were not in jeopardy. Farnham's party took shelter "under the lee of Mr. Kelly's wagons" to avoid a sudden prairie thunderstorm which broke over them that evening.—Farnham, *Travels* (Part I), 68; Robert Shortess, "First Emigrants to Oregon," *Transactions of the Twenty-Fourth Annual Reunion of the Oregon Pioneer Association for 1896* (Portland, Oregon, 1896), 95.

at discovering our white wagon tops. He and his companion were just about to sink exhausted, into a despairing sleep, as night descended, when our encampment appeared. The young man shouted, but the old man feared to believe, and when convinced, joy completed the work of fatigue, and his last strength left him. The old man was tottering when we met him, and could barely ejaculate, "White men! white men! God bless you!"—The poor old fellow feared we were Indians, though our wagons might have assured him to the contrary.

The next morning the sun shone out cheerfully, and the two travellers, refreshed, recruited, and with provisions replenished, bade us farewell, and departed to resume their journey home, while we moved from Council Grove to encounter again the burning heat of the prairie.

Cotton-Wood Grove

Between St. Louis and Santa Fé, a distance of some fifteen hundred miles,[27] it may be imagined there are some very beautiful places, and there are, but the loveliest place to be selected in all that long travel is Cotton-Wood Grove, a magnificent oasis about one hundred and fifty or sixty miles beyond Independence.[28] Council Grove has been spoken of in one of our earliest sketches, and is distant only from Cotton-Wood about two days easy travel. It resembles the Cotton-Wood in many respects, being an amphitheatrical enclosure around a beautiful bend in the creek; and for the hunter Council Grove is by far the best camping ground, as the creek running through is deeper, and a dense forest of some extent branches away on both sides, thus

[27] It was approximately 765–75 miles from Independence to Santa Fe via the Cimarron Cutoff. Adding the water distance from St. Louis to Independence and excess mileage of the Bent's Fort–Taos route to Santa Fe, the total would be closer to 1,200 than to 1,500 miles.

[28] Gregg placed the distance at 192 miles from Independence to Cotton Wood Grove; Sibley, by the route he took, put it at 206 miles beyond Fort Osage.— Gregg, *Commerce of the Prairies*, 207; Gregg (ed.), *The Road to Santa Fe*, 60–61.

affording shelter, pasture, and water, the three sure attractions for game. There is a wild beauty about Council Grove, beauty of an opposite cast to that of Cotton-Wood. There is grandeur and gloom in the solemn shadows of the thick wood, and in the dark stream that winds along beneath the overhanging banks, as if mourning that the sun may not peep down upon it.

The beauty of Cotton-Wood Grove is of a gayer and more sprightly character. The shade serves all the purposes of shelter from the scorching sun-beams without oppressing the spirit with a dreary aspect. At the shallow bend where the waggons cross, the chrystal water leaps merrily into the sunshine, plunging away again to boil against rocky impediments, and then at intervals beyond sleeping in shade or darting across spots where each ripple glances like flame in the light breaking through the forest boughs. A high green knoll projects over the crossing-places, from whence the eye wanders over a vast prairie stretching away to kiss the blue firmament, as if in that mighty solitude earth and heaven met in silent and majestic recognition, where the tall blade of grass never bowed down before the step of man.

When first approaching the place, upon our outward travel, two of us were far in advance of the caravan, and, engaged earnestly in contemplation of the beautiful grove, we came noiselessly upon the knoll. Beneath us, drinking from the cool stream, stood a noble deer, a tall, clean-limbed, graceful creature, while two fawn lay gambolling and frolicking with each other in the shade of an arbor formed by interlocking branches of the cotton-wood trees.—We paused and stooped from view behind the knoll, that we might peep at these innocent lords of the soil

In their assigned and native dwelling place.

Our rifles were loaded in our hands, and with leisurely aim we might have planted a ball in the creature's heart as it stood with its nose in the water, while another might have pierced both fawn as they rolled together on the grass. But we were young travellers, and as yet the love of Nature had not given place to the hunter's fiercer passion. The idea never occurred to us of what a treasure of game was there almost inviting our powder and shot. We never thought of firing, but paused in utter forgetfulness of aught save the rare beauty of the scene before us. The noonday stillness, the murmur of the glassy water, the delightful shade in contrast with the heat of the blazing prairie, and the living tenants of the solitude standing so fearlessly before us, all gave rise to sensations of pleasure really resembling a fairy influence. We were thus absorbed, when a sudden and very unromantic termination was put to our sport. An attendant in advance of the waggons came riding after us upon a mule, and when the long-eared quadruped came near enough to catch a glance of our horses behind the knoll, it lifted its nose in the air and commenced experimenting upon its organs of sound in a manner particularly musical and peculiar to the beast. The start of the deer was the most superbly graceful thing that may be imagined. The noble animal sprang with a sort of sideway bound from the edge of the creek, planting himself an instant in an attitude of exquisite alarm—

Wide-spreading his antlers, erecting his head,
The stag his enemies scorning!

He gazed an instant upward, just long enough to let us see the beautiful expression of inquiry in his eye and the alarm told of in his dilated nostril. Still we remained unseen, and he seemed uncertain from whence to expect the danger. The two fawn were with him, as if asking protection. An instant more, and three bounds brought him to the top of the knoll, as if seeking an observatory, where our presence was at length discovered, and like wandering stars seen only to be lost, the graceful creature wheeled instantly and was gone across the creek and into the deep wood, with the two fawn bounding swiftly after him.

We camped here, and, after two days of sultry and weary travel we threw ourselves into the creek and laved our bodies luxuriously in the running tide.[29] The enjoyment was a reward for the pilgrimage. We, poor, lone wanderers, deemed by our friends half crazy in leaving home, revelled there in the wilderness, and pitied, honestly pitied all who were cooped up in crowded places, totally shut out from pleasure such as ours. We seemed to feel swelling within the relief from thraldom, the proud free spirit of the deer we had driven from their home, and with our happiness there mingled a benevolent compassion for the hunters after dollars and cents, "cabined, cribbed, confined" in the benumbing atmosphere of dense communities. There is, perhaps, a wise and beautiful moral hidden in that story of Ponce de Leon's search after the fountain of youth, for we were all years younger when we stepped out upon the green velvet of the grove from a bath more delightful to sense than the patrician refinement of Roman luxury ever achieved. Many devotees of Mammon might be awakened to keener enjoyment of life, and many callous hearts might be expanded and rejuvenated by a half hour's plunge in the chrystal water of *Cotton-Wood Grove!*

The Sand Hills

We had been twenty-five days and nights upon the plains. The excitement derived from contemplating the vast ocean of grass had begun to yield to solitary and desolate sensations, and our thoughts more often reverted to home, the friends and the kind ones we had left. One afternoon, when the sun had commenced its evening's descent in the West, its glancing rays lit up an irregular display of silver in the distant horizon which attracted our attention. Ere we had time to broach any definite conjecture touching this new spectacle, one of the old travellers rode up and told us we were looking upon the *Sand Hills* which stretch hundreds of miles along the Mexican bank of the Arkansas.

With the sunlight the new scene faded away, but the next day brought it nearer, and on the third, from morn till evening our

[29] This creek is the north fork of the Cottonwood River, located one mile west and one mile north of Durham, Kansas.

eyes were fixed upon the singularly beautiful prospect. The irregular hills, presenting their declivities of sand to the sun-beam, assumed so forcibly the appearance of clustering domes, temples and spires, that it became all but impossible to reject the impression from our minds. A marble city lay before us in the desert, and our busy imaginations soon peopled the streets with bustling multitudes, and excited within us a strange yearning to press forward and look again upon our fellow men. Those who have looked upon the lime stone bluffs up the far Mississippi may conceive the hallucination which here came upon us.[30] There the precipitous cliffs irresistibly impress upon you the idea of ruined palaces and fortifications; here some ancient city of Eastern magnificence seems to rise, not as a mysterious ruin, but in life-like reality, tempting you to believe in fable and all the dear enchantments of romance.

The old traders with whom we travelled, doubtless smiled in their sleeves at our exclamations of surprise and delight, and, in or by way of parenthesis, we will just commit to type a remark touching this same self-gratulatory smile. We, knowing that we were yielding to a romantic conceit, yet feeling pleasure from the deception, fancied ourselves mentally favored above our rude companions; they, knowing that our fanciful city was a desolate region of sand, indulged no doubt in like dreamings of superiority; and thus each party yielded a sentiment of pity to the other; for we pitied the traders that they could not enjoy even the "base-

---

[30] One prominent explorer who saw the limestone bluffs of the upper Mississippi was Zebulon Montgomery Pike in 1805–1806. The map in his report refers to "handsome rocky cliffs" on the Mississippi a few miles above St. Louis. As he led his party northward between the Illinois and Salt rivers, "the eastern shore [of the Mississippi]," he noted, "is either immediately bordered by beautiful cedar cliffs, or the ridges may be seen at a distance." From St. Peter's River to the Falls of St. Anthony, "the Mississippi is contracted between high hills," and farther north, between Elk and Pine rivers, "the shores . . . presented a dreary prospect of high barren knobs, covered with dead and fallen pine timber."—Zebulon M. Pike, *Exploratory Travels* (Denver, 1889), 27, 59, 83. In *The Expeditions of Zebulon Montgomery Pike* (3 vols., New York, 1895), Elliott Coues has edited the bulk of the Pike material.

less fabric" of our pleasure; and they considered us simpletons, pitying us accordingly, for not knowing that sand hills were not marble walls.

Few have travelled these Western deserts, and those who have are not likely to trouble pen and paper about their journeyings. The green plains, the wild flowers, the nameless buds and blossoms that for untold centuries have scented the desert breeze, still wait the pen of poet and historian, and the humble scribbler of the present page, if ever known, will have been forgotten, ere the wild gardens of the West are intersected by the Macadamized walks of civilization. When Western enterprise pierces into the yet uncultivated regions of far Missouri—when the log cabin of the distant settler is seen upon the banks of the shallow Arkansas —when cities rise where now the advancing plough has not yet disturbed the sunflower of the tall green blade—then may we hear and listen with interest to the history of early pioneers, and our grandchildren will yet wonder why their fathers and grandfathers spoke not more fluently about the glorious inheritance left to the uncultured children of the West.

The sand hills of the Arkansas will be levelled, and the yet lingering red tribes will be swept away before the tide of emigration; and when the original owners of the soil are gone, then will such simple records as the present become valuable and perhaps be sought after in vain.—It may be told, perhaps, that a crowd of harum-scarum youths traversed the waste, but who they were who shall tell? What writer will picture to future generations the wild delight experienced by the first travellers who looked upon the sand hills of the Arkansas?

Our First Buffalo Hunt

We had been told in Independence that we would find buffalo in about the tenth or twelfth day of our travel. The tenth day passed, and the twelfth, and we saw none; the eighteenth day went by us, and still we looked in vain for buffalo; and the intense anxiety we had at first experienced began to fade away, wearied with continual disappointment, as a pleasing hope long deferred, yields at last to indifference.

But this state of indifference served to make our delight the greater, by making our surprise more sudden, when the next day (the 19th) our wishes were gratified, and we saw at last the far-famed monarch of the prairies.

It was about two in the afternoon. Four of us had ridden far in advance of the rest of the company, and we paused to rest at a spot known as "Round Mound" or "Plum Point," a little round hillock in the middle of the prairie, where we found plums growing very plentifully. Here we unsaddled our tired animals and suffered them to graze, with long halters round their necks, while we gathered the plumbs. One, in the meantime, descended to drink from a pond of good water, with a sandy bed, about fifty yards distant. He soon shouted to us that he had discovered the hoof print of a buffalo, and on looking at the spot we could distinctly perceive the trail of the animal where it had approached the pond to drink, and again departed. Our curiosity was not much excited by this, and we were reclining on the shady side of the mound, drowsy with fatigue and the heat of the day, when one more wakeful than the rest, attracted our attention to a dark spot in the prairie, which he declared was in motion. We had an excellent portable spy-glass, and by taking an observation distinguished plainly enough the hugh [*sic*] head of the beast slowly raising from the ground and falling again to crop the prairie grass. Our horses were saddled and we were mounted in a space of time that surprised ourselves; but the poor animals were tired, and after descending from the hill, we soon lost sight of the buffalo. After an hours wandering, we again discovered him; we approached as near as we could without his perceiving us, and there, dismounting, left one to guard the horses, while the other three started on foot for the slaughter. One of the three was a former traveller who understood the sport, and this method of killing buffalo he called "crawling." We approached slowly, bending our bodies and taking off our hats while on the high ground, to conceal ourselves from the beast, but when in a hollow where he could not see us, we ran with our best speed to shorten the distance between us as quickly as possible, for the day was growing late and a dark storm was thundering in the distance. Roll after roll of the prairie we traversed, until ascending one we perceived our object on the other side. Now the utmost caution was necessary, and the "crawling" commenced. Abandoning our hats we approached on our hands and knees, till our distance from the buffalo could not have been more than 120 yards. We were now prostrate upon the grass, with our heads raised to scan the curious monster. Our rifles were cocked, and our aim taken, but still we paused, for our aim was not good; we could distinguish only a dark mass, and it is necessary to hit the buffalo in a certain spot. Suddenly the animal rose—he had heard our whispering, and now looked directly at us. Click! bang! Three balls pierced his liver, and the hugh brute fled; at 20 yards he turned to look at us, and then disappeared over another roll in the prairie. We followed at leisure, for we had seen the blood streaming from his mouth—a sure sign that the work was done.

The Butchering

Away in the west dark clouds were gathering, and we heard the distant rumbling of

The immortal Jove's dread clamours.

In a few moments we stood beside the bleeding carcase of the beast we had slaughtered. Its dark, fiendish eye was rolling in agony, and it struck at the ground with it's short horns, exhibiting in it's dying moments the instinctive principle of revenge. But one of us had ever seen a buffalo before. He was instantly at work with his large knife, stripping the animal of it's skin in order to get at its flesh. Day was fast disappearing. In our pursuit of the buffalo we had completely lost sight of the road, and of our other

89

companions. The vivid lightning was flashing among the heavy clouds that came rolling in dark masses across the sky, and the loud pealing thunder sounded a "dreadful note of preparation." The writer of this started back in search of his hat, and after half an hour's fruitless search, found himself in the grey evening bareheaded and alone among the woe-like rolls of the prairie. He shouted aloud, again and again, uncertain which way to turn, till at last his call was answered, and he then soon found his companions. The buffalo was dead; his skin had been stripped from one side of his body, and large masses of flesh had been taken from the back near the hump ribs. Our companions who had staid with the horses now appeared, leading them to where we were, and we hastily prepared to depart. To butcher the buffalo properly was impossible even had we understood how to do it, which we did not; so we took what meat had been cut off, secured it well to our cruppers and started. The shadows of night were falling, and so were the heavy rain drops. We could see no sign of our main party, and were painfully uncertain as to whether or not we had taken the right direction. And now the "pitiless storm" came down. The surcharged sky burst over our heads a deluge! It came, not like the gentle descent of the earth-improving rain, but resembling more the angry plunge of the cataract. We were thoroughly drenched in a very few minutes; and the christian-like resignation of him who had lost his hat deserves to be recorded in letters of gold.

Our prospect now was neither more nor less than to lay down in the rain and pass the night where we were, for pitchy darkness had enveloped us, and being uncertain of the way, to proceed would be perhaps to lose ourselves more effectually. While pausing to debate this point we heard suddenly the report of a rifle. Here was another quandary. It might proceed from our own party, but we were in a part of the country frequented by the thieving Pawnees,[31] and we had heard many stories of their mur-

---

[31] Before the terrible smallpox epidemic of 1831, Pawnee-American relations were good. The tribe, however, blamed the white men for the disease and took

ders and depredations. Our impatience to reach camp was stronger, however, than our fear of the Indians, and we proceeded in the direction of the spot. The rain still poured in a steady torrent upon our heads, and as no camp-fire could exist in such weather, we had no guide to find our friends, until we were suddenly challenged by one of our own sentinels, and our perplexity was over.

The rain poured steadily down until ten that night; when it ceased we built a fire of "buffalo chips," dried our clothes, cooked our food, and with tolerable good appetites made our first supper of buffalo meat.

The Buffalo

We had as yet seen only small bands of twenty and thirty buffalo. The largest herd that had crossed us numbered about sixty or seventy; but these small bands fly in great fear at sight of travellers, and are soon out of sight. It was soon after commencing our morning travel, along the Arkansas on the American side, that we discovered a vast number of small black spots far away on the prairie before us. We had butchered two cows after a tiresome hunt the day before, and being well supplied with meat, we determined to recruit a little before we resumed the excitement of the hunt. Gradually, as we advanced, the dark spots grew larger and increased in number until our efforts to count them were rendered utterly useless. Still we pressed forward, and about noon day we found ourselves in the very centre of an enormous band that opened a path for us as we approached, and closed again behind us as we moved along. We were ourselves as much at a loss to judge of their number as the reader will be. It would have been as easy for us to stand still in a forest and count the trees, as then to have made a calculation, and the writer can

appropriate revenge. Regarded by many traders as the "Ishmaelites of the Prairies," the Pawnee frequently shadowed Santa Fe–bound parties, stealing supplies and livestock or attacking unsuspecting individuals.—Gregg, *Commerce of the Prairies*, 428; F. W. and A. E. Stearn, *The Effect of Smallpox on the Destiny of the Amerindian* (Boston, 1945), 79.

but say that they covered the earth in all directions. The natural green of the prairie was changed to black, and away to the horizon all around us spread a dense herd of the wild inheritors of the wilderness.

We travelled till evening with the same prospect around us. The next day it was the same. The enormous band had come from some region yet undisturbed by the hunter, and was then leaving the exhausted pastures to seek fresh provender. This day we resolved to enjoy the sport of hunting, and from morn till evening we chased the poor brutes about the prairie, killing the unfortunate animals in mere wantonness, as we were not in want of meat, and the dead carcases were left to feed the wolves in the night. Does not providence guide all our actions? The brutes that we killed to feed only our love of excitement, made food for the starving wolves.

The sounds emitted by these strange creatures are peculiar. They do not bellow so loudly as would be imagined for their enormous bulk and untamable wildness, but breathe or *blow*, particularly when in fright, something like the sneeze of a horse, but more sudden and not so sharp.[32] The noise made by the immense band through which we were travelling conveyed to the mind of the writer the distant surge of the Ocean, or midnight thunder when heard between sleeping and waking. It requires a swift horse to catch them when put to their speed, and yet they move most awkwardly, and it would seem with great labor. Their enormous shoulders and hump rise and fall, reminding one of a tired horse, with a drunken rider clinging to its neck, making a bad effort to canter.

The next day, the third that we passed in company with this great herd, we enjoyed a spectacle still more surprising than any thing we had witnessed. The animals commenced crossing the Arkansas. The strongest instinct with the buffalo, next to its quick

[32] Western travelers and naturalists report a variety of sounds, yet favor "squeals" or "bellowings"—deep, hoarse, or low—as the best description of a buffalo's voice.—Martin S. Garretson, *The American Bison* (New York, 1938).

sense of smell, is to press forward. One will follow the other, and never until the hunter is directly at its side will it break its track. Thus one instant one descended into the water ten followed, and fifty followed the ten, till the whole extent of the river, within our view, was black as the land with the buffalo. We nooned at this spot, and for *three hours* the Arkansas was filled with the buffalo, crossing so fast that they could not stop to drink, lest they should be overwhelmed by the crowd thronging behind.

Those who have paid no attention to the narratives already given to the public relative to this extraordinary animal, will think the writer is exercising the old traveller's privilege, and their unbelief will be perfectly excusable, for indeed the story must seem strange.

The writer only relates what he has seen, but now listen to what he has heard, and what he believes to be true. A party of mountain trappers once, descending the Missouri through a buffalo region with their flat-boats loaded with furs, were compelled to halt *four days,* to allow the passage across the river of a band of buffalo; and, the river being deep and the crowd so great, hundreds were drowned, and their carcasses were afterwards seen by the descending trappers lying among the logs upon the islands and along the banks. The space allowed for our sketch is overstepped already. This subject will require another chapter.

Indians Hunting the Buffalo

Silence, beneath the noon-day sun, is keeping
   Watch o'er the untrod prairies of the West,
Where myriads of buffalo are sleeping,
   Or grazing on earth's green and flowery breast;
And their low bellowing doth stillness break,
   As zephyr moves the lake.

Like the low surging of a distant sea,
   Or like the murmur of a storm retiring,
The sound the creatures utter seems to be;

Nor roar, nor bellow, but a short respiring,
Which, made by millions, low yet awful, seems
  Like thunder heard in dreams!

Count in the milky way each little star,
  Then number the wild monarchs of the scene;
Around the land, to this horizon far,
  The wilderness is black instead of green;
Millions and myriads, unseen, unknown,
  Rove the wild waste they own.

But hearken! Listen! Other sounds are near;
  See far away commotion speed along,
Like dark'ing waves; some wild and sudden fear
  Moves like a storm-lashed sea the mighty throng;
And lazy bulls, rising in sudden fright,
  Stretch their huge limbs in flight!

All that was still and peaceful only now,
  Now is a scene of terror wild and strange;
The solid earth is moving, trembling—how
  Appalling, how bewildering the change!
One vast, black, living mass, in headlong speed,
  Flying across the mead!

The cause! The cause! Look to the sky afar;
  See there the dust rising in sudden clouds;
Hear there the red man's piercing scream of war;
  Mark the wild steed mixed with the flying crowds;
See the swift arrows, flashing on the sight,
  Like truant stars of night.

A thousand hunters, on their fire eyed steeds,
  With barbed arrows, and with bended bow,
Shrieking as each new victim falls and bleeds,
  Are dealing death among the buffalo!
See the wild herds, swift crossing as they fly
  The verge of land and sky.

94

On! On! Now hither, thither wildly speeding,
  Their starting eyes in phrenzy glaring round,
Bends the vast throng, some staggering and bleeding,
  Goring the air and tearing up the ground—
Crossed, turned, cut off, and maddened by the foe—
  Ill-fated buffalo!

See the Camanches, with a fiend-like ease,
  Flying on half-wild steeds about the plain;
Their long, dark scalp-locks streaming in the breeze,
  Red as the sunbeam with vermilion stain;
Now distant far, then instant flashing nigher,
  Like mounted flames of fire!

And see the phrenzied buffalo at bay,
  After his savage hunter madly rushing;
Vainly he fights, or seeks to 'scape away,
  With the red stream from his wide nostrils gushing!
He pauses, staggers, pants, and glares around,
  Then headlong seeks the ground!

Goring the earth, gasping a feeble breath,
  And spouting blood, he falls upon his side;
And soon the quivering agony of death
Leaves his limbs stiff and eyeballs staring wide;
  But ere he yields his parting breath of life,
  He feels the butcher's knife!

Now mark the magic changing of the scene;
  Gone are the hunted myriads from the plain;
The earth again displays its carpet green;
  And some poor hundred buffalos remain;
Some fighting still, some struggling, gasping, dying,
  Around the prairie lying.

Around them see the red Camanches crowd,
  To the huge victim's horns their wild steeds tied,

With flashing knives and yells of triumph loud,
  Tearing the warm skin from his reeking side.
See the red devils, with the brutes' own hoof
  Knocking his hump ribs off!

Thus fall the untamed monarchs of the waste;
  But centuries shall seek eternal rest,
Ere the last, lonely buffalo is chased
  From the wild, grassy gardens of the West.
Then, like the mastodon, a ripped-up bone
  Shall be his funeral stone!

The Wild Horse

We were water-bound at "Walnut Creek."[33] The water was too high to admit of our crossing, and for three days we had remained listless and idle on the bank of the stream. The fourth day came, and still the water continued rising; and as we could not proceed upon our travel, three of us, weary of idleness, determined to start in pursuit of buffalo. We discharged the old charges from our fire-arms, and, having carefully loaded again, we mounted and rode off. As yet we had seen but one buffalo, and that was an old bull, with flesh as tough as leather. We started at eight in the morning, and rode two hours and a half without seeing a thing that had life, except the innumerable musquitoes and flies and ground insects. We rode through beds of sun-flowers miles in extent, with their dark seedy centers and radiating yellow leaves following the sun through the day from east to west, and drooping when the night shadows close over them, as though they were things of sense and sentiment. These beds are some-

[33] Walnut Creek should not be mistaken for Walnut River in southeastern Kansas. The creek joins the Arkansas, flowing into it from the west through an opening in the river's left or north bank. They join at the great bend of the Arkansas between Great Bend and Ellinwood, Kansas. Near by, Little Walnut Creek enters the Walnut from the right or southwest side. Fort Zarah (1864–69) stood near the Santa Fe crossing of Walnut Creek.

times beautifully varied with a delicate flower of an azure tint, yielding no perfume, but forming a pleasing contrast to the bright yellow of the sun-flower.[34]

About half past ten we discerned a creature in motion at an immense distance, and instantly started in pursuit. Fifteen minutes riding brought us near enough to discover by its fleetness it could not be a buffalo, yet it was too large for an antelope or a deer. On we went, and soon distinguished the erected head, the flowing mane, and the beautiful proportions of the wild horse of the prairie.[35] He saw us, and sped away with an arrowy fleetness till he gained a distant eminence, when he turned to gaze at us, and suffered us to approach within four hundred yards, when he bounded away again in another direction, with a graceful velocity delightful to behold. We paused—for to pursue him with a view of catching him, was clearly impossible. When he discovered we were not following him, he also paused; and now he seemed to be inspired with as great a curiosity as ourselves experienced; for after making a slight turn, he came nearer to us, and bounded off again, and still came nearer, till we could distinguish the inquiring expression of his clear bright eyes, and the quick curl of his inflated nostrils.

We had no hopes of catching, and did not wish to kill him;

[34] In July, the odorless western spiderwort (*Tradescantia occidentalia*), sky-blue or azure in color, grows intermixed with the sunflower in the sandy areas of mid-Kansas.—Letter of R. L. McGregor to John E. Sunder, November 15, 1958.

[35] The western wild horse is so encompassed with folklore that it is difficult to separate myth from reality. The earliest wild horse herds evolved from stray animals escaped from Spanish ranches and missions. A few, perhaps, came from exploring parties. Some wild stallions were superb animals, but not all. "The impression is general, however, that the heads of the western herds were those animals showing the characteristics of the best horses of Arabia." Frederic Remington, the artist, believed that "of all the monuments which the Spaniard has left to glorify his reign in America there will be none more worthy than his horse."—Walker D. Wyman, *The Wild Horse of the West* (Caldwell, Idaho, 1945), 27, 41, 305; Robert M. Denhardt, *The Horse of the Americas* (Norman, 1947).

but our curiosity led us to approach him slowly, for the purpose of scanning him more nearly. We had not advanced far, however, before he moved away, and, circling round, approached us on the other side. 'Twas a beautiful animal—a sorrel, with a jet black mane and tail. We could see the muscles quiver in his glossy limbs as he moved; and when, half playfully and half in fright, he tossed his flowing mane in the air, and flourished his long silky tail, our admiration knew no bounds, and we longed—hopelessly, vexatiously longed to possess him.

Of all the brute creation the horse is the most admired by men. Combining beauty with usefulness, all countries and all ages yield it their admiration. But, though the finest specimen of its kind, a domestic horse will ever lack that magic and indescribable charm that beams like a halo around the simple name of freedom. The wild horse roving the prairie wilderness knows no master— has never felt the whip—never clasped in its teeth the bit to curb its native freedom, but gambols unmolested over its grassy home, where Nature has given it a bountiful supply of provender. Lordly man has never sat upon its back; the spur and the bridle are unknown to it; and when the Spaniard comes on his fleet trained steed, with noose in hand, to ensnare him, he bounds away over the velvet carpet of the prairie, swift as the arrow from the Indian's bow, or even the lightning darting from the cloud. We might have shot him from where we stood, but had we been starving we would scarcely have done it. He was *free*, and we loved him for the very possession of that liberty we longed to take from him,—but we would not kill him. We fired a rifle over his head; he heard the shot and the whiz of the ball, and away he went, disappearing in the next hollow, showing himself again as he crossed the distant rolls, still seeming smaller, until he faded away in a speck on the far horizon's verge.

Just as he vanished we perceived two dark spots on a hill about three miles distant. We knew them to be buffalo, and immediately set off in the pursuit.

Pawnee Rock

Pawnee Rock is a precipitous mass of stone,[36] rising, with wild singularity, in the midst of a vast region of prairie, where not another object, tree or rock or shrub, or aught save here and there a white buffalo's skull, spotting the interminable green, appears in view. The effect produced upon the traveller by this solitary knoll, rising slowly as he approaches, until the base appears, and then the wilderness still stretching away beyond, has in it at once all that pertains to desolation, yet something belonging to its very opposite. We were part of an afternoon, and the greater part of the next day travelling with Pawnee Rock in sight before us. As its summit peeped above the horizon we found an object for the eye to rest upon, and this relief to one aching sense gave pleasure to all the rest. Yet when the Rock rose full in view and we saw the same prospect of far spreading green on the other side, our enlivening sensations shrunk back into a still deeper consciousness of our lonely and dreary separation from mankind. Leaving the wagons behind, our small crowd of leisure travellers rode forward to view the Rock. At the base we released our animals from their trappings, and haltered them to the tough roots of clustering plum trees, leaving them to graze while we sought around for an accessible pathway to the summit. This we reached with slight difficulty in clambering, a few scratched knuckles, and our pockets full of cold buffalo meat. Here we seated ourselves upon the rock for a jollification. We killed one rattlesnake and drove away half a dozen others, after which we quietly laid in our preemption right to the territory. From the eminence we glanced around the prospect, munching our cold luncheon with as much

[36] One mile north-northwest of the town of Pawnee Rock, Kansas, a thirty-foot shaft has been raised over this landmark on the Santa Fe Trail. Located just before the crossing of Ash Creek, on the north bank of the Arkansas, the rock is supposedly the site of an early Pawnee-Comanche Indian battle. The Santa Fe survey party of 1825 rode to the top of the "rocky point" for a view of the surrounding country, and it was common for travelers to marvel at the rock's "nearly perpendicular" face and commanding position.—Gregg (ed.), *The Road to Santa Fe*, 71; Margaret Long, *The Santa Fe Trail* (Denver, 1954), 89.

pure exhilaration and pleasure as ever was known by the most systematic gourmand seated at a groaning table of viands. Health and hunger are far more luxurious condiments than any French culinary *artiste* has ever yet invented, and our banqueting hall was of dimensions and beauty that art can never imitate without being lost forever.

Two objects now attracted our attention. Slowly along came the line of wagons, and the prairie breeze brought us, in sounds faint and far between, the drivers' invocations to their mules. From another point a herd of elk stood watching curiously this unusual intrusion on their wide pasture ground.[37] There were about twenty of these fleet and beautiful creatures and among them we could perceive the high branching horns of one noble fellow who seemed to be their leader. He would start away, followed immediately by the rest, speed like lightning for a few instants, and then suddenly turn to pause and gaze again. Nothing could be more beautiful than this sight. The line of traders' vehicles came slowly and steadily on, while the amazed animals would now bound far away, then circling nearer, pause to view the objects of their astonishment again and again, until a horseman darted from the caravan in pursuit, when their alarm was complete, and almost instantly they had disappeared beyond the verging horizon.

Pawnee Rock springs like a hugh wart from the carpeted green of the prairie. It is about thirty feet high, and perhaps an hundred around the base. One tall, rugged portion of it is rifted from the main mass of rock, and stands totally inaccessible and alone. Some twenty names are cut in the stone, and dates are marked as far as ten years back. A very beautiful little Indian legend connected

[37] The American elk is a misnomer. Properly speaking, the name "elk" refers to the European moose, whereas the American elk is of the wapiti group. Originally the American elk lived on the plains of Kansas, Colorado, Oklahoma, and in some parts of northern New Mexico, preferring temperate conditions to semidesert regions. The adult male may have an antler spread of six feet.—Olaus J. Murie, *The Elk of North America* (Harrisburg and Washington, 1951), 3, 20, 57, 80–81.

with this spot was told to us, which shall be embodied in some future sketch.

Legend of Pawnee Rock

The rock is cleft as if by the lightning, and one portion of it stands inaccessible, except by a dangerous jump from the other part. Thus dissevered, this solitary heap of stone bears some resemblance to the huge head of a buried monster, with its jaws open, gasping for air and liberty.

From the legend, as told, and even to this day believed by the Pawnees, it is evident there had been in practice among the Great Medicines a system of imposition very similar to the exploded religious charlatanry of ancient times in other countries. This petrified Gorgon was represented by the priests as the bad spirit who caused earth-tremblings, storms, and inundations of the land. He was at certain times of the year to be concilated [*sic*] with presents, and in hunting seasons especially plentiful stores of the finest buffalo meat were always placed in the jaws of Pawnee Rock before the hunters dared venture upon regaling themselves. When war was to be made, or sickness spread among the tribes, or any calamity or danger threatened the people, the first thing thought of was a pilgrimage to the rock, where prayers and present were duly offered up, and the pleasure of Manito was made known with mysterious solemnity by the priests. Malefactors were sometimes dropped into the bad monster's jaws, tied hand and foot, and left through the night to his [*sic*] fate. Then the next day the whole tribe would return and find the clean picked bones of the criminal scattered about the rock. Of course he had been eaten by the earth fiend, and none but the cunning priests themselves ever suspected the wolves of the unhappy man's death.

They tell also how this monster of stone was once free and used to travel about the land drinking the rivers dry, tearing up the trees, upon which he existed, and tumbling in the night great stones down the mountain side. It was him, they say, who caused the prairies, by eating away the trees and even tearing up their roots, so that they never sprouted again. At length Manito enchained him here in the earth lest he should destroy the red men, and now he is quite harmless, save that now and then he groans and spits forth storms and shakes the earth with struggles to be free.

A terrible punishment, it is said, is sure to fall upon any who are rash enough to interfere with the fate of a condemned criminal, and one little story is told, of deep and pathetic interest—doubtless, too, the relation of an actual occurrence—which we shall here set down, if possible, in the same simple manner in which we heard it.

A white boy, the son of a Canadian trapper who was drowned in one of the forks of the Platte, had fallen among a tribe of Pawnees, and lived with them until manhood found him one of the bravest and most expert of the young warriors of the nation. He loved the daughter of the chief in whose wigwam he had been nurtured, and the devoted Indian girl gave up her whole heart and being to the young American. Though Indian in all his habits and tastes, he yet possessed instinctively the superior intelligence of his own nation, and, though yielding obedience to the superstitious observances of the tribe, his lip curled in derision whenever called upon to practice them.—The priests read these thoughts in the young Canadian's mind, and his destruction was soon resolved upon. Being in high favor with the whole tribe, they could not proceed directly against him, but through the girl he loved, the old chief's daughter, they determined to inflict their first stroke of revenge.

An alarming visitation of the small pox soon afforded the vengeful Great Medicines an opportunity to carry out their designs.[38] They addressed the Great Spirit with mystic rites and

---

[38] Smallpox came to North America with the sixteenth-century Spanish and French and was transmitted by white men to the western tribes. Epidemics, beginning as early as 1778, swept away thousands of Indians. In 1831, there was a widespread outbreak amongst the Pawnee, and as a result an estimated 10,000, or

incantations, and then pronounced to the tribe the will of Manito that the old chief's daughter should be sacrificed to the stone fiend of the prairie. Disputing one of these decrees was a thing never dreamed of among the Pawnees, and the young Canadian knew that to offer even the slightest opposition would be to turn the whole nation against him, even to the very father of his betrothed, and inevitably stamp his own destruction. The priests expected him to oppose the decree, which was the end they aimed at, as then they would have pronounced the same doom upon himself, and nothing could have saved him or the poor Indian girl. So only despair or the alternative of some desperate stratagem was left for the young white lover.

The day of doom arrived, and a mourning train of warriors and women left the village and set forward to the distant rock. The song of sacrifice was chanted at nightfall, and the young betrothed of the white man was consigned to the rocky jaws of her lonely desert bridegroom, while the poor Indians turned back to their homes again, believing the angry spirit was appeased and they would now be released from the terrible disease under which they were groaning.

That night the young white man disappeared from the village and was never heard of more. The Indian legend ends here, and nothing further is told of the forest girl and her lover. But as the traders elaborate the story, it would seem that the lover sought Pawnee Rock in the night, released his betrothed, and, not daring to be seen again among the Pawnees, they wandered about the wilderness, seeking to reach the white settlements of Missouri. Not many years since a rude cross was discovered upon the bank of a small creek which the Santa Fé traders cross in their progress, and upon digging beneath it, the bones of a female were found, together with beads and ornaments such as are usually worn by a Pawnee girl.—This incident has been attached as a

one-half the Pawnee population, died. Stearn and Stearn, in their *Effect of Small-pox on the Amerindian*, declare that the disease was "the chief factor in [Pawnee] decline."

sequel to the Legend of the Rock, and the place is now pointed out as the poor girl's lonely grave. But the most ingenious story teller among the old travellers has never yet attempted to finish the narrative with the fate of the young white warrior.

The Deserted Village

Upon crossing Pawnee Fork we came in view of a deserted Indian town, and as we camped near the spot for the night, we had full leisure to look about and gratify our curiosity. From such dilapidated remnants as were strewed around we judged there must have been about one hundred lodges when the town was tenanted, which was certainly something less than twelve months before our arrival at the spot. Several skeleton wigwams were still entire, and we could observe the manner of their construction, which was according to the most primitive notions of aboriginal architecture. Long and slender twigs were planted in the earth, forming a circle of some six or eight square feet, and leaving a space open to serve as an entrance. These twigs or branches were bound together at the top, forming a frame work to be covered with blankets or buffalo robes as convenience served. This is an old and well-known method of erecting temporary wigwams. Wandering tribes who have no permanent locations, and hunting parties who ride into the buffalo country and camp during the hunting season, construct their habitations after this manner. There is then no necessity for the transportation of tent poles and the other usual conveniences of regular Indian towns.

The Choctaws about our own neighborhood here,[39] where

[39] Before Congress enacted the Indian Removal Bill of 1830, there were 2,000 Choctaws living in Texas, Arkansas, and Louisiana. The greater majority of those living in the lower Mississippi Valley moved west into Indian country during the thirties, but a small group remained near Bayou Lacombe, a few miles north of Lake Pontchartrain in St. Tammany Parish, Louisiana. Possibly Matt had seen them, since he accurately describes their bayou dwellings—rectangular three-sided homes crudely built of saplings covered with palmetto thatch. By the early twentieth century, however, their descendants on Bayou

large trees can be found and stripped, cover these frames with bark, but in the buffalo regions, where bark is not to be obtained, the rough skin of the buffalo forms a far warmer and more efficient thatching for the roof of an Indian's residence.

The fire places drew our attention. These were large holes in the earth, outside the wigwams, some eighteen inches in depth, over which twigs were bent and fastened in the earth on each side. The fire is built beneath the surface of the ground for two or three reasons. One is to keep the dry grass from contact with the flame, which, when once started, at certain seasons, spreads with a rapidity which utterly defies control. Another reason for this is to prevent the fierce prairie wind from carrying away or sweeping out the fire, for when these swift winds are blowing it is in fact impossible to make a fire upon the level surface. The hoops over the fire places were to serve in cooking, and we could observe how meat had been hung upon them to roast.—Feathers, buffalo ribs, a broken pipe or two, a worn-out mockasin [*sic*] and other trifles were scattered about, all of which we found interest in examining, though worthless and commonplace in the extreme. One of the old travellers knew and told us, by these signs and remnants, the whole history of the village. By one mark he knew that the people were Pawnees; another sign showed the object for which they had tenanted the place; again, why they had abandoned it; what was their number, &c. and the amount of his story was that a Pawnee hunting party, numbering some three hundred, had spent a season here chasing buffalo and drying meat for the winter.[40] This object completed, they had but to

Lacombe lived in log cabins covered with planks and shingles.—Grant Foreman, *The Five Civilized Tribes* (Norman, 1934), 22; W. Prichard, F. B. Kniffen, and C. A. Brown (eds.), "Southern Louisiana and Southern Alabama in 1819: The Journal of James Leander Cathcart," *The Louisiana Historical Quarterly*, Vol. XXVIII, No. 3 (July, 1945), 850–51; David I. Bushnell, Jr., "The Choctaw of St. Tammany Parish," *The Louisiana Historical Quarterly*, Vol. I, No. 1 (January, 1917), 11–12, 14.

[40] The Indians cut the meat of their "kill"—usually buffalo—into long thin strips which were hung on a pole framework in the sun. When the meat was

gather their blankets and skins, pack up their stores of meat, and journey home again to their squaws and children. It was a romantic spot, and one also well chosen for a camping place. A precipitous bluff of about one hundred and fifty feet elevation rose from the opposite bank of the creek, forming a natural observatory from whence the Indians could scan the vast plains around and watch for game, or obtain early notice of any hostile approach. The place is called by traders *Pawnee Fork,* from its being an abrupt elbow or point of land forming a turn in Pawnee creek. It has long been a favorite summer resort of the Pawnees, from which circumstance the water probably derived its name. The creek, or river as it is called, is thickly wooded, too, and deer and other game, as well as buffalo, abound in the vicinity. These advantages, wood, water, and game—the three things needful to the red man—make the spot also a usual camping place for travelling traders, no danger being dreaded from the quiet Pawnees in case of an encounter, though they will steal if by neglect any opportunity is left for them.

Huge skeletons of the poor, butchered buffalo lay about the prairie as we pressed forward resuming our journey. Enormous backbones and skulls, ribs and hoofs, and half demolished hides, were fast mouldering and whitening in the sun, speaking of the history of many a successful hunt performed by the wandering red man. Something mournful will touch our sympathies in looking at any spot deserted by the life which once belonged to it, and

Sweet Auburn! loveliest village of the plain,

has not attached to it a more pleasingly pensive interest than may be conceived for a scene like this, a solitary, melancholy, deserted Indian village.

---

dried (jerked), they folded it and stored it for winter use in skin (parfleche) boxes. A full-grown buffalo cow yielded about forty-five pounds of "jerky" and fifty pounds of pemmican, plus marrow and tallow. Pemmican was a mixture of pulverized dried buffalo meat and, if available, dried cherries (pits and all). It was packed in bags sealed with melted fat.—Hodge (ed), *Handbook of American Indians,* I, 170.

The Indian Fort

On the American side of the Arkansas, in a swampt [*sic*] bottom overhung by high limestone rocks,[41] we came upon a grove of tall trees, some still erect, others prostrate, some broken and leaning against others, some splintered from top to root, and all white, barkless, blasted, and dead. The tempest had evidently assisted time in hurrying on the work of desolation. The poor old trees stood like buried skeletons suddenly exposed to the air, looking as if the very sound of our steps would shake the crumbling branches down upon our heads. A singular awe crept over us while passing through this ghostly looking place, but sterner feelings took possession of our breasts when, in the very centre of the old grove, we discovered an Indian fort; a small apartment of about ten square feet, enclosed on three sides by rude walls, composed of trunks and fallen limbs of old rotten trees. The fourth side was left open, but the place was roofed securely with shrubs and branches, some of which were still green, contrasting strangely with the mouldering logs over which they were piled and interweaved.

Here we were told slept the bones of four white men killed by a war party of fifteen Pawnee Indians.[42] The four brave Americans were journeying to the States on foot from Fort William on the Arkansas, a distance of about four hundred miles, and the whole route lying over dreary and desolate prairies. They had with them a single horse to carry their bags of biscuit, their meat when they slaughtered a buffalo, and when the distance from

[41] This "swampt bottom" cannot be located accurately. Perhaps it was the Cheyenne Bottoms, immediately east of the junction of Walnut Creek and the Arkansas. The bottoms held a marshlike lake, drawing in the waters of two creeks. The swamp could have been much farther west along the Arkansas, possibly on or near Chouteau's Island or as far as Big Timber, where windfalls and log ruins were not uncommon.

[42] This story of four white men is a garbled rendition of one or more earlier engagements along the trail. In *Commerce of the Prairies*, Gregg relates several incidents (pp. 16–21); and Duffus, in his *Santa Fe Trail*, tells of others. (pp. 114–32).

107

creek to creek demanded it, also to transport wood sufficient to cook their lonely, melancholy meal. They had grown homesick living in the wilderness for years, and the four together had thus agreed to dare the dangerous journey for the sake of seeing once more their kindred and their friends. The fifteen savages were encamped at this fort in the grove when the Americans appeared, and the four unhappy victims were instantly attacked. One was instantly killed, the other three, by some ingenious stratagem, obtained possession of the fort. How this successful trick was played has never been ascertained, as the story has been derived from the Pawnees themselves, and upon this point they would give no satisfaction. But the Indians acknowledged that these three brave fellows took the fort and kept the fifteen assailants at bay for two days before the knife of the Pawnees touched their scalps. They placed their horse across the unprotected side of the fort, and from behind him two watched, with rifles cocked and levelled, every stump, log, tree, hollow, or rock where an Indian might conceal himself to fire at them, while the third peeped through the crevices among the logs, and guarded the fort from an attack in the rear. This was a wise precaution, for ere long an Indian approached with a blazing torch to fire the wooden rampart, and was instantly shot in the head by the watchful American. The Indians became intimidated by the sudden loss of their comrade, and withdrew to a distance for the night; but the besieged Americans were not aware of this, and with unceasing vigilance watched for their lives during the whole of that long, dreary night.

The next day the Indians were seen skulking at a distance, afraid to approach too near the fort. Horror now in a dozen dreadful shapes surrounded the unfortunate Americans. The stiff and bloody corpse of their slaughtered companion lay in the fort beside them; their biscuit bags and meat had been dropped in the confusion of the first attack, and they were now seen, Tantalus like, lying within a few yards of the fort; the pangs of hunger, the fears of death, each perhaps in turn subduing the other, were keenly felt by the doomed men; and added to this they doubtless lingered in the horrifying conviction that escape was impossible.

At length an Indian succeeded, unperceived, in climbing a tree near the fort, from whence he fired and killed the horse. The Indians say that it was at the death of this poor animal that the Americans showed the first sign of intimidation, and when their horse fell they groaned aloud. Well they might, for even had the unfortunate wretches escaped the Indians, what a task was before them to travel hundreds of miles, exposed to all the dangers of the desert, without even the assistance of their poor horse.

The hunger and despair of the besieged men now aided the savages in completing their work of slaughter. Late in the day one of the Americans rushed madly out from the fort and endeavored to secure the lost food, but, as might have been expected, he was shot down while snatching at one of the biscuit bags. After this the two remaining men were seen by the Indians cutting the flesh from the dead horse, and tearing it raw in their teeth, and while thus employed, abandoning themselves as it seemed to utter desolation, the miserable men were shot dead, and the scalps of the four victims were taken in triumph by the blood thirsty savages.

It is impossible in so small a space to do justice to such an incident, and much of the intense interest with which the writer listened to this story must necessarily be lost in so brief a relation.

The Blind Buffalo

These animals, although numerous, are seldom seen by the travellers, and their strange peculiarity of running in a circle is but little known.[43] Old hunters, who were with us when we hap-

[43] Matt's account of a blind buffalo is one of the few available firsthand records of the phenomenon. Frank Gilbert Roe believes that most of the pitiable creatures were blinded by prairie fires. In *The North American Buffalo: A Critical Study of the Species in Its Wild State* (Toronto, 1951), he notes that Blind Bull Lake in Canada's Northwest Territory derives its name from a buffalo bull which drowned there in 1923.

pened to cross one, declared that it was the first they had ever seen, and their fright was as great as the most inexperienced among us, when the huge beast suddenly left its circle and dashed headlong towards us.

It was soon after commencing our afternoon travel, one warm day in August, that we discovered one of these singular creatures, directly in our path. When it first appeared we were much perplexed to determine what it could be, seeming in the distance no larger than a wolf or an antelope, yet being so deeply black we concluded it must be some other animal. As we approached, however, we soon distinguished the enormous hump and peculiar motion of the buffalo. Still we knew not how to account for the creature's running so continually in a circle, and we supposed it must be battling with wolves that were seeking to slay and devour it. Six of us rode forward, and when about two miles in advance of the caravan we were sufficiently near the buffalo to perceive that there was no other animal, small or large, in sight. We now slackened our pace and advanced slowly, wondering at the extraordinary fancy which seemed to have entered the huge noddle of this wild monarch of the wilderness.

We approached to within three or four hundred yards of the brute, and our surprise still increased at finding that it did not run from us, but all heedless of our presence kept on coursing and widening its circle. The curious sight caused much merriment among us, and, cracking jokes upon the poor beast, we continued to advance, wondering how near his eminence would suffer us to approach before he would take to his heels. Our jests continued until within less than a hundred yards of the solitary old bull, and then our merriment was suddenly changed to utter consternation, for the beast made a quick pause in its circular race, gave the peculiar blow with its nostrils, and then, instead of taking to flight, as we anticipated, it broke from the circle and came running with full speed towards us, with its wild, fiendish looking head bent downwards, ready to gore with its short, thick horn, any object in its path. Our little party, riding so compactly together, was instantly scattered far and wide, and the enraged beast, when it could no longer snuff our presence, resumed its circle as before.

The old travellers who were with us, now remembered the stories they had heard of the blind buffalo, and it was very evident that the creature before us was in this condition, by which its singular conduct was accounted for. The animal was old, its meat was not good, we did not want its skin, and we were tired of the game of killing the poor beasts for mere sport; yet the wagons were advancing, and should the furious beast rush among the mules, great mischief might ensue; so that it became imperative upon us to kill the old blind bull in self-defence.—This, however, we found to be a more difficult task than any we had yet undertaken in the way of hunting, for, though we could without danger, get sufficiently near the animal to strike it with our balls, yet its movements were so uncertain that a dozen shots were lodged in other parts of its body before we planted one in its liver, the most vulnerable spot about the buffalo, and that at which the arrow of the Indian, and the rifle of the American are always aimed. The thick blood gushed now from the bull's mouth, and we gathered near to see the poor brute die.

Weak, and choking with blood, it would pause an instant, start again and run a few steps, stagger, strike at the air with its horns, drop upon its fore knees, and then again rise and dash furiously at the hunter who had ventured nearest. This beast died harder than any that we had killed during the whole journey. It lived full half an hour after the blood spouted from its mouth, and would have lived longer but that we determined to end its sufferings with another shot. A rifle was levelled at the spot directly beneath the shoulder blade, about four inches from the bone, and almost instantaneously with the report, the poor bull gave a short blow from its nostrils and fell, boring its horns into the ground and tearing up the earth in great fury. We dismounted to examine more nearly the sightless orbs of the beast. The head of no other creature that the writer ever saw, resembles so clearly the idea that we are apt to conceive of the devil. Short, thick, curling horns, almost hidden in masses of black wool; eyes that glare like balls of polished ebony, whose very want of expression excites fearful imaginings; and, added to this, the desolate region which is its habitation, where it seems neither to herd or have sympathy with any other creature of God's creation. The eyes of this old bull were not black, but white, and sightless, and issuing humours which seemed to us like tears, as the poor beast lay upon its side, stretching out its limbs in death, and yielding its last sigh to the prairie that it was leaving forever.

Two reasons are assigned for the bull buffalo's loss of sight; the cows are never seen in this condition. One need not be mentioned; the other is, that they are attacked in the night, when they stray alone, (which the bulls often do, but the cows never) by the hungry wolves, and while defending themselves with their horns, their eyes are torn out by their ravenous assailants. When blind, it is only by accident that they can find their companions again; and their habit of running and gradually widening a circle, is probably its means of ascertaining how much ground it can pass over in safety, as were it to press forward in any one direction, it might plunge into a river or swamp. Its singularity of rushing at danger instead of from it (so opposite to its conduct when possessed of sight) probably arises from the influence of despair; not knowing which way to escape, it seeks at once to destroy its enemy.

An Old Bull

One afternoon when the slanting sun-beams were blazing upon the white sand hills, making them seem like onward rolling waves of liquid silver, we came upon a solitary bull that was drinking in the Arkansas. The camp was richly stocked with fine, fresh cow meat, and we were tired of hunting, so that not one of us felt the slightest disposition to start in pursuit, and most magnanimously we resolved to let the bull escape.

Our caravan continued to advance, and still the buffalo remained standing in the water, seeming to feel none of the usual alarm at our approach. Our surprise at this was increased when at last the brute, with that headlong stupidity for which it is remarkable, instead of making for the opposite side of the stream, moved forward and ascended the bank directly at a point from whence it could not possibly escape without crossing our path. Our course lay along the shallow and sandy Arkansas, where the beast might have crossed in water scarcely above its knees, yet it turned, seemingly with a disposition to confront us. We continued to advance, and observed with still increasing surprise the strange leisure which the buffalo seemed to take in mounting the bank, until it stood at last in the path before us, exhibiting not a single symptom of fear. The consequence of this was that the alarm which we did not find as usual in the buffalo, instantly took possession of ourselves, and, not knowing what to expect, we, in some trepidation, drew up our animals and halted.

We were within two hundred yards of the beast, and might have killed it with a single shot, but curiosity withheld us from firing, for so strange a sight we had not witnessed before. A few days previous we had seen a blind buffalo, which is a most dangerous creature to cross, and very seldom met with, but the animal before us was not blind, for its head was partly turned towards us, and its position clearly indicated its possession of sight. After pausing an instant, almost anticipating a charge from the huge brute, we became ashamed of our hesitation, and rode forward. The animal then started into motion and ran from us, but so slowly as still to impress us with much wonder. The cause of this strange conduct now began to be perceptible as we approached, until, having advanced to within thirty yards of the object of our curiosity, as pitiable a spectacle burst upon us as ever caused the chords of sympathy to vibrate within the human breast. The poor buffalo was feeble with old age! It could run no further, and was now walking, tottering along, while we rode within fifteen paces of its side. We gathered around the poor, helpless creature, and he paused in the midst of us. His old limbs were stiff, and he could not move another step.

There, surrounded by his deadly enemies, each with a weapon of death in his hand, forlorn and helpless, stood the monarch of vast leagues of land. The poor old bull was emaciated almost to a skeleton, and the hair had nearly all forsaken his hide. There he stood, turning his head feebly from side to side, looking at his enemies but incapable of moving from them; for the few hundred yards which he had managed to run from the river, had exhausted every remnant of strength left in his fleshless bones.

We had a dog with us which invariably accompanied us when hunting, and we had often seen him outstrip the horses and run barking under a flying buffalo's legs. This dog now came up, and, perceiving the old bull, instantly commenced his favorite amusement of barking furiously and biting at the buffalo's fetlocks.— But the feeble bull could not lift a foot to punish his tiny foe. It seemed as though terror and his late exertion in running (for in all likelihood years had passed since he had before made an attempt at speed) had wrought upon him like a paralysis, and there he stood, showing only by his wildly rolling eyes and the slow turning of his head from side to side that life still remained in his carcase.

There were those among us who could feel and whose hearts were touched with the spectacle; others found only subject for loud jesting and obstreperous mirth; and one, before he could be prevented by the more merciful, with a heart callous as stone, or rather possessed by a fiend, dismounted, bent down before the beast, and discharged a pistol up the unfortunate creatures nostril. His cruel and heartless temerity was within an ace of leaving us a comrade to bury in the wilderness, for the bull's fore knees bent and he plunged forward burying his right horn, with frightful and unexpected strength, in the very spot from whence his heartless tormentor sprang. The shot and plunge were like electricity itself, and it always seemed to us a miracle how our rash and imprudent companion escaped. He rolled away upon the grass many paces before he could regain his feet, and then rose, pale as though he had received the stroke and the life blood had indeed forsaken his heart.

Scarcely less terrified were we, ourselves, and we hastily divided to afford room for the convulsive struggles of our miserable victim. Even human tones of utter and despairing wretchedness could not have been so thrillingly mournful as were the low moanings of this poor tortured animal. The sound conveyed to our senses such misery as we sometimes know in unhappy dreams and nightmares, from which not speedily to awaken seems like certain death; and we would spurn any reality of affliction as a simile inadequate to express the acute oppression which we experienced upon hearing it.

A rifle was levelled at the creature's heart to end its sufferings, but before sight could be taken it rose again, and, with the strength of approaching death, fled wildly toward the setting sun, whose burning disc already kissed its green couch in the far horizon.

The poor buffalo ran full a hundred yards before it staggered sideways and stumbled upon its fore knees, supporting itself in this position by planting its horns again in the earth.—We rode after it resolved to release it at once from such horrid suffering. As we came near, it tore its horns from the earth once more, and struggling to its feet, it turned and approached the foremost horseman. Poor thing! there was no more danger to be feared. The hand of a child then laid upon its side would have pushed it to the earth. A skeleton with a hide thrown over it would have presented as formidable an appearance. It paused, stepped feebly again and paused, and its eyes closed while it yet remained erect. No sound came from it now; its huge head swung loosely on its shoulders, and with a motion scarcely perceptible its horns seemed still goring the air. The muzzle of a rifle was placed against its heart, and with the shot the poor brute fell, venting its last breath with a hollow sigh as the heavy carcase rolled over on the earth.

The wolves had but a poor feast that night, but the old bull's bones were gnawed white enough, no doubt, when the next day's sun rose upon them.

Lazy Hasey

We had a character along with us; a man so strikingly different from every other ordinary mortal, and whose individuality stood out in such bold relief, that his presence added not a little to the novelty and interest of our far excursion. He was a man of gigantic frame, standing full six feet eight or nine, and with an expanse of chest that seemed, as he moved, a small mountain in commotion. There was not one among us who had ever seen such a lazy mortal as this Hasey was. Laziness was his study, and he was really industrious in reducing it to a system. He was a nice connoisseur, too, in the way of creature comforts, and the sole aim and entire reach of his ambition was to excel others in securing most ease at the least cost. He had an old hat, over which he had coarsely stitched and pinned an oil-cloth covering, and when our hats, bought in St. Louis expressly for the journey, were worn out of all shape and rendered nearly useless by soaking rains, he would contemplate his old chapeau in contrast with our ruined beavers, and chuckle with as much satisfaction as a broker would over a favorable fluctuation in stocks, or a conqueror scanning a victory won. The hat had cost him nothing, he had *made* it in some former bargain; the oil-cloth he had begged from somebody; he had been in possession for years of a needle that he once obtained from a Blackfoot squaw; and he boasts of remarkable skill in picking up thread and all such useful trifles here, there and any where. When he got home to Toas [*sic*], (for, though an American, he calls Toas his home and has lived there some fourteen years) the oil-cloth was taken off, and his hat was good as ever, while our expensive beavers were just in that uninteresting condition which fitted them to be thrown away.

Upon approaching a camping place, Hasey's eye was on the lookout for the snuggest shade for himself and the freshest pasture for his old blind horse. He had a horse with only one eye, and he delighted in making the poor beast serve all his purposes, while others were wearing down noble and expensive animals. Slow and easy as he was in everything, Hasey would yet be first man on the camping ground, and before another of the party would be out of the saddle he would have his old horse at stake among the tallest and greenest grass, and himself stretched out in the only shady spot that appeared, if there was one at all to be found about the prairie. In case of a waggon stalling, and a stop being put upon progress, the force of Hasey's philosophic system of laziness would be observable in its fullest perfection. He was himself owner of one light waggon, which contained his entire capital, about $500 worth of merchandise, and this vehicle he knew was always quite certain to pass safely where others, more heavenly [*sic*] laden, were just as sure to stall.

Upon an occasion of this kind occurring, Hasey would take an observation of the difficulty, note what time was likely to be consumed in surmounting the obstruction, and then deliberately dismount, put his old horse to grass, and stow himself away in the shade until the trouble was over, when the extent of his exertion would be to slip on the bridle of his blind Bucephalus, mount, and move off. The admirable coolness of this conduct can only be appreciated when it is remembered that every other individual of the party, except those who might be out hunting, (Hasey never hunted, his old horse was opposed to it) would be dashing about in the sun, and laboring energetically in assisting the traders, anxious that the travel should not be interrupted. But Hasey had plenty of time to spare, and, in fact, he had travelled the road often and knew that he could be a great deal lazier upon the prairie than he could be at home, where now and then, while smoking his pipe, he would be called upon by a bare-footed Señora to get up and cut off a yard of domestic. The Señoras of Santa Fé and Toas invariably wear veils over their heads, manifesting at the same time a most enduring contempt for shoes and stockings. Yet notwithstanding his ineffable laziness, Hasey possessed such prodigious strength of limb and muscle, that when by any miracle he was induced to put his shoulder to the wheel a stalled waggon was as sure to jump from the mire as though a double team of mules had been put into harness.

At a buffalo slaughtering Hasey's manoeuvring to escape labor was especially ingenious. He never went out with the hunters, but whenever a good fat cow was killed in sight of camp he would amble his blind nag along to the spot as though anxious to assist in the butchering. His assistance then amounted to securing for himself such morsels as by old experience he knew to be most delicious to the palate, after which he would remove his huge carcase out of the way and leave room for others to dig in as they pleased. After this the meat, and such parts of the hide as were needed for ropes, &c. were obliged to be carried to camp, and to avoid this duty was of course a part of Hasey's system. So, he would generally remove himself and his old horse to a respectable distance, and there lounge quietly on the grass until the others had packed the last piece of meat and were ready to move, when seeing there was nothing left for him to carry, he would mount leisurely and join the hunters.

Nobody disliked Hasey notwithstanding all this, for he was blessed with an imperturbable equanimity of temper that through every disagreement and reverse always left him quietly in the ascendant, and, while none were at all anxious to quarrel with one of his herculean proportions, his conduct was so invariably free from offence, and he suffered himself with such mild composure to be laughed at and made a butt of for his laziness, that we were bound to afford him regard rather than any harsher sentiment, and while we might laugh at him freely it would have been exceedingly dangerous to salute him with a frown. So Lazy Hasey continued during the whole travel on as good terms with the rest of the party as he managed to maintain with himself, and a very sociable general understanding among us all was the very natural result.

Guarding at night, the worst annoyance of all, was the only one that Hasey had not ingenuity to evade. But still he managed to make himself comfortable on guard, and his skill in doing so exhibited the refinement of his philosophy in a very nice degree. In the first place he would consume one quarter of an hour after he was called before he would get wide awake; then he required another quarter to get his arms in order, the camp fire fixed, and his pipe lit; then he would take a large double blanket, roll it round him, walk about two yards from camp, and there sit down in the grass and smoke his pipe out. Another half hour he would spend fussing about the camp fire, and in this manner manage to be full two hours out of his two hours and a half of duty inside camp, while the companions of his watch were far outside maintaining their proper stations. Still he boasted, and truly, that he never *slept* upon his post, and had a prowling Camanche crept near the encampment, the danger, in all likelihood, would have been first detected by the quick and experienced eye of *Lazy Hasey*.

A Storm

It had been an unclouded day, and the heat was so intense that the flies and musquitoes seemed to have been scorched out of existence, for we were not annoyed by them.—We had been since sunrise travelling a desolate region with not a tree or a sign of water to cheer us. When a buffalo wallow or a marsh appeared, we rushed to the spot and sucked up a mouthful of the stagnant moisture through the little reeds which we carried in our pockets for that purpose, but we could not venture to swallow without instantly ejecting the nauseous liquid. We found swampy places where, in the deep footprints of the buffalo, a little yellow water existed, with which we would moisten our parched lips and pass on. As the sun descended, the clouds began to gather in the west, and the sight of a cloud was refreshing. We prayed for rain, and watched the gathering of dark masses of vapor in the sky with delighted eagerness. From the far western horizon where the sun was sinking, the storm came hurrying on, and the distant thunder rolled like notes of war, while the lightning played among the clouds. It is very possible that such storms had often passed over our heads before, when, sheltered in christian habitations, we took no note of them, but never before had we looked upon the sky with half the wonder and admiration with which we now observed it. Thus every change in life produces its lesson and its wrinkle. We wonder today at our ignorance of yesterday, and deem that we have learnt wisdom, when to-morrow again lays bare new errors, and it is only when life is closing, that our pride bows down to the humbling truth, that all is vanity—vanity—vanity. Some of the preachers will pirate that last sentence from us without a doubt, and they might as well, for to say the truth, it has very little to do with our "storm."

The ragged edges of the driving clouds were red with the fiery rays of the sun, and a vast volcano seemed to be flaming in the sky, that every moment raged more furiously. Louder and nearer the thunder rolled, and as the sun disappeared, the lightning darted more vividly among the clouds, that now spread darkly like an angry demon band, half across the sky. A few heavy drops fell. The swift wind that was driving along the storm above our heads came down, and as it whistled wildly past us, we pulled off our hats to experience a refreshment far, far more delightful than was ever yielded by perfumed breezes wafted by art through oriental halls of luxury. A few moments more, and the black storm had spread far and wide around the sky. Day had departed, and the deep gloom that overshadowed the land, was only relieved by the fearful blaze of the lightning that shot in long quivering flashes all about the horizon, one stroke scarcely expiring ere another illuminated the sky. The heavy clouds hung lower and nearer to the earth, and the sharp rattling peal of the thunder broke so near to us as to leave a singing in our ears for moments after.

The storm burst, and the o'ercharged sky poured forth its torrent over the grassy plains. The wind increased to a hurricane, and drove the falling rain almost horizontally before it. In a very few moments the earth was as soft as after an ordinary rain of several days, and during the night, being upon a very soft prairie, we walked about while on guard, ankle deep in the water. The night was now black as the regions of death, and the rain poured steadily down, but the lightning ceased to flash, and the wind died away. We had now all the disagreeable qualities of the storm, without any of its wildness and grandeur. The burning thirst that had tortured us through the day was now thoroughly quenched, for we were thoroughly drenched, and we wished no more for water. But nature herself is deeply imbued with the characteristics she has given her children, and she is as fond of extremes as the wildest enthusiast that ever lived. For ten hours we had been travelling over a tract of country, and under a burning sun, where not a drop of moisture was to be found, except such as was repulsive to sight and taste. Now a deluge of the longed-for element was around us, and we sighed for the sun to dry the earth, as vehemently as before our parched lips had prayed for rain.

In the course of our five months' travel we had but one other such storm, and that occurred on our return travel on the Mexican side of the Arkansas. But then the icy step of winter had intruded on the green, and the wind from the mountains swept across our path, making real hardship of what before was only a night's annoyance. We were compelled to halt and camp, from the exhaustion of our worn-out animals, at a spot where not a stick or shrub could be found to kindle a fire, and, rolled tightly in our buffalo skins, we lay shivering in uncomfortable dozes until morning. Ten of our mules died during the night, and many of the remaining animals were so broken down the next day as to be incapable of service. The heavy rain pelted upon us through the night, and the thunder rolled dismally in the distance. The lightning gleamed faintly, not blazing through the sky as on the former occasion, but struggling in vain at intervals to light up the deep gloom of the sky. Nothing was heard but the constant dash of the rain, and the desolate moaning of the cold night wind, except when now and then arose the low rumbling of the far-off thunder, as if the angry spirit of the storm was curbed in his wild career. In our camp all was most dreary silence, and our poor animals, hungry and tired as they were, cropped not a blade of grass from the barren spot on which we were compelled to rest, but stood in the darkness, forlorn and dejected, enduring

The pelting of the pitiless storm.

Storm on the Prairie

Clouds are gathering, fierce and black,
O'er the trader's prairie track.
Night is closing, dark and fast,
Round the desert wild and vast.
Sudden stops the caravan
As the sky the traders scan.
Down the west the sun is dashing,
   O'er the head are thunders pealing,
Round the sky are lightnings flashing,
   Wild sublimity revealing!

Down upon the prairie land,
Like an angry spirit band,
Press the thunder-laden vapors,
Quenching even's starry tapers.
While the far off mutter comes,
   Louder still and nearer swelling,
Like the battle-call of drums
   From the storm-fiend's misty dwelling.
By the lightning's fitful lamp
Soon is formed the trader's camp.

Now above the fearful yell
   Of the tempest, wildly shrieking,
In successive roar and swell,
   Jove is heard in terror speaking!
Lurid lightnings, far and nigh,

Flash and quiver round the sky.
Mute the desert pilgrim stands,
Awe-struck and with clasped hands,
While above his shrinking form
Breaks at last the prairie storm!

Now like hail-stones on the plain
Heavy beats the pelting rain—
Driven far before the blast
   That goes howling on its course
O'er the lonely region vast
   With a voice so wild and hoarse.
Darkness like the pall of death
   Yields an instant to the flash
Of the lightning; human breath
   Pauses for the coming crash!

Like a phantom through the sky
Hear the peal go rattling by,—
Sharp and loud, and wildly clear,
Ringing on the trader's ear,
Rending earth, and bursting near,
Like a thing of death and fear!
O, how brightly morning beams
Over plains and over streams
When the prairie storm is gone,
"When the hurly burly's done!"

Night Guarding

It is midnight, and the moon does not rise till one. A hand is laid upon the shoulder of a sleeper, who, stretched upon a buffalo robe, with a saddle beneath his head and a blanket above him, is enjoying that slumber which is the attendant only of true weariness. After a shake or two and a name being called, the sleeper utters a grunt expressive of dissatisfaction, and then exclaims, perhaps, with a pause and start,

"Hallo? Who's that?"

"Come—guard!" is the reply.

The aroused sleeper, after a stretch and a roll and perhaps a hearty oath, throws off his blanket and pulls his rifle from beneath his buffalo robe. After securing his arms, and belting, perhaps, a thick blanket coat around him, he moves toward the expiring camp-fire, when he examines his watch to see that he has not been called too soon, or perhaps pulls a pipe from his pocket, which having duly filled and lighted, he places in his mouth, and then off he goes, disappearing in the gloom to take his station outside the camp. An instant or two elapses, and the relieved guard is heard whistling some merry dancing tune as he comes from duty, to amuse himself a few moments, throwing fresh sticks on to the fire, perhaps exchanging a joke and a laugh with some messmate who has been awakened by the disturbance of changing guard, or perhaps he digs into the ashes for an ear of corn which he had left there to roast when he went out to guard, and now he plumps down cross-legged before the fire to enjoy a delicious midnight lunch.—Half of the hot ear is probably broken off and thrown in generous sportfulness at his waking messmate, who instantly seizes and devours the favorite morsel, throwing back in return, perhaps, a pocket liquor flask by way of "acknowledging the corn." This little affair being arranged, the returned guard draws his solitary buffalo bed a little nearer to the fire and disposes himself for the remainder of his nights slumber, talking facetiously to an imaginary wife, telling her to lay over and not use both pillows, to give him more room, draw the curtain, and behave herself. Such are very apt to be his closing words as he drops to sleep, and in a few moments the camp is again wrapped in silence.

Now let us pay a visit to the guard whom we have just despatched [*sic*] on duty. There he stands in the dark, leaning upon his rifle in utter silence, by the side of the farthest mule staked outside of the camp. What can the eye distinguish in the darkness? Knowing the wagons are there, you can discover their

white tops, but otherwise you might fancy the faint light came
from some clearing away of the clouds in that direction. In addition to this, you recognize a man's form and a few of the nearest
horses and mules, all else is black. What is heard? The mules
munching the grass; if it is near a water course, the ripple or rush
of the wave; if buffalo are near, you hear their low bellowing,
like a distant ocean surge, or like wind moaning through hollow
caverns; perhaps an opposite sentinel whistles or sings a merry
air, but this might serve to guide an enemy and is not often indulged in; these sounds you *may* hear, but at times death itself
is not more solemn or more still.

Hush! Observe! The mule beside the sentinel lifts its head
from the grass, gives a short blow with its nostrils, pricks back its
ears and stares before it into the darkness. Mark the sentinel!
The instant he observed the action of the mule he crouched upon
the ground and cocked his rifle, and now observe with what intent
watchfulness he peers into the pitchy depth in search of danger.
Suddenly a foot step is heard approaching, and instantly the stillness is broken by the quick challenge of the sentinel.

"Who goes there? Speak!"

The answer shows the person to be the captain or sergeant of
the guard, taking his solitary walk round the encampment; and
now the sentinel is sure to want a dry cap for his rifle, or a bit of
tobacco, or the loan of a pipe, any thing to detain the sergeant a
few moments in conversation; and should the sergeant be in a
sociable humor, perhaps they may both sit down upon the grass
and while away fifteen minutes in guessing how long the travel
will continue to be through the dangerous country, where the
disagreeable duty of guarding is considered necessary.

The sentinel is again alone, and, hush! Again the grazing mule
shows tokens of alarm! You hear the faint click of the rifle as the
guard suddenly cocks it, and again he prostrates himself in the
grass, with his head cautiously raised and his eye fixed in the
direction indicated by the gaze of the startled mule. Something
moves—no: the silver moon is rising, but the light is yet so indis-

tinct as to be even more perplexing than the darkness; but something *does* move. It is not the waving of a tuft of grass in the night breeze, for it has changed its position. The guard is certain of this, and steadily keeping his rifle aimed at the moving object, he gives the challenge,

"Who goes there? Speak!—Speak!"
and his forefinger is curled around the trigger to fire, when he takes an instant more to pause, and as the moonlight falls more clearly upon the earth he becomes aware that the intruder is a wolf prowling around the camp in search of food. Relieved from his alarm at the same moment that the cheering moonbeams come to enliven his solitary duty, the sentinel laughs at his mistake, and perhaps examines his watch, peering closely at it by the moon, or feeling the hands with his finger, to see how long he has got to remain on guard.

And how gloriously does the moon rise upon the prairie! How beautiful is the moon, rising in any clime or upon any scene! But that sympathy, that notion of companionship which some spirits seem to find in the silver night Queen, can never appear so like a real and actual influence as when you are removed far from your fellow men, and feel yourself alone in the wilderness. Then you see that heaven still smiles on you though man is distant, and your soul whispers that the God that made you can be as near, perhaps nearer, to you there than when walled around by a circle of friends and kindred. The moon is a sweet chastener. It may be a silly love, yet it is harmless to love the moon.

Death of Bernardo

Poor Bernardo was a Mexican youth of about twenty-two, who sometime before had left his relatives and his home in the beautiful valley of Toas to traverse the wilderness and look upon the great republic of the United States. This was all we knew of him. He joined our party at Independence, and in the capacity of cook travelled with us to seek his home again. He attracted little attention at first, for we were all absorbed in new thoughts and sensations, created by the daily changing prospects, as we slowly receded from civilization into the wild regions we were about to traverse. When however the novelty began to wear away, when the prairies stretched before us day after day the same, then poor Bernardo became an object of much interest. He never uttered a word, but performed his duties daily in melancholy silence. We could never learn whether he was ignorant entirely of English, or what other reasons caused his reserve, but it was evident that sickness or melancholy, or perhaps both, were preying sadly upon his spirits.

When about twenty-nine or thirty days from Independence, Bernardo, who had ridden all day in his usual silence, dismounted from his mule in the evening when we stopped to camp, and rolling his blanket around him lay down upon the grass. *"Mala! Mala!"* sick, or bad, was all he would answer to our inquiries. We gave him medicine, which he swallowed without uttering a word of objection or approval. The next morning his mule was saddled for him, he mounted without assistance, and with not a moan or syllable of complaint he journeyed on before us in the same gloomy silence. We watched him during the day hoping to learn the true nature of his ailment, and in the evening we gave him medicine again, such as we supposed would be of service to him.

The next day a region of prairie lay before us where water was not expected. Ten gallons was all we could carry with us, and that was exhausted before noon. 'Twas a day in July, and the scorching heat seemed as though at each moment it would kindle the grass into flames. Bernardo drank from our supply of water as long as it lasted, and soon after it was gone we missed him from among us. As the sun was setting we reached the Arkansas, and there we found poor Bernardo sitting at the water's edge, with his pale face turned to the west, and his glazed eye fixed upon the departing day. We spoke to him in the gentlest tones of kindness, yet "Mala! Mala!" was the only answer he would give us.

That night we were aroused by a confusion among the sentinels, and upon inquiring we learned that they were alarmed by a figure moving in strange haste through the camp. Some excitement, of course, ensued, and we soon discovered Bernardo sitting again at the water's edge drinking. *"Agua! Agua!"* Water, in feeble, melancholy tones, was now his reply to our questions. He had rushed to the river to quench the raging thirst of the fever that was destroying him.

He lingered two days longer, and expired.—*"Mala"* had been his only cry of complaint, *"agua"* was his last word. We buried him near Choteau's Island on the banks of the beautiful Arkansas.[44] Poor Bernardo! Among strange men, speaking a strange tongue in the lone wilderness, he breathed his last. Where had been his thoughts in that long silence he had kept during our thirty days travel? He had doubtless felt the approaches of death, and in lonely hopelessness had brooded over remembrances of a mother's tones of love, a sister's kind caresses. Perhaps some young affection blighted lay in his heart like a withered leaf preserved in the pages of a favorite book. Many sweet thoughts are daily buried in the grave that have never yet been enshrined in song.

Yet poor Bernardo has a glorious grave. The murmur of the Arkansas sings his requiem by day and night; the wild flower of the prairie shall bloom over him uncultured; and though no mother's tear shall fall upon his grave, yet the rude foot of man will not disturb it. He needs no recording stone to tell the roving buffalo his name, and, alas! alas! perhaps the wolves discovered him without the aid of chiseled marble! It may be that his own whitened bones mark his resting place, and the creeping worm must wait for existence until the hungry animals that were feasted yield their own bodies to the scythe of time. Poor Bernardo!

---

[44] Choteau's Island was at the upper crossing of the Arkansas (Hartland, Kansas). Named after a French trader, the "forested island" was well known to Indians and whites alike.—Riddle, *Records and Maps*, 50; Hulbert (ed.), *The Santa Fe Trail*, 31.

The spot known as the *"Cache"* is about three hundred or three hundred and fifty miles from the last log house in Missouri, and about one day's travel from the "Crossing," which is the fording place on the Arkansas where the traders cross to take the Semirone road to Santa Fé.[45] Two stories are connected with this spot, either of which is sufficient to render it one of especial interest to the traveller. From the first of these stories the place derives the French name by which it is known, and interesting evidences of both stories still remain upon the spot; one being a deep hole in the ground, and the other an iron cannon broken into two parts, either of which is as much as a strong man can well manage to turn over.

The road or track, running parallel with the Arkansas, crosses at this point a dry sand creek, and in a high knoll which projects into this creek the hole appears which is called the *Cache*.

Here, five years ago, a caravan of traders were surprised by the appearance on the other side of the river of a large marauding party of Pawnees.[46] An encampment was instantly formed, and every preparation for defense made which the time and the nature of the ground would permit. In the night, while the camp was carefully guarded by sentinels, the cache was dug in the knoll, and their most precious goods buried and hidden in case

[45] The Cache or Caches were approximately five to six miles west of Dodge City. Santa Fe traders James Baird and Samuel Chambers, in the autumn of 1822, dug at the Caches large, jug-shaped holes and hid their goods in them. The outlines of the holes remained as landmarks for later travelers, and Forts Mann, MacKay, and Atkinson were built close to the site. Susan Magoffin, who traveled to New Mexico in 1846, described the Caches as "situated about a quarter of a mile from the River, on rather an elevated piece of ground, and within a hundred yards of the road, which runs at present between them and the river."—Magoffin, *Down the Santa Fé Trail*, 53–54.

[46] This is another of Matt's embellished versions of some earlier action. Since the article was written in 1840, the attack, five years before, must have been between 1834 and 1836. Those years, however, were not violent ones on the Santa Fe Trail. Most of the men killed on the route were killed earlier. Perhaps the attack should be placed in an earlier period.

of defeat. Day dawned, and the Indians had crossed the river, and were spread around the prairie, completely surrounding the camp of the Americans. During the whole of that day, each man stood rifle in hand, watching with perpetual vigilance, the Indians hovering at a distance. Night descended, and not daring to sleep, the besieged Americans watched until day again appeared. No fires were kindled, as lights in the camp would enable the Indians to steal near undiscovered and take sure aim at any form too carelessly exposed. And thus the night dragged on in dreary silence, broken only now and then by the sudden report of a sentinel's rifle discharged at something in the darkness which his excited imagination shaped into an enemy. Toward morning, however, one of these shots was followed by a sharp stifled scream which told the traders that they had at least one red skinned enemy the less.

The horses and mules of the Americans were confined within an enclosure formed by the wagons, and as the main object of the Indians was to get possession of the animals, they could not be suffered to graze and receive their natural sustenance. This day passed off as the day before, the cowardly Indians not daring to advance to the attack until advantage favored them. When night again came the traders ventured to lead out the poor brutes to graze, as to allow them to starve in confinement would be as bad as to be robbed of them by the Indians. Under a strong guard the animals were led forth, while the most spirited beasts were secured by long halters and held by the armed sentinels, who with cocked rifles watched around for any approach of danger. As was anticipated the Indians soon became aware of this movement and resolved upon an effort to secure the booty. Mounted upon their half wild horses a hundred Pawnees approached the camp in silence, until within a sufficient distance to distinguish the position of their prey and the best plan of securing it; then raising their blood freezing war whoop and striking their spurs into their horses' sides, they dashed past the American camp, endeavoring to terrify the animals and drive them off before them. But the

Courtesy George F. Green and the Native Sons of Kansas City, Missouri

MAIN STREET, INDEPENDENCE, MISSOURI, IN FRONT OF COURTHOUSE, 1845

"The town of Independence is the principal meeting and starting place from whence traders set off for Santa Fe." After a contemporary sketch by W. L. Pynchon.

From a daguerreotype in the Missouri Historical Society Collection

MATTHEW C. FIELD AND WIFE

Matt married Cornelia Burke Ludlow, the daughter of his good friend and theatrical sponsor, Noah Ludlow.

traders understood this mode of attack and were prepared for it, and while one half of the men held in the frightened animals, the other half levelled their rifles at the flying forms of the Indians, and many a death scream arose in the night air, mingling frightfully with the yells of the red assailants.

Emboldened by this successful defence the traders next day determined at all hazards to proceed upon their journey, as starvation stared them in the face to remain thus besieged where they were. So, leaving their valuable goods concealed in the cache lest they should still be conquered by the Indians, they struck camp and moved off toward Fort William. For three days the red robbers of the prairie followed upon their trail, harassing them night and day; but they eventually succeeded in reaching their destination with but the loss of two men, who rendered desperate by thirst, ventured too far from camp in search of water. Some months after the traders returned and opened the cache, from which the goods were removed and the deep hole remains open to this day, warning the traveller of the perils which surround his path.

The story of the broken cannon is as follows. A large caravan, comprising nearly two hundred souls,[47] was moving along the Arkansas, when early in the morning a party of twenty left the main body to go in pursuit of buffalo. The caravan journeyed on and camped at this spot, when in the evening nineteen of the hunters returned, having spent the latter part of the day in a fruitless search after their other companion who had strayed away and was lost. While daylight lasted the wilderness was scoured in every direction by the traders, but when night lowered and still

---

[47] According to Gregg's statistics in *Commerce of the Prairies*—the best figures available—it was rare for two hundred or more men to be engaged in the trade in any one year. Prior to 1839, such large numbers of men participated on two occasions only, in 1828 and 1831. The Smith-Jackson-Sublette party of 1831—eighty-five men, not two hundred—carried a small cannon—and encountered a large band of Blackfeet and Gros Ventres near the Arkansas.—John E. Sunder, *Bill Sublette: Mountain Man* (Norman, 1959), 95–98.

there appeared no signs of their lost comrade, it was determined to discharge the cannon that the report, if possible, might reach him and give him token of their whereabout.—This was done, and the cannon exploded, flying into two pieces in the midst of the camp, yet fortunately and almost miraculously, not a soul was injured. It served the purpose, however, for the lost man heard the report and soon after found his way into camp on foot.

He had killed a cow near the river brink, and while taking the meat was surprised by the appearance of five Indians, from whom he happily escaped by plunging into the river before he was discovered, and concealing himself among some rotten logs. The Indians found the newly slaughtered cow and instantly commenced searching for the concealed trader, who would soon have been dragged from his hiding place, butchered, and scalped, but that they in turn became alarmed by the appearance of the other American hunters, searching for their companion, and the Indians now fled, taking with them the horse which they found tied by a halter to one of the horns of the dead buffalo. The unfortunate hunter, not daring to peep from his concealment, was wholly unaware of the flight of the Indians or the near neighborhood of his own companions, and supposing that the five savages were watching for him, he remained all day up to his chin in the water with his head concealed among the drift wood. Even when night descended, knowing the deliberate and persevering cunning of the Indians, he did not dare to leave his hiding place, and in this miserable situation he still remained, when faintly the distant explosion of the cannon reached his ear, and he crawled from the water, chilled and sickened by five hours intense terror and watchfulness. By speeding as fast as his weakened limbs would permit him, in the direction from whence the sound came, he soon caught sight of the camp fires; and the poor hunter, who it is said was one of the merriest and most light-hearted of men, knelt down and wept when he found himself once more among his companions.

Crows and Arrappachos

During a fierce and bloody contention which raged a few years since between the two Indian tribes mentioned in this caption, the following rascally and treacherous deed was perpetrated by the Arrapachos [*sic*].

Crow messengers, carrying overtures of peace, were received with every manifestation of honorable treatment by their sanguinary and villanous enemies. Still it was demanded that the ten Crows coming to offer peace should be met by only the same number of the opposite party, and the requisition was acceded to at once in a manner seeming to promise the utmost honesty of purpose.

The ten warriors of each side met upon an appointed spot, the peculiar location of which forbade the possibility of a treacherous collusion with ambuscaded numbers belonging to either party. The Crows really and honestly longed for peace, which the Arrappachos needed quite as much; but the poor Crows, harassed to extremity themselves, were not aware how far their fierce enemies might be in the same predicament. The red Arrappachos, however, could not resist an opportunity of gaining advantage by treachery, and their savage cunning could not fail them on an occasion like this.

Arriving at the ground, they walked to a distant tree, depositing their rifles against it, and, by action, demanding that the Crows should do the same. The example was immediately followed, and the twenty men met and sat down together, apparently in anticipation of nothing but calm and honorable council. The subtle Arrappachos then pointed to the knives still in possession of the Crows, flinging their own, at the same time, to the foot of the distant tree. This example was, also, instantly followed by the Crows, and now the party sat together, stripped, as it seemed, of every instrument of mischief. But it was not so.

The scheming and dastardly Arrappachos had each an extra knife concealed under his deer-skin hunting shirt, and, having cunningly taken positions alternately between their unsuspecting foes, every one had his opponent at advantage, and only waited for the previously arranged signal to strike.

The signal was not long in coming; and the ten Arrappachos, (each snatching out his concealed knife and seizing a Crow by the throat) with a simultaneous and diabolical war-scream, plunged the steel up to the handle in the hearts of their miserable and unfortunate enemies! The horrid and wholesale murder was effectual and instantaneous, and the villanous red rascals returned to their war-camp, with yells of triumph, and bearing away the rifles, knives, and scalps of their miserably misled victims!

Adam and Eve

We "nooned" one day at a singularly wild and beautiful spot. Two tall trees, with intertwining branches, stood in the bend of a shallow creek, and all around the vast prairie there was not another shrub or any vegetable sprout taller than a grass blade to be seen. None of the old traders could tell us any name by which the spot had ever been distinguished, and a merry companion, who has been named before in these sketches, rode up to the bank beneath the trees, and, flinging the contents of his canteen among the branches, he called out *"Adam and Eve,"* and we all said "Amen!" to the christening.

The creek was nearly dry, and what water we could find was warm and sickening to the taste from lying without motion in the sun. We had scarcely, however, unpacked for nooning, when the sky, that had been some time clouding, let fall a smart dash of rain, while the sun still peeped out brightly through broken scud and cumuli. Few will conceive the exquisite and refreshing sensations we experienced in lounging passively on the grass in the midst of this summer shower. We turned our mouths upward and received the raindrops fresh from Heaven to quench the thirst of our parched throats. Iced wine, drank while luxuriating upon an ottoman in a chamber fanned by perfumed winds, was

never half so delicious, half so delightfully yet harmlessly in-
toxicating. Had a palace been open to us we would not have left
our grassy resting-place, and we looked up at the glorious canopy
above us with hearty and sovereign contempt for the most gorgeous shelter that art ever created.

We came in view of these desolate trees the day before reaching them, and during ten or fifteen hours they formed a singularly interesting point in the prospect before us. At first there
appeared a little bush peeping above the far horizon's verge, and
as we advanced it seemed to grow until the two trees stood in full
relief against the sky, and the embracing arms of *Adam and Eve*
formed a wild and romantic arch, beneath which the prairie pilgrims passed upon their road to Santa Fé. There was sublimity
in the spectacle. It was neither a triumphal arch of costly marble,
erected in honor of a conqueror, that he might pass beneath in
his victorious car; nor was it a rustic interlacing of boughs to form
a passage for the procession attending on a rural May Queen or
a village bridal party; but the two trees seemed to stretch out
their meeting branches as though to shake hands in the wilderness! In the midst of the wild and trackless plains an arch arose
curiously woven by the queen of architects, Dame Nature. And
the trail of the adventurous traders from the States to Mexico
passed beneath this desolate and lonely gate-way. Not the faintest sign of another tree could be detected all around the vast land
scape, and a strong feeling of desertion and loneliness was forced
impressively upon us by the distinct and unusual character of the
scene.

The sky cleared again, after a brief and lively summer shower,
and almost like the flashing of powder, went up the moisture in
steam again to the sky to be drank by the thirsty sunbeams. We
eat then, and slept, and awoke to find our drenched garments as
thoroughly dried again as though we had only been dreaming of
a shower and our refreshment was only visionary. The fancy was
good in our companion to christen the trees as *Adam and Eve,*
though a longer thought might, perhaps, have suggested a still

more appropriate sponsorial; the spot, however, is likely to retain the name, as we not only placed a document recording the event in a safe place, but marked one tree deeply with the name of *Adam* and the other with that of *Eve*. If our valuable record has not yet been found by any passers, it may, perhaps, have been eagerly devoured by some literary squirrel, and if the squirrels have left it alone, then any future traveller, who may happen to glance at this sketch, can climb up *Adam* and look in a hole under his left arm, where he may, perhaps, "hear of something to his advantage."

After the christening, the rain, the dinner, and the nap, we packed up and packed off upon our travel again, bidding adieu to Adam and Eve, and leaving them there, locked in a lonely and life-long embrace in the wide prairie. Often and often did we turn to look back at this singular spot, and indeed the idea of the banished children of Eden was irresistibly called up by the sight. The utter desolation of the two trees, clinging together in the wild solitude, was so like the picture of man's fall—the disobedient couple, wandering out upon the yet unpeopled earth, when the gates of the garden were closed upon them forever.

> *Both in subjection now*
> *To sensual appetite, who from beneath,*
> *Usurping over sovereign reason, claimed*
> *Superior sway.*

If the traders do not take our hint and call the place *Adam and Eve*, they will display a shocking absence of taste and fancy, and it will serve them right if the trees wither away and the creek dries up completely, leaving them without wood and water, and so spoiling one of the prettiest camping places between Little Blue and the Arkansas. Catlin,[48] it is to be supposed, has never

[48] George Catlin (1796–1872), celebrated western artist and interpreter of Indian customs, went west as early as 1830. Although trained in the law, he turned to painting and in 1839 took his Indian collection to Europe, where he remained for many years. He returned to the United States as an old man and died in New Jersey.—George C. Groce and David H. Wallace, *The New-York*

visited the spot, but any artist of pencil, whose love of the sublime can lead him to make a pleasant little pilgrimage, should see these two trees and place them upon canvas, when he will be master of a treasure worthy to accompany Dubuffe's celebrated work of *Adam and Eve*.[49]

A Night Scene

Dark and heavy masses of vapor are floating about in the near atmosphere, while the depth beyond seems like a vast illuminated palace of gems. Now the moon rides into a blue gap, and the shadowy earth is bathed at once in a flood of silver radiance.— What objects are now discernible? There, with their white tops glancing in the moon beam, see the traders' wagons clustering in a group. See the dark forms of the mules and horses grazing near the wagons; and hear the sounds, the stilly, subdued sounds, so expressive of content, which they make in tearing the green pasturage from the earth, and chewing the juicy mouthful, with their noses lifted in the air. What form sits yonder? Something is crouched in the grass, and muffled in a blanket. Does it move? Hark!

Click! It is the sound produced by the sudden cocking of a rifle, instantly followed by the abrupt demand of "Who's there? Speak!"

"Guard;" is the answer. "Your time's up; go in."

"Is it half past one?"

"Exactly. At what time does day break?"

"Four o'clock. Don't go to sleep now."

"Go to thunder. Jerry, lend us your pipe."

Historical Society's Dictionary of Artists in America, 1564–1860 (New Haven, 1957), 115–16.

[49] The French painter Claude Marie Dubufe (1790–1864) had a successful early career in Europe and in 1835 exhibited a number of his works in New Orleans. He may have had a studio there, but no direct evidence "has been found to support this assertion." Matt's familiarity with Dubufe's work suggests that he saw the painter's exhibit of 1835.—Groce and Wallace, *New-York Historical Society's Dictionary of Artists,* 191.

"Well now take care of it, Jim; you see its the same old thing, and Charley broke the bowl off yesterday; you see I've tied it on again and plastered it up with clay: if you don't handle it monstrous cautious you'll have it to pieces again."

"Don't get yourself in an uncomfortable situation now, Jerry; I'll take care of your old broken necked pipe, and be hanged to you. Go and creep into your blanket and shut up."

"Well, Jim, don't be frightened if a Camanche should invite you to part with your hair; just call me; you know I promised your mother to take care of you."

"Yes, Jerry, come when I call you, do; be sure you take hold of the right end of your rifle, and don't forget to cock it before you fire; taking care not to shoot more than two of the wagons at the first shot!"

"Don't waste your ammunition, Jim: you have charged your wit with wet powder, and it has got off at half-cock now. You know your rifle kicks, and you're always hurting yourself."

"What's that?"

"Yes: put it in your pipe and smoke it:—good night."

"Hallo! Jerry!"

"Hallo!"

"Don't forget to put your boots outside the door."

"No: and see you clean them better than you did yesterday; good night; we'll go to supper in the morning."

And in three minutes Jerry was couched on a soft place in the grass, snoring in his blanket; while Jim was anxiously engaged trying to join the bowl and stem of the pipe, which he had already broken in an effort to get in a charge of tobacco.

Again the heavy shadow of night enshrouds the scene as the full-orbed moon plunges behind the dark masses of rolling vapor. The camp fire, replenished by Jerry ere he lay down in his blanket by its side, is now crackling and sparkling in the midst of the vast prairie solitude,

As shines a good deed in a naughty world!

Jim has come to the fire, endeavoring by its light to reunite the old pipe, but, finding the attempt fruitless, he at last, with a subdued oath, puts the bowl in his pocket, the stem into sleeping Jerry's open mouth, and then contentedly walks back, whistling, to his station on guard.

Night on the prairie! How peacefully sublime, how sternly beautiful is night, even when the thickly clustering tenements of men are round us, 'troops of friends' near us, behind us the memory of well spent days, and meek-eyed Hope still beckoning in advance! But in the desert, where the circling horizon kisses the land around, and the stars are seen peeping from the very verge —at times causing the gazer to hesitate, lest the distant light should prove to be a red man's camp fire—there the majesty of night thrills solemnly that still, small questioning, which, when listened to and received into the heart, proves the source of our best and noblest qualities. There in the wild solitude the voice of man's doom seems speaking in the thunder tones of eternity. The battling of the elements is not half so solemn as the stilly moonlight; the canopy of azure mellowed by the moon; the ever preaching stars; the bending heavens, that seem here nearer the earth, as if guarding the lonely wanderer more closely in his desolation.

Beauty is here shrined in sublimity; and so Jim was probably thinking, as he sat upon the grass, muffled in a red double blanket, nursing the lock of his rifle from the dew, and gazing sentimentally upon the sky. A half an hour passes in grave-like silence, and the three men on duty walk round the camp, counting the animals as well as the light will permit, greeting each other, stopping, perhaps, to chat, wondering how many days of travel are yet before them, and so on, until the round is made and their solitary stations are resumed again.

Hark! (See Jim cock his rifle, drop on his knee and listen!) It is the murmur of the buffalo, like spent echoes of thunder, sounding near. Some travelling herd is approaching; they have discovered the white wagon tops and are halting in alarm. When day dawns there will be sport for the hunters.

The heavy clouds have left the sky, perhaps attracted by some storm that is gathering far away; and now look to the east. Is light appearing, or does the hopes of the weary guard cheat him into belief that he sees the dawn?—

You need not pause to answer, for see, already the grey light is marching up the acclivity of heaven.

> *Streaks*
> *Do lace the severing clouds in yonder east:*
> *Night's candles are burnt out, and jocund day*

stands, not tiptoe upon the mountain, but comes blushing from a prairie couch of green, gemmed with the starry tears that hang quivering upon every blade.

Bang! "Wake snakes, day's abreaking!"

"Hallo, what's the matter? What did you fire for?" asks Jerry, popping out his head from the blanket.

"For you to get up and see daylight," replies Jim, catching up the corner of Jerry's blanket, and rolling the sleeper out on the grass.

The camp was soon alive; and just as the burning disc of the sun displayed its edge in the east, we, with our faces still westward, were pressing forward on our journey.

Big Timber

Within a days travel or so of Bent's Fort, upon the Arkansas, we reached an oasis to which we had long been looking forward. For weeks we had been revelling in anticipation upon the charms of this delightful place known to the old traders as Big Timber.[50] When exhausted beneath the blazing heat of the prairies, the older travellers would tell us of Big Timber, of the ancient trees,

[50] See article footnote 18.

the cool stream, the gushing spring, and the near neighborhood of Fort William, where we would meet the hospitality of Christian brothers.

From a dreary waste where we had encamped the night before, where a stagnant yellow pool furnished our drink, and the grass, closely cropped by the buffalo, left our poor animals starving through the night, we started, with the distant trees of Big Timber just in sight. The want of pasture for our poor, four-footed servants had broken their energies, so that our progress was slow in the extreme, but about two in the afternoon we arrived at the long promised land of rest and refreshment. Here the expedition with which we released horses and mules from harness and turned them loose upon the rich grass, and flung ourselves, some into the stream, some beneath the trees for slumber, displayed an alacrity surprising after our long hardship. Vast sunflower beds spread far and near around the spot, and tall carpets of juicy grass contrasted their emerald hue with the bright yellow of the sun-worshippers. A thick forest of venerable trees sheltered us from the heat, and beneath them wandered a stream yet cool with the mountain snow.[51] From the bank a spring gushed, shooting its crystal water far across the hurrying tide of this young tributary to the Arkansas. We saw the wild deer bounding from shore to shore and scarcely wetting a foot; and among the sunflower beds the huge back of a buffalo here and there was seen, as the ponderous brute broke down the stalks before him while pressing forward to a fresher pasture ground.

We were wearied down to the last gasp, and recklessly abandoning all ordinary precaution, we drank and bathed, and in the luxurious languor that followed we dropt beneath the trees and slept.

From this delicious slumber we were all simultaneously aroused by a long, shrill scream *a la* Camanche, and we sprang to our feet

[51] Any one of several streams could be the one in Big Timber, but most likely it is a branch of the Rush Creek–Big Sandy Creek network near Lamar, Colorado.

to find ourselves heartily laughed at by our good natured Captain, who had himself been sustaining a solitary guard while we spent two hours in sleep. The sun, a vast blood-red ball of fire, was just about to plunge over the western precipice, when we hastily rubbed our eyes and stared about us. Perceiving the animals quietly grazing, the Captain heartily laughing, and feeling ourselves wholly unharmed, our momentary alarm soon gave place to sundry well understood hints from our craving inner man. A fine cow was in sight among the sunflowers. Three of us, rifles in hand, soon determined upon fresh meat for supper, and in less than ten minutes, the ground affording us every facility, we "crawled" upon the cow and tumbled her over among the sunflowers.

That night we had a glorious feast. We toasted our distant friends in hot coffee with as much exhilaration as we could have derived from the pure juice of the grape itself. The choicest meats of the cow were subjected to extra culinary touches, and there was not one among us who would have changed his seat upon the grass for a place at the most sumptuous board in Christendom. Here was revelry in its gayest and brightest form, smiled upon by heaven through the silver glances of the moon, and not a draught was drained that could return a sting upon the morrow. We laughed, sung, and jested until midnight, when, leaving the cows hump to boil over the fire, we raised an extensive cloud of smoke from burning "buffalo chips" to keep off the musquitos, and couched ourselves for the night.

Our late supper gave us no nightmare, and, having resolved to waste the next day in rest, we slept until the morning sunbeams kissed off the dew from our blankets, when, after a merry bath in the creek, we made short work of the poor cow's hump, which was sweet as sugar, while it cut like new cheese.

If any reader of this little sketch should ever visit Santa Fé, let him cut the Semirone track and visit Fort William, just stopping one day to luxuriate at the little garden bower of the West, Big Timber.

Robbery of Fort William

A party of some three or four hundred Camanches succeeded in robbing Fort William of a valuable stock of horses and mules a few months before the time of our visit.[52] Fort William was founded six years ago by William Bent, of St. Louis, after whom it is called.[53] To afford facilities in the extension of their mountain trade, and to lend them security against the Camanches and Pawnees, William Bent and his enterprising brothers commenced and completed this remarkable stronghold, far away upon the banks of the Arkansas, four hundred miles from an American settlement, and in the very heart of the great wilderness of the West. Although built of the simple prairie soil, made to hold together by a rude mixture with straw and the plain grass itself, the strength and durability of the walls is surprising and extraordinary. Though Indians should come in swarms numerous as the buffalo, Fort William would prove impregnable, for the red devils would never dream of scaling the walls, and if they should their sure destruction would follow, for the building is constructed with all the defensive capacities of a complete fortification. Round towers,[54] pierced for cannon, command the sweep

[52] According to Farnham, who was there in July, the robbery occurred in mid-June. He estimated the Comanche force at sixty warriors and believed the Bents lost one man plus fifty or sixty horses and mules. A passing trader, E. W. Smith, stated: "Mr. Bent had several horses stolen from the fort . . . by a party of the Comanchee [*sic*] Indians, nine in number."—Farnham, *Travels* (Part I), 164–66; J. Neilson Barry, "Journal of E. Willard Smith While with the Fur Traders Vásquez and Sublette, in the Rocky Mountain Region, 1839–1840," *The Quarterly of the Oregon Historical Society*, Vol. XIV, No. 3 (September, 1913), 258.

[53] Although Charles Bent reputedly planned the fort, his brother William (1809–69) built it and was principal manager, and from him the post took the alternate name of "Fort William." Upon the retirement of William's partner, Céran St. Vrain, in 1848, William became sole owner of the post. Ten years later he gave up the mountain trade and ranched at the mouth of the Purgatory River, but, when his second wife died, he returned to Missouri. In 1867, he married a third time and two years later died at Boggsville.—Ghent, "Bent, William," in the *Dictionary of American Biography*, II, 206–207.

[54] The towers, each probably sixteen feet in diameter and thirty feet high,

all around the building, the walls are not less than fifteen feet high, and the conveniences to launch destruction through and from above them are numerous as need be. Two hundred men might be garrisoned conveniently in the fort, and three or four hundred animals can be shut up in the corral. Then there are the store rooms, the extensive wagon houses, in which to keep the enormous, heavy wagons used twice a year to bring merchandise from the States, and to carry back the skins of the buffalo and the beaver. Besides which the great wall encloses numerous separations for domestic cattle, poultry, creatures of the prairie, caught and tamed, blacksmith and carpenter shops, &c. &c. Then the dwellings, the kitchens, the arrangements for comfort are all such as to strike the wanderer with the liveliest surprise, as though an "air built castle" had dropped to earth before him in the midst of the vast desert.

To the hospitable courtesy of Robert Bent we were indebted for several days courteous and really delightful entertainment.[55] The fatted calf was killed for us and the hoarded luxuries of Fort William were produced. The tenants of the fort were merry fellows, we were a set of youths well worthy to shake hands with them, and as such meetings, to the lonely sojourners in the desert, were indeed much like "angels' visits," the time was mutually appreciated, and by no means suffered to pass unimproved.— Among many stirring incidents pertaining to this adventurous life, related to us while at the fort, Mr. Bent told us of the death of one of his men and the severe loss he had sustained by the Camanches a few months before.

---

stood at the northeast and southwest corners. They were "properly perforated" for cannon and small arms and commanded the adjoining plain. Excavation reveals that the tower walls were over two feet thick.—Dick, "The Excavation of Bent's Fort," 194–95; Farnham, *Travels* (Part I), 162.

[55] Robert was sixteen when he went west in 1832 with his brothers Charles, George, and William. He served loyally the family business on the Arkansas and was killed by Comanches in the autumn of 1841 while accompanying a wagon train bound for the fort.—David Lavender, *Bent's Fort* (New York, 1954), 131, 189.

The brothers were at the time absent on one of the upper forks of the Platte, trading with the Pawnees, and the fort numbered only twenty tenants. It was just at sultry noon day, when the full flood of heat and light poured over the scene, the voice of the wind was mute, the insect ceased to hum, the wave of the Arkansas to murmur, and mid-day rivaled the night in hushed and breathless repose. The huge gate of the fort swung wide upon its hinges, and the whole stock of valuable animals—swift horses for hunting buffalo, strong mules for labor, etc., under care of a single Spanish guard—grazed in confident security, at some distance, but within sight of the watchman on the battlement. Demonstrations of danger had been of late unusual at the fort, and a degree of carelessness had grown upon the inmates, which, combined with the rapid movement of the marauders, was the cause of the fatal result which followed.

Suddenly the dozing inmates of the fort were startled by the war shriek of three hundred Camanches, who appeared upon the opposite bank of the Arkansas. This was exactly in the wrong place either to attack the fort or capture the stock; but the cunning Indians had skilfully laid their scheme. Almost in the same instant a faint cry reached the fort from the cattle guard, and before the alarmed tenants of the fortress had issued from the gate, all the animals were seen in full flight down to the green bank, over the Arkansas, and away, driven before some twenty red devils on wild horses, while the hapless Spaniard who had been on duty was seen to stagger towards the fort, and fall with three barbed arrows quivering in his body. These twenty Camanches, on their swiftest horses, had cautiously gained a position unobserved from the fort, from whence they could pounce upon the stock; and at the instant that the wild yell was raised by the main body, this smaller band broke from their concealment, shot down the brave fellow who would not fly his post, and successfully drove the frightened animals across the shallow bed of the river, and then swiftly out of sight.

We were shown the three arrows plucked from the body of the

145

dying Spaniard. The point of one of them had pierced from breast to back, and only after death was the murderous missile extracted. The iron point—the long, tough stick—the feather, bound tightly in a slit with deer sinew—all were red with the victim's blood, and as sad mementos of the unlucky event, they were preserved within the fort.

Seventy-five valuable animals were thus swept away from the fort, and five minutes scarcely elapsed from the first cry of alarm until the receding Camanches disappeared with their booty on the far horizon. The men at the fort were left without an animal to mount in pursuit, and so like a swift stroke of lightning came the misfortune, that, save bringing in the dying Spaniard and closing the gates, not another action of the inmates followed the alarm.

Sham Indians

Great merriment was excited one day in camp by a capital joke that four of the drivers played off upon a fifth. The young fellow upon whom the trick was practiced had made himself remarkable in camp, and somewhat disagreeable among the men, by an assumption of more than ordinary daring, amounting at times to an offensive affection of superior metal. Some indications at length appeared which gave rise to suspicions that the young Missourian was not quite so formidable an individual as he seemed anxious to pass for, and these growing stronger, the opinion was soon whispered round that Joseph (for so was he called) was decidedly the opposite of what he set up for. This idea was no sooner broached than its truth seemed evident to every one, and a prospect of fun immediately presented itself.

We had crossed the Arkansas at Bent's Fort, and the labor of the animals having been most severe, dragging the huge vehicles through the soft bed of the river, (eighteen mules were required to one wagon) we camped for rest upon the opposite side at a little after noon. Here was a clear half day of leisure for the men, and they had not lounged upon the grass long after dinner

BIG TIMBER, ON THE ARKANSAS RIVER

"When exhausted beneath the blazing heat of the prairies, the older travellers would tell us of Big Timber."

BENT'S OLD FORT

"Two hundred men might be garrisoned conveniently in the fort."

From Commerce of the Prairies, *by Josiah Gregg*

ARRIVAL OF A CARAVAN AT SANTA FE

"The arrival of a caravan from the States is an affair of much en-livening interest."

before they began to feel uneasy for some excitement. Mischievous glances were cast sideways at the blustering Joseph, and it was very evident the men were dying to extract some fun from him by drawing out and exposing his real character. Jo was a round cheeked, fresh and innocent looking young farmer, who, it was said, had run away from some log village on the outskirts of Missouri, on account of a girl who had not treated him ill, but whom he wished to tease for loving him too well.—He was lusty, and about nineteen or twenty, with a large mild eye, soft cheek and downy upper lip, and

> *That alluring look,*
> *'Twix man and woman,*

which is very apt to make a young fellow impudent and a coquette among the girls. We found out afterwards that he loved the girl sincerely and sorely repented of his folly. His disposition was naturally soft and kind, but unguided impulse had suddenly plunged him into waters very different from those he was wont to navigate. He had probably been told, as young travellers in these regions always are, that reckless daring and desperation was the only protection upon the prairies, that might was right, and pistol and Bowie-knife made up the only law. So, with the same rashness which had urged him to abandon his home, he now suddenly resolved to adopt a new character, and endeavor to make up by impudence for his conscious lack of moral stamina.

Joe was observed to be gazing wishfully at a dense cluster of trees on the river bank, darkened with a thick undergrowth of shrubbery, and he presently said he thought plums were there and he would like somebody to go with him and see.

The idea that was wanted came like a flash at this moment, and the wink was exchanged almost simultaneously among the men, who, from constant knowledge of each others habits and thoughts, seemed at once to jump upon the same conception. One indolently volunteered to accompany Jo in search of plums, while three others started off in a different direction, with their rifles of course, as if in search of game. These three men were no sooner removed from view than they took advantage of a hollow in the prairie to turn back, and moving briskly along, concealed themselves in the wood before Jo and the other driver, who managed to gain time for the scheme by delaying his steps, arrived at the place. Jo carried a musket,[56] which his companion had contrived to relieve of its load, lest he should by accident turn out a hero and hurt somebody.

"Jo," said Charley, the driver, a facetious fellow, "what would you do first if a war party of Camanches should break out here upon us from the woods? We are out of sight of camp, and here we are, you and I all alone."

"I aint afraid of any six Camanches that dare come before me," said Jo, "I only want to see a few of the red devils once, that's all, and I'll show you what I'll do first!"

A short conversation of this nature was continuing between them, and Jo had got entangled among the bushes hunting for plums, when a loud shrill scream arose, followed by half a dozen terrific yells, and several dark, naked figures were seen bounding directly toward the two drivers from the wood. Poor Jo jumped as if he was shot, and making a dart, he tripped in the tangled underwood and fell heavily upon his face. Up he scrambled with his nose streaming blood, and leaving his musket upon the ground, he ran for camp, bellowing as if a dozen arrows were already quivering in his body.

The best of the fun is to follow. The three drivers had stripped of their clothes and daubed themselves from head to foot with mud, so that they resembled Indians completely. They had charged their pieces without ball, and now seeing Jo flying, they fired after him, accompanying the report with another volley of wild screams. Nothing had been preconcerted, and the joke now turned on the driver, Charley, who was with Jo, for it not oc-

[56] The musket, a hand firearm, was a weapon common to both military and civilian use. Early muskets were fired by a match or matchlock; later designs used a wheel lock, flintlock, or improved percussion lock.

curring to him how his friends had managed their disguise and loaded their pieces, he could not account for the firing, and concluded real Indians were actually at his heels. So, in undisguised terror, he started after Jo, and ran for camp, expecting to catch a bullet or an arrow in his back at every step.

Again the fun took another turn. We had been dining at the fort, five of us, and had just rode across the river when the firing took place, and Jo came rushing into camp covered with blood. We made instantly for the wood with our rifles in rest, and the three drivers seeing us coming, were filled at once with the utmost consternation, fearing to be shot down for Camanches before they could make themselves known.

Explanations were soon arrived at and the joke understood, but to Jo the trick was never revealed, and during the remainder of our travel we were continually amused with poor Jo's recital of the perilous adventure; he assuring us upon his honor that he distinctly saw seventeen naked Indians, and showing us a wound upon his ear where a ball had whizzed past and scratched him.

Pueblo de Leche

The Milk People are a community residing in a mud fort on the Arkansas about four hundred miles this side of Santa Fé.[57] They are composed of the dark skinned, half Spanish half Indian tribe, who inhabit Toas and the Department of Santa Fé,[58] and

[57] *Pueblo de Leche* (El Pueblo or Milk Fort) was located four or five miles above Bent's. Matt's description of Milk Fort, given in this article, is one of the best available. F. A. Wislizenus, E. Willard Smith, and Farnham all passed the settlement the same year as Matt and left accounts. Wislizenus remarked that the settlement was called "Peebles Fort," and Smith explained that the inhabitants "procure flour from Towse [*sic*]" and "raise a small quantity of corn for their own use." Farnham added that the community's homesteads consisted "of a series of one-story houses built around a quadrangle, in the general style of those at Fort William."—F. A. Wislizenus, *A Journey to the Rocky Mountains in the Year 1839* (St. Louis, 1912), 141; Barry, "Journal of Smith, 1839–1840," *The Quarterly of the Oregon Historical Society*, Vol. XIV, No. 3 (September, 1913), 259; Farnham, *Travels* (Part I), 173.

[58] In July, 1824, the Mexican Republic granted territorial status to the

there cannot exist in any nook or corner of the wide universe, a wilder, stranger, more remarkable collection of human beings for a civilized eye to look upon. The pencil of old romance would fly from forest cave and daring freebooters, and find here in real life a scene more full of all the best ingredients for its colors. A rude mud built fortification rises in the very center of a trackless wilderness hundreds of miles in extent, and a part of whose confines are even yet unknown, and here a knot of beings of so wild a race as to create in the beholder ideas of what men were long centuries ago, men

> *Who look not like the inhabitants of earth,*
> *And yet are on it,*

reside, unknown to the world, and seeming to claim neither knowledge or kindred with any tribe or nation in existence.

Milk Fort is so termed from the number of goats possessed by its tenants, and the quantity of milk so procured, which is always sure sustenance when buffalo or other game cannot be found. In case the fort should be besieged by the wandering hordes of Indians, these milk people could exist a far greater length of time than the marauders could be content to remain in one spot. But of this there is no danger, for the men are brave and daring as the Camanches themselves, of whose wild nature, indeed, they seem to partake, and they could sally forth and battle successfully with any war party of ordinary numbers. They possess the fleetest horses, and sit them as though they had been cradled in the saddle, and to say they were would perhaps be but a literal fact, for the writer saw once a Mexican woman making a little naked infant cling and balance itself on a horse's back, with its arms and

---

Santa Fe region. Twelve years later, under the constitution of 1836, the area was given departmental government and remained a department until the end of Mexican rule. The departmental governor had extensive powers. The departmental council (*junta departamental*) was a small, elected body.—H. H. Bancroft, *History of Arizona and New Mexico, 1530–1888* (vol. XVII of *The Works of Hubert Howe Bancroft* [39 vols., San Francisco, 1882–90]), 310–11; Twitchell, *Leading Facts*, II, 54.

legs, while the animal was walked about by the bridle. The poor little innocent creature could not yet walk, and its little fat fist grasped instinctively the horse's mane with ludicrous earnestness. The men of Milk Fort are also full as expert with the bow as the Indians, and, although provided with fire arms, they kill more buffalo with arrows than with ball.

How to describe this strange fort and its nondescript inhabitants is somewhat perplexing.—There are about thirty houses, of small dimensions, all built compactly together in an oblong square, leaving a large space in the centre, and the houses themselves forming the wall of the fort, into which there is but one entrance, through a large and very strong gate. Some of these houses have an upper story, and the rooms are generally square, twelve feet from wall to wall, more or less, with the fire place in the corner, where it is found most convenient to construct the chimney up through the mud wall. These rooms are whitewashed and look enough like Christian apartments to surprise us, while we remember that they are constructed of mud, and, in the way of comfort, they are really desirable, being cool, like cellars, in warm weather, and in winter close and warm. The best way, perhaps, to convey an idea of the people will be just to describe our entrance through the great gate and the scene that then presented itself.

Half a dozen boys and men ran and took our horses, pulled off the saddles and head gear with swiftness that excited our wonder, and in an instant our animals were haltered and led into a corner of the fort, where a feast of corn shucks lay piled upon the ground before them. We looked around us, and the first thing that took our attention was the women suddenly appearing at every door and window in the place to look at the strangers. They were generally rather neat in their appearance, though the men, with scarcely an exception, exhibited the reverse.—Their dress consisted of just three articles, a common domestic undergarment, a coarse petticoat, and a long, narrow shawl thrown over the head. They were combed and seemed to take delight in showing off their raven hair to advantage. Most of them were blotched and disfigured with vermilion, their cheeks, nose, forehead, all horridly daubed with it, but some, who had taste enough to abstain from this vile Indian custom, were really pleasant looking females. They were all much taken with us, however, and crowded about us chattering Spanish in a manner most bewildering to American ears.

But the men held aloof from us, perhaps not liking the attention bestowed upon us by the women. They kept their eagle eyes bent upon us from under their dark brows, but did not rise from the ground, where they were chiefly lying outside the doors, smoking their clay and stone Indian made pipes. Dogs, goats, cats, tame coons, tame antelopes, tame buffalo calves, kids, and jack asses were about in all directions, and little children were on their backs kicking up their heels and playing with the animals. A stout little rascal near us was bellowing "Madre! Madre!" to come and punish a juvenile buffalo who had hit him a butt and knocked him against the wall.

The men generally had beards at full length, and long hair flowing over their shoulders, which, together with their dark skin and piercing eyes, gave them a truly wild and ferocious appearance. They were armed also, some with, some without pistols, but not one was without his large knife; and as they lounged about the ground they were employed filing up arrow heads from bits of sheet iron, cutting and trimming the long sticks and fixing the delicate feather at the end.

We remained one night in this fort, that we might note all its singularities, though not without experiencing some awkward sensations relative to the black-looking fellows who were around us. We had been told, however, at Fort William that these men were not to be feared, being of peaceable character, and living entirely by hunting and trading now and then with friendly Indians. Once or twice a year they travel to Santa Fé, sell skins, and buy necessaries. Just before night closed in a confusion was heard, and a man with a tremendous voice called out for the corral to be cleared. Instantly there was a rush among the women to catch up the children, and run with them into the houses, and the next moment the whole stock of horses and mules, "full of the pasture," the rich pasture of the prairie, was driven through the wide gates and into the center of the fort. Here was a scene! Before we knew it we were wedged in among the animals, and had no small work to extricate ourselves, for the stock completely filled the corral. The heavy gate was now strongly barred and fastened, and we found ourselves secured for the night within the walls of *Pueblo de Leche.*

The Salt Pond

We had started on our travel at day-light, having breakfasted at half past three A.M., in the dark. Our prospects now were dreary, for from this spot, former travellers had told us we would have no certainty of water for four days. Our ten gallon keg was accordingly filled and packed carefully for transportation. We travelled comfortably enough until the sun began to pour upon us at 10 A.M. Frequent applications were made to the keg, and by four in the afternoon our last drop of water had vanished. Our party here consisted of eighteen efficient men—we say efficient, because, although there was another member of our party, he was in the most frightful stage of the consumption, and, heaven rest him, poor fellow, he is since dead. To stop and camp where there was no water was out of the question, and our only course was to travel while light lasted. The sun was low in the heavens and still the desolate prairie stretched before us. The mountains, the gigantic hills crowned with their caps of snow that for ten days had been slowly rising on our sight, were now towering before us, and the sun went down behind them.[59] Worn and weary as we were, enduring the pangs of hunger, thirst, and

[59] These would be front ranges of southern Colorado and northern New Mexico (the Spanish Peaks area). Since Matt's party was going south-southwest, the Raton Range—snowy peaks visible sixty miles north of Raton Pass—was directly before them. To the west-southwest they saw the Sangre de Cristo Range.

bodily fatigue, we paused in silent wonder to view that glorious scene. The golden god sunk down behind a peak of snow that reared its towering head in solitary grandeur over the surrounding ridges; and as he disappeared the live rays shot high into the heavens, making the cold mountain resemble a fiery Vesuvius. Slowly the flame-like brilliance faded away, and we watched the varying tints of the floating clouds as we rode along, until, forgetful of our desolate situation, Cynthia had risen into the heavens and starry night had flung its silver mantle over the green prairies of the west.

Long endurance makes men callous to suffering. We were not at this moment half so hungry as we had been at noon. But a dull sensation of pain in the head began to steal upon us, and though we felt not the raging thirst we had experienced during the day, yet we longed for water. Few, very few know what it is to feel the pangs of thirst. We had lived long and never before had conceived the most distant idea of the torment. A mine of gold would have been freely exchanged for a pond of water, and yet on, on we went with the same dull, dreary prospect before us.

We separated, and rode about in different directions in hope of finding water. Again and again we met and parted with the same success. Nine o'clock was near. Our jaded animals could scarcely crawl, and we were ourselves fit to drop from our saddles, when we heard a loud shout before us; one of our companions had found water—it could be nothing else. We struck our spurs cruelly into our stumbling beasts, for we felt no pity then, and dashed forward to the spot. We found our companion prostrate upon his face drinking from a shallow, whitish looking pond. We flung ourselves from our saddles and instantly imitated his example, while the mules and horses rushed over our very heads into the water. Long and deeply did we drink, and paused and drank again, taking the water in swift, hurried draughts that we might avoid tasting it, for the first swallow had told us it was brackish, sickening, and salty.

Our thirst was quenched; and we sat by the side of this filthy swamp pond, gazing at it while we rested, as though it was a thing to love and admire. The deep foot prints of the buffalo were thick in the soft soil around us—they had been the last visitors before us. And perhaps never before, since the green grass carpeted the wild prairie, had the step of man been on the spot; or had the lip of human being quenched its thirst in the briny water of *The Salt Pond!*

The River Styx

We have fair reason to presume (as we are not aware of any former penman having touched upon the same portion of far western travel with which our sketches are connected) that it will be a new thing to tell how the waters of Acheron[60] flow through the Mexican prairies. One hundred and seventy-five miles this side of Santa Fé we crossed the river Styx;[61] and the son of Erebus and Nox, old Charon,[62] culpably neglectful of his duty, was not there to attend us. The low stage of the water may have been the occasion of his absence, as we had not the smallest need of a ferry, and scarcely sprinkled our stirrups as we rode across.

We were puzzled to think how such a stream could ever have been christened with such a name, for every thing about it was decidedly the opposite of gloomy. The water rushed and sparkled over rock and pebble, and the sunbeam glanced freely through

[60] The River of Woe in Hades or, more generally, any rivers associated with the lower world.

[61] The Spanish name for the river was, originally, *El Río de las Ánimas Perdidas en Purgatorio* (the River of Souls Lost in Purgatory). It took its name from the near-by Indian defeat of a Spanish expedition. The French called the river the *Purgatoire;* modern maps prefer "Purgatory." The early Anglo-Americans in the area, however, pronounced it "Picketwire." The stream flows in a general northeastwardly direction and enters the Arkansas about fifteen miles east of Bent's Fort.

[62] Erebus was a "deity of the lower world, sprung from chaos." He married Nox (or Nyx) his sister. Old Charon, their offspring, "conducted the souls of the dead in a boat over the river Acheron to the infernal regions.—Harry T. Peck (ed.), *Harper's Dictionary of Classical Literature and Antiquities* (New York, Cincinnati, and Chicago, 1896).

the overhanging boughs, irresistibly conjuring up images of life and gladness, while it was impossible to look upon the scene and form an associating idea of darkness or of death. The name was used, we observed, in Spanish, and from that we concluded that some wanderer from Santa Fé had journeyed to this point in early times, and, looking upon the unknown bourn at which we had arrived, and the trackless region that lay beyond, stretching away to limitless Missouri, he named the water Styx, and made his way home again as fast as possible.

It was an hour past noon when we arrived at this place, and, the crossing being extremely awkward for the wagons, we, travellers of leisure, dismounted and bathed in the lethean waters, truly forgetting all former hardships in the refreshing enjoyment. Our description of this spot may furnish interest for some, perhaps, but only those whose warm natures kindle with novelty and delight, as did our own, may appreciate the heighth [*sic*] of our captivation.

With some difficulty we descended a rocky and precipitous bank to reach the water. An old tree rifted by the lightning was there; and there, clustering around the dead trunk in beautiful contrast, spread a luxuriant bed of flowers. A beetling cliff hung above us, and beneath, the very image of a sportive child, rolled the merry chrystal stream. Hours of leisure were before us, and around us spread the loveliest scene in nature. The shallow water and scattered rocks made swimming impossible, but we couched in the tide and suffered the swift, cool current to rush over our limbs. We thought then of dear ones far away, not sighing to be with them, but wishing that they could be with us. We footed up our accounts with fortune and chuckled with the thought that the balance of enjoyment was in our favor. There we were, a set of reckless, aimless wanderers, floundering in the river Styx, as happy a set of care-for-naughts as ever drank rapture from the eye of beauty or the bowl of Bacchus.

A long, striped snake glided past us in the water, and slipped in among the flowers upon the green bank. So poison is ever creeping through the regions of delight, watching a chance to sting.

Within the infant rind of this small flower
Poison hath residence, and med'cine power!

We quickly abandoned our aquatic sports, but health and gladness followed our noonday plunge in the merry waters of Styx.

Imallahokes

At a western military post bordering on the great prairies, and in the near neighborhood of several Indian tribes, the following laughable adventure occurred.

A young officer was famous for his power of imitating Indian character, and had practised many humorous jokes among his friends, by means of the remarkable skill he possessed. On one occasion, when relating an exploit recently accomplished, a lady boasted that he could not impose upon her. She had seen enough of the Indians herself, and understood their character and manners too well for any white man ever to deceive her by an imitation. The young soldier bowed, and changed the subject.

The lady, not long after, was hostess of an entertainment, to which, of course, our hero was invited. He could not attend;—an unfortunate call of duty summoned him away upon a journey of many miles, and he was compelled reluctantly to decline being present where his heart, at any rate, was certain to remain. The husband of the hostess was our hero's superior officer, but quite as ready to join a bit of fun as to serve his country in the face of death and danger. He was made a party in the plot. The young officer had lived much among the Indians, seemed intuitively to conceive their very ideas, and could, in fact, by dressing, painting, and acting, make himself so perfect a resemblance of an Indian, that neither Indian or white man would dare to say, at three yards distance, whether he was one or the other.

The lady was informing her husband of her great regret that

the entertaining young officer was called away, when he took the same occasion to say that an Indian delegation, headed by a celebrated chief, was expected to arrive immediately at the fort, and he had some idea of introducing the red aborigine into the company, as he might amuse and fill the vacancy caused by the other disappointment. The fair hostess went into ecstacies at once. Nothing could be more delightful. She entreated her husband to invite the warrior by all means, and also, by way of a novel surprise, she requested that no intimation of his coming should be given the company until the moment of his appearance. This, of course, was agreed to, and preparations for the evening went on. The party assembled, and all was getting on agreeably, when the host, who was the officer in command at Fort L——, was suddenly summoned to meet an Indian delegation which had just arrived, the great chief *Imallahokes* desiring to see him immediately. The lady hostess instantly created a great bustle and excitement among the guests, by requesting her husband not to leave the company, but to have the big Indian brought in, provided he was not really dangerous. The ladies all agreed to this, manifesting a great deal of delightful trepidation and curiosity to see the distinguished savage. None were in the plot but the hero himself and the master of the house, and the penetration of the lady was not called into action by even the faintest shadow of suspicion.

The grand introduction of illustrious *Imallahokes* into fashionable society took place, and never was a debut more successful. The young man entered, painted and dressed completely—silver ornaments hanging about him, vermilion streaks upon his face, feathers in his hair, and every point of Indian character attended to with nice elaboration. The warrior was offered a chair, which he took up and curiously examined, seating himself upon the floor in the meantime, and preserving a solemn silence. The company was next entertained by a very serious conversation, in the purest Pawnee lingo, between the host and his red guest; for the commanding officer at Fort L—— was understood to be a proficient in several Indian tongues, and on this occasion he was of course expected to be polite to his red friend. The ladies listened to every sound that fell, as though each gutteral accent was a gem to be stored away in memory.

Supper was announced, but *Imallahokes* could not be prevailed upon to sit at table. He accepted a turkey, and sat down in a corner to demolish it, tearing off legs and wings with his teeth, in the most scientific method of Indian dissection. The young officer all this time was enjoying with intense satisfaction the remarks in relation to himself that were passing about among the company. Every body spoke with perfect freedom, judging, of course, that they were not understood. This, however, was nothing to what occurred soon after, for it happened that the supper party adjourned to another apartment to dance, while a group of some half dozen ladies remained to see *Imallahokes* digging the stuffing out of the turkey with his fingers. So well was the character sustained, that all idea of suspicion was still as distant as ever.

"Won't you take a glass of wine with a pretty white squaw, Indian?" said a jocose young lady, disposed to have some fun, and presenting a glass to the sham chief.

He took the glass, tasted the wine, drank it off, and then "grinned horribly a ghastly smile," frightening the fair wag half out of her wits.

"What a well-made fellow he is!" remarked the hostess—she who had boasted that no white man could impose himself upon her for an Indian. This was such particularly fine fun for the young officer that he could not resist chuckling, and then, to disguise the laugh, he broke out with a war whoop, upon which the ladies ran screaming out of the room, leaving him to enjoy the merriment with which he was bursting.

One thing annoyed him;—he was passionately fond of dancing, and his disguise completely prevented his joining in that part of the sport. He had intended to carry the thing through without disclosing himself, but this was too great a trial for his firmness. He bounced into the dancing room, and commenced a fantastic display of Indian contortions, placing himself in the middle of a cotillion, while the dancers moved aside in amused astonishment.

Here a serious termination was put to the affair. His own wife was in the room, as utterly unconscious as the rest that the supposed Indian was her husband. Growing excited with the successful trick he was playing, he thought to give a finishing touch to it by kissing his wife, intending to disclose himself in the alarm and consternation that would follow. The thought was rashly conceived and as promptly executed. He seized his wife, kissed her, and she fainted stone cold in his arms! He then tore the feathers and disguises off, exposing his white arm to show his true identity, and with frantic earnestness called out in English the name he had been using. "My love! my love! don't faint!—it's me—'tis a joke! *I'm all a hoax!*—do you not understand?—*I'm all a hoax!*" It was a hoax, and so serious a one that he never played another of the same kind.

The Ratone

Not the most beautiful, but certainly the wildest and most romantic scenery which we saw in our whole travel, was while making our way through a range of hills which formed, as it were, a younger growth of the high mountains we saw beyond. In performing this part of our journey, we were obliged to follow the wandering of a clear, pebble-paved stream, called the Ratone;[63]

[63] Raton Creek, Colorado, empties into the Purgatory a short distance southwest of Trinidad. The creek runs south-southeast above Trinidad and turns sharply east just above the New Mexico line. The trail, leaving the Purgatory, ascended Raton Creek Canyon, crisscrossing the stream at least fifty times. Near the upper end of the creek the trail left the canyon to strike across Old Raton Pass (in New Mexico). The trail at that point was east of the railroad tunnel entrance built later at Wootton. Once over the pass, the trail met the upper part of Willow Creek (Old Willow Creek, Willow Spring Creek, or the Raton Creek of New Mexico) in Railroad Canyon. The descent was steep and difficult.— Long, *The Santa Fe Trail*, 230–31; Henry Inman, *The Old Santa Fe Trail* (New York, 1897), 485; Colorado Drainage Map of 1922; Elmoro, Colorado,

and sometimes, where cliff and precipice utterly barred our way, the wagons were obliged to be drawn along in the bed of the creek. At one place, so difficult was our progress, that we advanced but a mile and a half in a day. Overhanging branches and projecting roots were obliged to be cut away, and heavy rocks removed, for the creek was barely wide enough to admit the wagons between the rugged banks.

The day mentioned was perhaps the most wretchedly uncomfortable of our whole journey. When we struck camp in the morning the sky was clouded, but we hoped to get through this ugly looking place and find good grazing ground for a noon encampment before the storm would break. In this we suffered as complete a disappointment as the hardest luck could impose upon us; for a cold, heavy, drizzly rain commenced falling just after we started, and continued without cessation the whole day. One unfortunate wagon was upset three times, and once right into the creek. A shelving ascent had been prepared with sticks and stones to enable the wagons to leave the water, at a place where no further progress in it could be made, when the body of this unlucky vehicle turned directly over, leaving twenty-five hundred weight of merchandise in the water, while the relieved mules dashed up the bank with the wheels. A surly and dissatisfied driver had charge of this wagon, and it was strongly suspected that he occasioned the mischief by design. The place was truly most awkward and dangerous, but still, while he met three disasters in one day, the other wagons all came through safe.

Fortune seems sometimes to take delight in making sudden contrasts of good and evil. The whole of the next day we lay camped on a wide green lawn, closed in by trees and hills,[64] and

Quadrangle (1909); Raton, New Mexico, Quadrangle (1914); Starkville, Colorado, Quadrangle (1951).

[64] As Matt descended the Raton Creek of New Mexico, he saw Bartlett Mesa to his left. The hills behind him and somewhat to his right were foothills of the Raton Range. Immediately to his right (west) he could see lava-capped outcroppings below the Culebra Mountains.

around which glided the same purling river which was at once the source of all our pleasure and all our trouble. The Ratone wanders and winds like a silver snake among the roots of these half grown mountains, and we crossed and recrossed it full twenty-five or thirty times before we finally found ourselves upon the level plains again. To repair the disabled wagon we remained upon this green eminence closed in by the higher hills around, and the day was as delightful as the preceding one had been disagreeable. The place was thickly covered with the greenest and richest pasture, and twenty feet below, purling and sparkling and tumbling over impediments here and there, overshadowed now with thickly clustering branches above, and again glancing full in the sunbeam, rolled the tiny waves and ripples of this infant tributary to the majestic rivers of the West.[65]

Just from the scorched prairies, we here couched upon the green carpeted bank and luxuriated with chrystal draughts of the cool mountain water. While noon-day blazed above, we lounged beneath the hoary trees and dipped our limbs in a tide so clear that not a living tenant of the water could move and not be seen. The whole scene was a most admirable mingling of the lovely with the wild and terrible. Splintered and rifted trees and tottering rocks above, hung beetling over the ravine, while, like a very laughing child sporting unconsciously near some object of fear, the bright little stream danced gaily over the pebbles. Huge stones were lying around, from whose forms we could trace the gaps above from whence they had fallen. Dark and tangled thickets were near, where hung the berries sought for food by the grizzly bear. Like the lion and the lamb lying down together seemed this singularly fascinating yet unsafe retreat. We thought

[65] The Raton of New Mexico joins Chicorica (Chico Rico Creek) southeast of the pass. Chicorica, in turn, flows south-southwest to enter the South Canadian River, which, far to the east, joins the Arkansas in eastern Oklahoma. The Raton of Colorado enters the Purgatory, and the Purgatory enters the upper Arkansas. Ultimately the Arkansas, receiving the water of both Raton creeks, reaches the Mississippi and the Gulf.

of paradise, where woman and the snake, man's best good and greatest ill, breathed the same air together. Still those very features in the scene which lent us in perspective something to fear, gave a keener zest to our enjoyment of what was beautiful. So true it is that we ever appreciate a good better when the opposing evil is in sight.

We encountered another spot upon this Ratone which formed the subject of a journal note. At one of the crossings the banks were so steep that the wagons were obliged to be roped around the trees and lowered, and again upon the opposite side a half a day was consumed in dragging the loaded vehicles up the precipitous ascent. Several lives were here placed in imminent danger. One of the wagons was half way up the ascent when the tongue and traces broke and the enormous vehicle with its heavy and closely packed contents, rushed back into the creek. It seemed like a miracle how those who were behind the wagon escaped. One man flung himself upon his face, seeming to gather himself almost into nothing with terror, as he shrunk between the four wheels, and the wagon darted over his head. He was in the act of placing a stone behind one of the wheels to prevent the wagon from slipping back, when the accident occurred, and the rapidity of his action alone saved his life. Another fellow was straining at a wheel to assist it forward, and he was saved by suddenly seizing the root of a tree. Though only slightly hurt, his clothes were nearly all torn from him, for by some means they were taken hold of by the descending wagon, and he, himself, would have been dragged down, had he not grasped the tree and escaped at the expense of his dress and a sprained arm.

Our whole travel through these hills was most difficult and tedious, and but for the delight of cool shade and clear water it would have been insupportable. These, however, more than counterbalanced the vexations we met with, and long afterwards our remembrance dwelt with pleasure upon the three days we spent slowly winding among the hills and along the green banks of the Ratone.

The Night Guard—The Alarm

The lonely desolation of the American prairies conveys to travellers, of an imaginative temperament, a wild excitement and exhilaration not to be conceived by those who live, move, and spend the term of their being in crowded communities. We were told of one young man who became a raving maniac in fifteen days after leaving the town of Independence. Some disappointment in business prospects, or perhaps in love, had caused him to start in search of adventure over the vast plains of the West, and the frightful solitude preyed so heavily upon his already wounded sensibilities, that his mind wandered and his reason was lost. It will not appear strange, then, that incidents, which might be considered trivial in cities, are rendered vividly interesting and impressive when occurring far away from the habitations of men among trackless plains and dreary solitudes.

Twenty-five miles was known to be the distance between the creek where we last camped and the next point where water was to be found. The sky had been clear during the day preceding, and a heavy storm seemed to be gathering in the sky; yet we determined to proceed, hoping to accomplish our day's travel before the slowly accumulating elements of the tempest should burst over our path. We were disappointed. We had started with the daylight. About 10 A.M. the heavy drops began to fall, and we travelled through a soaking shower during the four hours following. The prairie became soft; the mules gave out; the wagon wheels sunk in the soft ground; and, willy nilly, we were compelled to halt. That night we did not experience much privation, having carried with us ten gallons of water, and sufficient wood to cook a comfortable meal. The next day our wood and water were exhausted, the rain continued, and we were in the centre of a smooth flat prairie. Our only course was to start and make what progress we could, which we did, and at two in the afternoon we had accomplished about three miles, taking the wagons forward one at a time with double teams. We could see the timber of Red River five miles away to our left.[66] Two men were despatched with mules to bring wood, and at eight in the evening one of them returned. The mule of the other had taken fright and ran away in the dark with its load of wood fast upon its back. The man himself had lost his rifle while endeavoring to catch the mule, and had determined to remain and sleep on the spot, lest he should never find the place again when daylight came. With the wood brought we built a fire, the rain had abated, and after a twenty-four hours' fast, we enjoyed a hearty and delicious meal. Our guard was always stationed at nightfall, and changed every two hours and a half till daybreak. Three men only stood at a time, our party consisting of but eighteen in all. We had grown somewhat careless, having not encountered a sign of danger, or an alarm until this night.

We had grown gay over our jolly supper after two days vexation, and were merrily laughing over song and anecdote, sitting cross legged around the fire, when one of the sentinels shouted loudly from the pitchy darkness where he stood, *"Look out!"* Our rifles and pistols were all in the wagons to be kept dry from the rain.—The night was dark as the confines of Erebus. We sprang from the ground and hurried pell mell to secure our arms, expecting momentarily to hear the blood-chilling yell of the Camanche. Great confusion ensued, for we were in the very heart of what was considered the most dangerous part of the country, and we were well aware of our weakness and inefficiency to compete with danger. A moment sufficed for us to get possession of our arms, and we hurried toward the sentinel who had given the alarm. We found him upon his knees, with his rifle cocked, peering into the darkness. He told us that the animals which were grazing quietly near where he stood had suddenly taken what is called a stempide [*sic*], which is a headlong racing in company, caused by fright.

[66] In 1839, the Canadian River was called commonly the "Red." Matt's party was just below Raton Pass, traveling south between the upper Canadian River, meandering five miles to the east, and the foothills to the west. The party was north of Cimarron Canyon.

The sentinel was a brave fellow, and had not moved from the spot, but calmly crouched upon the ground and awaited the on-set of the Indians. That there was a foe prowling around us, probably creeping nearer every moment, seemed certain; and having disposed ourselves in separate stations around the camp, we paused in silent expectation of a deadly struggle. Thus we would probably have stood the whole night, not daring to sleep, had we not, after a half hour's watching, discovered the cause of alarm. The lost mule with its heavy load of crooked branches on its back had found its way to camp, and its sudden appearance with its mysterious burden had occasioned the fright of the other animals. Few of us will soon forget the impression we received when we that night started from our camp fire at the simple words, *"Look Out!"*

The Ascent—The Night Camp

Our sketches are given at random. It is of no importance to our readers whether we follow a regular succession of incidents, or skip here and there to suit our fancy. It is seldom now-a-days that we read a book fully through; but turn over the pages and read where we find our interest most excited. These papers were written in pencil among the peaks of the mountains, and under the blazing sun of the prairies; and are now chosen at random from a careless Journal.

At nine o'clock A.M.—no matter for dates—three of us bade the main party good-bye, and started to cross the mountains into the Toas Valley.[67] The company we had travelled with were bound directly for Santa Fe, and had no mountains to cross in their way. We arrived at the foot of the first ridge exactly at noonday, and camped on the bank of a cool mountain stream,[68]

[67] These are the Cimarron Mountains, generally part of the Culebra Sangre de Cristo ranges.

[68] Cimarron Creek flows through Cimarron Canyon. It rises in the region of Eagle Nest Lake (Reservoir) immediately east of Taos Valley.—Ute Park, New Mexico, Quadrangle (1955); Cimarron, New Mexico, Quadrangle (1955).

with a very romantic name, which is unfortunately forgotten. Here we roasted one side of a sheep, and with the addition of some crumbs of Spanish sweet bread, which we procured from some wandering smugglers whom we chanced to meet, we made a luxurious repast. Our wine was the chrystal water; and our desert, the crumbs of sweet bread. After our repast we slept in the cool shade of the trees till half past two, when we saddled our animals and commenced the ascent of the mountains. The path—if path it might be called—was the dry track of a mountain torrent; and our poor, worn out, unshod animals stumbled at every step as they struggled to mount the steep ascent.

When at the altitude of about one hundred yards we turned to look at the green prairies we had left. The slanting rays of the descending sun threw their tints of gold over the prairie green; and their lovely hues mingling together caused us all to regret that we were not painters. As we were admiring the prospect, a deer sprang from out the shadow of the overhanging precipice, and darted across the green plain beneath us; one of our rifles was instantly discharged at him, and the ball struck the ground at his feet; had he been a thing of wings he could not have sped more swiftly out of view. We toiled on up the mountain. Old trees, thrown down by the blast, or crushed by falling rocks, constantly impeded our progress; others stood in desolate grandeur, splintered by the smiting hand of the storm flame. Again and again, as we mounted higher, we looked back at the prairies. The sun had passed over the mountains we were ascending; and now, while ourselves were involved in shadow, we could see far away the last rays take leave of the plain; then the glory that had left the earth, gave brighter hues to the clouds; these too grew darker; and by the time we had found a favorable spot on the mountain side to camp, night had flung its sable mantle around us. A spring was bubbling from a crevice in the rocks; and meandering over a clear grassy spot that was quite clear of brush and shrubbery. Here we camped; having in plenty the three necessary requisites of the traveller, wood, water, and grass. The air was

167

cold, and a thick mist came rolling down the mountain side. We kindled a large fire, and, gathering our blankets around us, were soon as comfortable and warm as we could wish. Our solitary pipe was filled, and passed from one to the other in true Indian etiquette. Having dined well, and being obliged to be sparing of our provisions, we eat nothing; but filled the pipe again, and sat talking of friends far away—calling to mind how our young fancies used to be excited by tales and histories of the very mountains on which we were now reposing, till completely weary we dropped our heads upon our saddles and slept. And the fair Mab came down in the mist to sport with our dreaming thoughts[69]— painting to us faces that were dear, and telling us fanciful tales of home.

The Fairy Lake

On the second day of our journey over that spur of the mountains which encircles the valley of Toas and stretches away to Santa Fe, after ascending a dry water course so precipitous as to render our progress extremely slow and dangerous, we reached at last the summit of the gigantic hill we were climbing. Here we rested an hour by the side of a spring, the water of which was so intensely cold, that to decide a wager previously made with one of the Spanish smugglers, we attempted in vain to swallow three draughts of it successively. Tall, white, cotton wood trees grew here, straight and arrow like, piercing into the sky; the aspen with its delicate leaves fluttering eternally, when not even a zephyr sighed around the mountain top; and low thickets of

[69] Mab the fairy queen, in Shakespeare's *Romeo and Juliet*, is a busy midwife:

> "... *Queen Mab hath been with you.*
> *She is the Fairies' midwife; and she comes*
> *In shape no bigger than an agate-stone*
> *On the fore-finger of an alderman,*
> *Drawn with a team of little atomies*
> *Athwart men's noses as they lie asleep.*"
>   —Act I, scene 4.

pine and scrubby oak formed a singularly pleasing contrast to the lofty and majestic trees which soared above them. From this place we pursued our way, now winding around the side of some towering peak, now descending, and again ascending, now in the full light of glorious day upon the summit and again plunged in the deep shadow of the ravine, until in the very heart of the mountains a scene opened before us as beautiful as the brightest dream of fancy ever framed.

The rough Spaniards who were our companions had eyes for beauty; and though they could not understand our exclamations of surprise and pleasure, yet they had looked in our faces for tokens of admiration, and they now told us that we were actually treading *la tierra de los duendes,* or fairy land. Well did it deserve the name, and had we been asked to christen it, we would never have thought of giving it any other. A circular hollow of some three or four miles in circumference,[70] lay like a shallow cup in the breast of the mountain, and in the center slept a lake without a solitary ripple on its glassy surface. Swans, white as the snow flakes on the distant crags, were floating on the silent water, and a dreamy repose hung over the scene, which, like the influence of a spell, subdued our voices into whispers, as in wrapt admiration we gazed upon the fairy lake.

The Fairy Lake! Strange how vividly that beautiful sheet of water rises before the writer's vision at this moment. From the summit, as we descended, it was a sheet of burnished gold; nearer, it was an unruffled mirror, reflecting back the heavens. All around the lake and down to the waters edge, and beneath the water, grew a carpet of grass, silken, soft, close, and green as the sea. It was about a foot and a half high when lifted to its length, but as it fell gracefully over its height from the ground did not

[70] Deer Lake, at 8,300–8,400 feet, is located in a circular indentation to the left of the entrance to Cimarron Canyon. The body of water, now somewhat elongated, was then almost a round lake in a bowl-like valley of approximately four miles circumference. Pack trails crossed the region in several directions.— Tooth of Time, New Mexico, Quadrangle (1956); Ute Park, New Mexico, Quadrangle (1955).

exceed ten or twelve inches. Here our path was completely lost, but the Spaniards knew well how to regain it at another point. Two parallel horse tracks, worn by hunters from the valley who were in the habit of crossing to the plains beyond in pursuit of buffalo, formed the guide by which our steps were directed, and here in fairy land, as if forbidding the approach of mortal foot, the tracks were hidden by the gorgeous green carpet of the fairies dancing ground, and indeed it seemed to us as savoring of sacrilege to disturb the beautiful grass with the rude hoofs of our horses and mules.

We rode in silence to the edge of the lake and there paused in mute admiration of the sun-lit sky we saw beneath us. The white swans sat motionless upon the water with their graceful forms shadowed in the glassy mirror below,[71] until a wild bird screamed from a blasted pine whose twisted root clung to an overhanging rock upon the opposite side of the lake, when they hastily moved away, yet so gently that scarcely a ripple was seen upon the water as they swam. When the bird screamed a deer, that would other wise have remained unobserved by us, sprang from the waters brink with hasty bounds across the velvet grass and up the cliff behind us. Two rifles were instantly discharged at the poor "native burgher of this desert city," and instantly, like the shifting of a kaleidoscope, the scene changed. From behind every rock and cliff an echo sprang, and hundreds of creatures that were before unseen, now started from the emerald couch where they had been basking in the noontide, and sped with startled haste up the surrounding ascents. The scene which a moment before

[71] If these were true swans and not geese, then they were whistling swans or trumpeters (*Cygnus buccinator*), also called whoopers or bugler swans. Now rare and confined to the Northwest, the trumpeters, a century ago, frequented the plains and far western interior, perhaps ranging as far south as the Gulf.— John C. Phillips and Frederick C. Lincoln, *American Waterfowl* (Boston and New York, 1930), 285. In her *Birds of New Mexico* (Washington, 1928), Florence Merriam Bailey states that "the Trumpeter Swan, now nearly extinct, was formerly known as a rare migrant [to Colorado], and it is almost certain that these migrants entered New Mexico, although there are apparently no New Mexico records." Matt's observation may be the record proving her surmise.

seemed void of life and spell-bound in silence, now for a moment exhibited the reverse, and again in the next moment sound and life were absent, and lonely silence had again usurped her reign.

Like a plate of gold laid upon a circumference of emerald, lay the Fairy Lake—a lake formed from the melted snow of the mountain peaks and existing hundreds of feet above the level of the sea. An impression seems to be prevalent that our "Sketches" are colored somewhat with the warmth of imagination, but any reader who forms such an opinion is as unjust to himself as he is to the writer. All descriptions of scenery contained in these hasty reminiscences are literally correct, and the writer only regrets his inability to find expression sufficiently vivid to convey the surprise and delight of actual observation.

The writer is not aware of any former traveller having ever spoken of this particular region of the western wilderness, and though he wishes to depart from the ordinary form of narrative, he is very loth that his scribblings, rude and unconsidered as they are, should be deemed unworthy of confidence.

This lake, which the coarse smugglers designated as the "fairy water," lies high among the summits of the mountains, between the great plains and the Toas valley, and doubtless when swelled by the melting of snow in the spring time, it helps to form those mountain torrents which leap the rocky cliffs and traverse the wilderness to mingle with the Missouri and the Mississippi, and wash the streets of New Orleans as at this present writing.[72] It is sadly destructive to the poetry of the thing to be sure to think so, yet the humble journalist now often thinks, while making a long step across a muddy gutter, of his summers wandering in the far

[72] In the spring of 1840, the Mississippi River in Louisiana reached its highest crest in nearly sixty years. " 'Like the fountain of an infant sea' " the water poured past New Orleans in late April, backing up the slough on Poydras Street, inundating the crossings. A dangerous overflow was predicted, but, fortunately for the city, the river bent its fury on upstate parishes and, after several days of fluctuation, started to fall in mid-May.—*The Daily Picayune* (New Orleans), April 28, 30, May 2, 5, 1840; John Smith Kendall, *History of New Orleans* (3 vols., Chicago and New York, 1922), I, 152.

west and that beautiful sheet of water in the mountains known as
the Fairy Lake.

The Grizzly Bear

We met with few remarkable adventures ourselves, but we
heard of many "hair breadth 'scapes," which will be found full
of interest, at least if we may judge by our own warm excitement
in hearing them. The following anecdote we had from a wild
young fellow who spent five years among the mountains. He
told us the story by our camp-fire at night, when the winds were
shrieking over our heads among the cleft mountains, and darkness hung around us like a funeral pall.

With a single companion he had been five days away from his
party, searching for some new stream on which to trap beaver.
As the sun was sinking, on the fifth day, they stopped at a spot
where wild berries were growing very plentifully, and a little
mountain stream was trickling over the rocks. They alighted,
unsaddled their horses, and placed their rifles leaning against a
tree. Our hero then turned toward the bushes to pick some berries, and being well pleased with their flavour, and withal being
somewhat hungry, he did not at first notice that there was a
rustling among the bushes. When he did, however, he sprung
for his rifle, and had scarcely turned again before an enormous
grizzly bear broke through the bushes and dashed directly at
him. His own rifle was a single trigger, that of his companion's a
double, and in his confusion he had seized his companion's instead of his own, so that when he attempted to fire, the trigger
not being properly set, his effort was useless. A deadly faintness
thrilled him, and an instant and terrible death stared him in the
face. The furious animal was crouched to spring upon him; his
companion was too far from the spot to render him any assistance,
and bewildered with terror, unable to account for the state of
his rifle, and faint with fear, destruction seemed inevitable. The
animal sprung, and despair proved the poor trapper's salvation,

for with the motion his strength returned, the strength of desperation wrought up by the last extremity of peril, and giving his rifle one wide swing he struck the infuriated beast upon the head with the heavy barrel, while in the very act of descending upon him. The bear was stunned; one of his fore paws fastened on the shoulder of the trapper as he fell, and they both came to the ground together. The trapper described his sensations at this moment as having undergone the most wonderful change. All fear had vanished, and a savage delight seemed to have taken possession of his soul. He felt a consciousness of strength equal to that of the enormous brute with which he was struggling; and as the grizzly beast opened its huge jaws to fasten its tusks upon him, uttering most appalling growls, and while he was inhaling its strong, sickening breath, he plunged the barrel of his rifle down its throat, and springing to his feet, endeavored to force the gun completely into the animal's stomach. His arm had been dreadfully lacerated, and his deer-skin coat entirely torn from his body by the sharp fangs of the bear, which now rose to its feet, and gripping the rifle barrel firmly in its teeth, endeavored to wring it out of the trapper's grasp. The bear had been stunned and hurt, and was now in a high phrenzy of rage. The trapper clung for life to his rifle, and the next instant, by a furious effort of the enraged beast, he was lifted from his feet and dashed to the ground at the distance of some four yards from the spot. The fall bereft him of power to move, and here his fate had been sealed forever but for his companion, who, the instant he saw the separation, discharged the other rifle, and broke one of the bear's shoulder bones. The shot would have been more effectual, but he also having the wrong rifle, and not being aware of the mistake, had fired when he thought he was only setting the hair trigger. The bear fell, however, still holding the rifle fast in its teeth, close to where the first trapper was lying, who had barely strength to seize the butt end of the rifle once more, set the trigger, and fire the contents down the animal's throat. The grizzly bear was then soon despatched, and the unfortunate rifle is now to be seen in the museum at Chihuahua, with the heavy barrel bent, and the marks of the bear's teeth distinctly visible.

Camping Out

We were three. Night was fast approaching, and we began to fear we should not reach the town of St. Fernandez,[73] to which we were hastening, in time to secure our evening meal. Night came on, black as the caves of Erebus. We were in a deep gulley of the mountains which opened into the valley of Toas, and through which rolled a headlong current of deep water.[74] The track was plain, and in many parts presented no obstruction to our progress while we had daylight, but when the night came down our travel became difficult in the extreme. At times the path wound high up the bank along shallow ledges overhanging the deep ravine. At others we would have to penetrate the abyss where our animals would scarcely dare the descent. At length we reached a point where it became necessary to cross the stream, and here our progress for the night seemed to be at an end. We crossed it, however, with considerable spurring and splashing, and got over safe and wet on the other side. But here we were stopped again. We encountered a precipitous ascent, and the animals absolutely refused to proceed. We judged the time to be about 8 o'clock. No blacker night ever obscured the face of the earth. We were in the very bottom of a cleft which divided two gigantic mountains. They towered above our heads in most awful

[73] The Spanish town of Taos, today's county seat of Taos County, in earlier days was known by a variety of names: Don Fernando de Taos, Fernando de Taos, Fernández de Taos, San Fernández de Taos, and St. Fernández. The name originated from either the near-by river (*Río de Don Fernando de Chávez*) or from the landholding Fernández family. The town was an agricultural trading center and trail junction for generations before Matt's arrival. Spanish missionaries were there early in the seventeenth century, although Indian troubles hampered settlement for decades.—Fray Angélico Chávez, *Archives of the Archdiocese of Santa Fe, 1678–1900* (Washington, 1957).

[74] Matt is most likely referring to the *Río Fernando de Taos,* which enters the valley from the east.

grandeur, and even in the day the light of heaven was excluded for the scrubby oak and pine; the tall cotton wood and the aspen grew upon their cragged sides, with their green arms stretched out to meet each other across the noisy torrent below.

Here we were at a nonplus. We dismounted and endeavored ourselves to climb the ascent and draw the poor jaded animals after us, but it wouldn't do. We had to climb by the aid of the branches, and our four-footed friends planted their hoofs and said No. We had exhausted our provisions at ten in the morning, expecting to reach our destination before night fall. We had ridden all day in high spirits, for it had been sixty-five days since we had seen a christian habitation, and this night we hoped to sup and sleep under a roof. But, alas, though hope is a delightful creature, she is a woman and not to be trusted. We could get no further; we had nothing to eat; we were afraid to make a fire, and we were afraid to go to sleep; we were all fond of romance, but none of us liked to feel uncomfortable, and upon a fair survey of our situation we unanimously determined that though extremely romantic, it was decidedly disagreeable. Our last two days' travel had been through a chill, drizzly atmosphere; every one knows how pleasant that is. The clouds hung about the mountain peaks, and the September wind that had been wantoning with the snowy breasts of the mountains more northerly now came whistling the song of winter about our ears, and making somewhat free with our noses also.

The mountain mist began to thicken around us. To proceed further was impossible. We had heard of difficulties between the small settlements in Toas and the Apachus [*sic*] Indians,[75] and

[75] The Apaches were a constant menace to the valley settlers. An early, well-remembered raid in 1761 brought death to many Spanish settlers and slavery to fifty women who were carried off. The Spaniards never were successful in putting down the Apaches, and even after the establishment of Mexican control, warfare continued. Both sides took scalps, the Apaches brazenly approached and entered settlements, and the Mexicans fought back with trickery and greater vigilance.—Erna Fergusson, *New Mexico: A Pageant of Three Peoples* (New York, 1951), 107; Earle R. Forrest, *Missions and Pueblos of the Old Southwest* (Cleveland, 1929), 91.

being now almost on the very ground, to have kindled a fire would have been madness. Another vexation was we had no pasture for our poor jaded beasts; we were in the midst of scrubby cedar and thick brush; scarcely a blade of grass peeped from the barren soil; yet here we must remain; and being worn down with fatigue we were soon pillowed upon our saddles and rolled up close in our thick Spanish blankets. Never did the light of morning appear more lovely than when we rose from our damp beds next day and proceeded into Toas.

Maria Roméro

Poor Maria will never know that the story of her sorrow is told beyond the little village where she lived, and loved, and learned to weep. Her friends will never learn that an English pen has given a brief record to Maria's story, and that in a far strange land many eyes will glisten with the tear of sympathy for the lot of the poor Spanish girl. For in all lands the heart is the same; and that delightful sensation of pity, that sweet pain so near "akin to love," is not fettered by distance, but like the chrystal water that gushes from Maria's native mountains, it roves abroad over the land to gladden all mankind.

Toas is a beautiful, a very beautiful valley. Hemmed in by the mountains, and its carpet of bright green, crossed and divided by the waters from the high hills that go rippling over the pebbly beds all about the vale. We spent several days in this valley, roving from town to town, delighted equally with the novelty of the strange people we saw, the mountains, those gigantic hills of stone, of which we had so often read with eager curiosity, and which we now stopped again and again to gaze upon, towering away in enormous black masses high into the clouds above our heads—delighted equally with the novelty of these, and the surpassing loveliness of the green valley through which we were roving. In the morning, we would saunter out to see

Jocund day
Stand tiptoe on the misty mountain top,

and the sun peep into the valley. We loved to see the bare-footed, and sometimes nearly naked children drive their sheep and goats out from the towns, into the rich pastures, before the sunbeams drank away the dew. But to the story. One morning while thus employed, a young female started suddenly up from before a door where she had been sleeping, for in the warm months the inhabitants spread their blankets and mats outside the houses, under

That majestical roof, fretted with golden fire,

and sleep in the cool night air. She rolled her blanket hastily, yet modestly about her, and advancing to where we were, she twined the fingers of each hand together, and standing before us in a most plaintive and imploring attitude, she spoke.

"Americanos?"

We told her we were Americans. But it is necessary that we give her other interrogatories in English.

"Where is John?" she asked. Her manner, although singularly wild, had in it such a touching tenderness that our disposition to laugh was instantly checked, and we paused in silent admiration of her sweet, melancholy countenance, and most impressive attitude.

"Where is John?" she continued. "He did not die, you know; that was all a joke, and he means to come back to poor Maria."

We could not understand the poor girl, and knew not what answer to make her. She came nearer, and placing her slender fingers upon the writer's arm, she looked into his face, and said,

"Good American, did you not see John in the great United States, and did he not give you a Spanish letter for Maria?"

Had we known her story at the moment, we could have humored her, but as it was, we could but shake our heads and say

177

we knew nothing of John. She turned to each of us alternately, grasping our hands with energy, as if she would force from us the answer she wished. She said we were Americans, from the United States, and that of course we must know John. She described him, and in such tones and terms of glowing affection, that either of us would have given the best horse in camp to have been John for her sake.

"Good Americans," she said, "I am a poor Spanish girl, but John loved me, and he told me that the American ladies are not more beautiful than Maria. Do handsome young Americans ever tell lies? Do you think John deceived me? Are the American ladies handsomer than I am?"

We answered this latter interrogatory sincerely, and told her that we thought she was as beautiful as any American lady; for though it seems strange even to the story-teller, that beauty could exist linked with madness, rags, and ignorance, yet was poor Maria a most lovely creature. Her complexion was dark, it is true, but she had sprung from a morning slumber, and a strong excitement was working at her heart that sent a kindling color to her cheeks; added to which, the natural lustre of her eye was heightened by that fascinating brilliance conveyed by a disordered intellect.

The interview filled us with deep interest, and when we returned to the house of Mr. Branch, the only American resident in the village, and to whom we were greatly indebted for courteous hospitality, we related our adventure. He told us that five years before, a wild, dissolute young fellow, after involving himself desperately in fashionable society, had crossed the wilderness to hide himself from the world. He was a young man of very remarkable personal attractions, besides being possessed of an elegant address, and fascinating manners. He had but to smile and lift his finger, and poor Maria, the child of nature, and the charmer of the village, flew into his arms. His name need not be told. He is now back among his early friends, and not unlikely his own eye may peruse this sketch. Suffice it to say, that after a time he returned to the States, and Maria was told that he had been killed by the Camanches. This affliction the poor girl bore only in melancholy, bending over her infant in silent anguish; but when subsequently she heard that he had designedly abandoned her, and had gone forever back to the United States, her reason failed, and poor Maria, the beauty of Toas, became a lunatic. When traders were leaving the valley for the States, she invariably came and entreated to be taken with them; and when she found her pleadings useless, she would pray that John should be brought back with them when they would return. Poor Maria! Death she had heard of before; she knew that it was an affliction sooner or later to be expected, but the idea of desertion never entered her mind until it came to dethrone her reason. In real life stories are occurring every day which shame the pen of fiction, and never did the most exquisitely woven romance touch us with so captivating an interest as we experienced in hearing the simple history of the poor Spanish girl, Maria.

Ojo Colorado, or Red Eye

Ojo Colorado, or Red Eye, was the name of an Indian we encountered in Toas. He was the great chief of a small tribe that have a settlement near the Spanish town of *St. Fernandez.*[76] A sort of Justice of the Peace over the community, he settled all disputes, and was, doubtless, a very great man among his two hundred people.[77] These people are under the Spanish rule, and said to be christianized; but their christianity, and the Spanish

[76] The Taos Valley Indians were Pueblos. Their settlement was the northernmost of the Pueblo towns of New Mexico and Arizona.

[77] In other words he was the *alcalde* of the Pueblo community. The Persian and Arabian *kadi* and the Saracen and Moor *alkaid* were forerunners of the Spanish term which was brought to the New World. The Spanish *alcalde* was town judge and a type of mayor of the town council. His wife was the *alcaldesa*, and to receive *alcalda* was to be given "the protection of some powerful citizen or great nobleman."—Charles H. Shinn, *Mining Camps: A Study in American Frontier Government* (New York, 1948).

christianity in this place remind us very strongly of the blind man carrying the cripple.

Ojo Colorado was a jovial fellow, spoke Spanish after a fashion, and was received in the first society of St. Fernandez. This, however, did not make him proud; for he would help any body that would ask him, to drink a pint of whiskey and he treated us with the greatest condescension when we offered to treat him. He was a man fifty years old; fat, funny and pock-marked. He told us he was, *"un amigo al Americano—un amigo al Espanole"*; and said he could, *"Habla Espanole muy bien"*; but his Spanish was about as good as a strange Frenchman's broken English. In fact, the best language of the country is but a mongrel mixture of Indian and Spanish.

Ojo favored us with his company to dinner; but he wouldn't stand the table and chair. He would eat with us, drink with us, sleep with us if we liked, but when it came to making him sit at a table his good nature gave out, and he would indulge us no more; so we gave him his plate and knife and fork on the floor. He looked at the knife and seemed pleased with it, but after examining the fork curiously, he laid it aside, and went to work with his fingers. He would visit the fandango's in the evenings, where he was a great lion. The *señoritas* liked to coquette with him; and indeed he was a very shrewd, amusing, humorous fellow. He would treat the girls to an Indian dance, accompanied with a song, and wind up with a yell. Some idea may be formed of the melody of the song by fancying a duet between a funeral drum and a hurdy-gurdy. Yet withal, he was very dignified, and would suffer no freedom which he considered derogatory to his high station.

He was called *Red Eye,* from the fact of his eyes being of that color; caused, no doubt, by long indulgence in his favorite beverage of whiskey. We do not know whether or not Catlin has taken a portrait of Ojo to show to Queen Victoria;[78] but certainly

[78] For a sketch of Catlin's life, see article footnote 48. Catlin sailed for England in November, 1839, taking his Indian paintings and curiosities with him.

that artist could have chosen no countenance of a more strongly marked character to exercise his pencil upon. In his youth, it was clear Ojo had been handsome; even now, with red eyes and pock-marked visage, his original good features took away everything disagreeable from his face; and he excited our interest the more by his bearing a most striking resemblance to a very learned Judge, residing in one of our large Western cities. We told him of this resemblance, and afterwards distinguished him by the name of *"Judge,"* which pleased him very much; and he endeavored to learn the word, that he might teach his people to call him so likewise. We had a very amusing scene instructing him, his efforts to pronounce the word were so ludicrous. *"Ugh!"* *"ugh!"* he stuck to for a long time; then he got as near as *"Hoosha!"*. The *j* puzzled him, sounding like *h* in Spanish, and also in his own language. At last he said *"Fudge!"* very distinctly, and we told him he had it right.

A Burial in Toas

While we were sauntering about the streets of St. Fernandez one delightful afternoon, the church bell commenced tolling, and we remembered we had been told of a burial which was to take place. We hurried to the church,[79] and arrived at the gate just as the funeral procession was entering. The body of a female was in a rough uncovered pine box placed upon a barrow carried by

Two months later he opened an exhibit at the Egyptian Hall in London and, in the autumn of 1841, published his two-volume *Letters and Notes on the Manners, Customs, and Condition of the North American Indians.* Queen Victoria and Prince Albert subscribed for the first edition, yet they did not meet Catlin until after it was published.—Loyd Haberly, *Pursuit of the Horizon* (New York, 1948), 116, 119–20, 124–25, 133; George Catlin, *Catlin's Notes of Eight Years Travels and Residence in Europe* (2 vols., London, 1848), I.

[79] *Nuestra Señora de Guadalupe* (Our Lady of Guadalupe) stands on the *Plaza de San Fernando.* It was built shortly after 1800 and at the time of Matt's visit was under the care of Padre Antonio José Martínez, who brought the first printing press to the valley.—Forrest, *Missions and Pueblos,* 92; L. Bradford Prince, *Spanish Mission Churches of New Mexico* (Cedar Rapids, 1915), 255–57.

two men. A concourse of some forty or fifty persons, men, women and children, followed the corpse into the church, wailing and screaming in a manner that made the blood run cold. The church of St. Fernandez, like all the other buildings in Toas, is constructed of mud, and has no other flooring than the earth over which it is built. Sixty dollars is the price charged by the priest for the privilege of burying a body within the walls of the church, and the relatives of the deceased will beggar themselves even to starvation, rather than suffer the departed clay to rest without the sanctuary. Upon entering the church we found a new made grave yawning near the altar, and the box containing the corpse was placed beside it. Over the coffin bent a young female upon her knees, kissing the cold features, and grasping the hand of the dead body in painful agony. She was the daughter of the departed, and at the foot of the corpse knelt the father, not wailing loudly as were the others of the group of mourners, but with his white head pressed to the cold naked feet of the body, and giving vent to low moans and heart-breaking sighs.

With unceremonious haste the coffin was lowered into the grave, a rough board placed over it without nail or screw, and that desolate sound of the earth falling upon the coffin succeeded. At this a confusion ensued that was most appalling. Piercing screams from the female drew forth echos from the terrified children, and the men gave way to loud and passionate wailing. The old man tottered away from the grave and knelt before a crucifix at the side of the altar. He could not have been less than seventy-five or eighty years old, and his hair was white as the snow of winter. His body was so shrunken and withered that it seemed strange that life should exist within it, and the glassy eyes that stared in unspeakable terror from their deep sockets conveyed to us the chilling idea of an animated skeleton. The feeble old man bent before the crucifix, muttering prayers and moaning pitifully, until all sense and strength seemed to have forsaken him and he fell motionless upon his face. Not one of us will soon forget the extraordinary scene—the group that rushed from the grave to surround the old man—the sobbing daughter —the screaming children—the snowy hair of the old man contrasting so remarkably with the dark hue of his shrivelled countenance. The sun was setting and the red light streamed through the windows above, giving a wild and unearthly coloring to the scene. And there were we, three strangers in a wild country, two thousand miles from home and kindred. The curiosity our appearance usually excited among the natives was now lost in their absorbing affliction, and our presence in the church attracted no attention. They placed the old man upon the same rude bier which had conveyed the dead body to the church, and the crowd of mourners departed as though following a second funeral.

We paused behind to make a hasty examination of the church. Coarse paintings, crosses, and figures of saints lined the walls;[80] and in niches skulls and crossed bones were placed, producing a most sad and desolate effect. Dirty and ragged drapery covered the images and the altar. Basins of clay, made by the Indians, and containing the holy water, were also fixed in niches in the wall. Not a bench or seat of any description was in the church, the people always kneeling or standing during service. The old grave digger completed filling the grave while we were observing the uncouth ornaments of the altar, and after beating down the earth with his feet and smoothing the earth with his spade, he signed to us to go. No mound was raised over the corpse, no board or stone was placed upon the spot, and simply sprinkling a few drops of water upon the floor the old man muttered *"a Dios!"* and led the way to the door.

This incident occurred in one of the six small Spanish towns that lie scattered about the beautiful valley of Toas.[81] The high

[80] The *santos*, made by folk artists, were carved of wood (*bultos*) or painted on panels (*retablos*). Matt was in New Mexico during the latter days of the greatest period of the *santeros* (*santo* makers). The simple, oftentimes gaily colored figures were present in every religious edifice.—E. Boyd, *Saints and Saint Makers of New Mexico* (Santa Fe, 1946).

[81] The six Spanish towns in the Taos Valley are probably the following: Cañón, one-half mile southeast of Taos; Fernando de Taos; El Prado, also

black mountains tower within a mile of the town, and as we left the church the sun was sinking behind them. The sky was still bright with golden hues, but in deep shadow lay the valley, and as we turned a corner not far from the church we heard the continued wailing of the bereaved family proceeding from the house of woe. We left St. Fernandez the next morning, and as we rode by this house we saw the old man sitting upon a stone at the door. From the other houses the tenants came out to see the strange Americans depart, but the old man never raised his head. There he sat with his face buried in his hands, and his snowy head uncovered, like a sculptor's model of Despair; and his melancholy posture haunted us for many miles as we rode in silence up the side of the mountain.

Montezumas Treasure

Like the abode, or like the spirit itself of some fabled Genii enchained among the rocky hills, appears that enormous pile known as the mountain of Toas.[82] A perpetual gloom hangs round it through day as well as night, and even when the sun is brightest, it assumes no livelier appearance, but seems ever to be involved in shadow. When a storm gathers, the lofty peak of this mountain is soon hidden, and the heavy laden clouds roll down the dark sides as though poured forth from a crater at its summit. The voice of the storm seems to rumble within its breast, and the inhabitants of the valley peep from their dwellings at the black mountain, with fear, and curiosity and wonder. From the valley the snow upon this mountain is only seen in winter, but in the middle of August, when crossing a high ridge a few miles

---

called Los Estricoles and located three miles from Taos on the Pueblo grant; Placita, about one and one-half miles north of Taos; Talpa, in the southeast corner of the valley; and Pilar, or Cieneguilla.

[82] Taos Peak is northeast of Taos and rises to a height of 13,145 feet.— Henry Garnett, *A Dictionary of Altitudes in the United States* (Washington, 1891).

distant, among its more northerly cliffs and crags we saw the snow glittering like molten silver beneath the gleams of the mid-day sun. The appearance of this gigantic black pile is eminently calculated to rivet attention and excite wonder, and therefore it is not surprising that the superstition concerning it should exist among the simple minded people of the valley.

Many, very many years ago, it is said, the lofty summit was accessible, but all who achieved the ascent immediately after became lunatics, and could never tell what they had seen. This fact spread great alarm and awe among the people, and the opinion was soon entertained that the black mountain was the spot chosen by Montezuma for his re-appearance.[83] After this no more attempts were made to scale the summit, which was now held to be a hallowed and sacred spot, until a wealthy young Spaniard in the city of Mexico laughed at the popular superstition, and declared that *he* dare make the ascent of the Sacred Mountain. He was carousing when the boast was made, and one of his companions instantly proposed him a princely wager upon the adventure; which was accepted, and a few days after, in spite of the warnings of the priests, the prayers of his relatives, the entreaties of his friends, and the earnest persuasion of the young man with whom he laid the wager, and who now offered to relinquish it, the resolute adventurer bade good-by to all and started for Santa Fé.

He travelled to Chihuahua, crossed the prairies and sand plains that lie between it and Santa Fé, and arrived at the base of the

[83] Most of the Pueblo people near Taos and Santa Fe called "themselves descendants of Montezuma, although it would appear that they could only have been made acquainted with the history of that monarch by the Spaniards. . . . A tradition was prevalent among them that Montezuma had kindled a holy fire, and enjoined their ancestors not to suffer it to be extinguished until he should return to deliver his people from the yoke of the Spaniards. In pursuance of these commands, a constant watch had been maintained for ages to prevent the fire from going out: and, as tradition further informed them, that Montezuma would appear with the sun." Warriors kept the fires going in subterranean rooms, and the Indians stood watch on their pueblo roofs for Montezuma's coming.—Gregg, *Commerce of the Prairies*, 187–89.

black mountain in Toas. He told the people what he meant to do, and here again he was warned and entreated, but in vain. After resting two days he commenced the ascent, followed by a crowd of the most daring spirits of the valley. The extreme summit was reached by climbing a splintered crag and proceeding for some distance along the edge of a dangerous cleft, which is always filled with snow, but known to be very deep, as a man once fell into it and his body was never recovered. Here the people paused, and the young Mexican laughingly proceeded to climb the fearful and difficult ascent. With undaunted resolution and iron nerves, he toiled up the splintering pinnacle, reached the narrow ledge, and, with his small axe, working holes in the ice to cling to, he disappeared slowly upon his hands and knees over the high summit of the mountain.

He had been gone but a few minutes when he returned to the sight of the people, and called to them to ascend, for he had discovered a wonder to astonish the world; a magnificent cavern, through which ran inexhaustible veins of gold, and lit into the blaze of day with the glare of precious stones. The whole interior of the mountain, he declared, was one immense cavern, down which, from the entrance, ran winding galleries of easy descent, leading to various brilliant apartments. He entreated some one to follow him up and confirm his story, or when he returned no one would ever believe his words.

Scarcely had this announcement left the lips of the speaker when a whirlwind came shrieking around the mountain peak, and the young man was seen to fall upon his face, and cling to the edge of the rock to preserve himself from being blown over the precipice. The terrified people called to him to descend instantly; but the sky darkened, and a thunder bolt suddenly struck the pinnacle by which he had ascended, which fell with a frightful roar into the deep cleft, and his retreat was cut off forever. Filled with consternation and terror the people fled away down the mountain side, abandoning the wretched victim to his fate, and shutting their ears against his screams for assistance. From rock to rock, and down the steep ravines; along brinks beneath which the headlong torrents roared; over chasms crossed by fallen trees; struggling through thickets of brush and scrubby; and sometimes treading the water courses of the mountain, the awe-stricken people hurried, until, when night had closed over peak and plain, they reached the valley. The reckless young Mexican was never heard of more; and this is the legend told and believed by the simple people of the valley, of the black mountain of Toas, and the cavern of Montezumas Treasure.

The Indian to the Rainbow

Manito! Hark! Manito! Hear!
  Manito's voice is in the sky!
Manito's children quake with fear,
  For fire is in his eye!
The storm-wind moves the mighty water;
The waves, like warriors mad for slaughter,
  With battle yell and angry roar,
Start from their solemn ocean sleep,
To bound across the darkling deep,
  And lash the Indian shore!

Manito! Hark! The Shivered rock,
  And blasted oak upon the ground,
Follow Manito's lightning shock,
  And the deep thunder sound!
What has the stricken red man done?
Why does Manito hide the sun?
  Why does the frowning fire-cloud come,
To tear the red man's hunting ground,
And scatter desolation round
  His happy forest home?

Prostrate upon his wigwam hearth
  The dauntless warrior heaves a sigh;

Angry Manito shakes the earth,
  And the Indian fears to die!
Now faint and distant murmuring
Tell of the storm-cloud's wandering,
  And the warm light breaks forth again;
Kneeling upon a jutting crag,
The forest child views heaven's flag
  Arching the peaceful main.

Great Father of the forest tribe,
  The strong chief is a little child;
And his poor words may not describe
  Thy power and terrors wild!
Why does the red man's heart grow glad,
That even now was pale and sad?
  Doth the glad spirit through the eye
Enter within his soul to glow,
That thus he joys to view yon bow
  Of beauty in the sky?

Father! The Red Chief lowly kneels—
  Strange hopes and fears perplex his soul;
Father! The Indian lonely feels—
  Teach him his own control!
When does his hand or heart go wrong?
Does hunting cry or battle song
  Awake Manito's vengeance dire?
How shall the poor red hunter know
To chase the deer or strike his foe,
  And not displease his sire?

Why does Manito's anger wake,
  His lightnings flash, his thunders roll,
Causing the solid earth to quake
  And awe the red man's soul?
And what has calmed Manito's ire?

Whence came yon bow of happy fire?
　Does good Manito's wondrous hand
From spirit lands bring lovely dyes,
And fling them o'er the troubled skies
　To glad the forest land?

Manito is a god of power;
　The great Chief of the Spirit Land—
The burning sun, the mountain shower,
　Obey his high command!
Perchance yon bended lines of light
May mark Manito's pathway bright,
　When the loud storm was wild and black;
The Spirit Chief is wandering
When the big cloud is thundering,
　And fire lines mark his track!

The Paleface came—Manito hear!
　The Paleface from the isles afar;
With arms of fire, and words of fear,
　And wondrous arts of war!
The Red man now looks vainly round
For wigwam, home, or hunting ground;
　He turns, a stranger sad and lone,
Taking his wife and infants' hand,
To lead them from the bright green land
　That once was all their own!

Where the red sun sinks down in night,
　The Red Race lay them down to rest;
Where the glad day takes wings for flight
　Over the ocean's breast!
And as the lingering rays depart,
Sorrow falls o'er the warrior's heart
　As darkness o'er the slumbering wave;
Darkness shall mark the Red man's fall;

Darkness shall be his funeral pall;
Oblivion be his grave!

Battle of the Ranch

The people of that part of Mexico known as the "Department of Santa Fé," have for many years been harassed and annoyed by the depredations of the Apachus Indians. An American by the name of *Kurker* [*sic*], at the time of our visit, had just entered into a contract with the Government to whip the Indians and bring them to a permanent treaty, for the sum of one hundred thousand dollars, five thousand dollars of which was paid to him in advance to commence operations.[84] Kurker is now carrying on the war, and his first skirmish occurred while we were in Toas, within two miles of the town in which we were sojourning. He is a man of daring and reckless disposition, who has himself suffered from the villainy of the Indians, and he now hunts them as much in revenge for the injuries they have done him as in prospect of emolument.

The battle which forms the subject of the present sketch, occurred close under the black mountain of Toas, in the valley of the same name, near to a small town called the "Ranch."[85] Kur-

[84] Max Moorhead, in his recent *New Mexico's Royal Road* (Norman, 1958), estimates there were about one hundred hunters, teamsters, and civilized Indians in James Kirker's employ. Kirker came originally to the United States from Ireland in 1810, at the age of seventeen. Several years later he moved to St. Louis, drifted into the fur trade on the Upper Missouri, and in the mid 1820's was in Santa Fe. For a while he mined at Santa Rita but was involved in politics, Indian difficulties, and, supposedly, an assassination plot. Despite his unstable political allegiance, the New Mexican authorities were willing to have him undertake his anti-Apache campaign of 1839–41. In the mid 1840's, he returned to Sonora; then served as a United States scout during the Mexican War. In 1849, he led a party to California and died there in 1852 or 1853.—Ralph P. Bieber (ed.), *Southern Trails to California in 1849* (volume V of The Southwest Historical Series [Glendale, 1937]), 357–58; Moorhead, *New Mexico's Royal Road*, 148.

[85] *Ranchos de Taos*, located four to five miles south-southwest of Taos, was the Indian agricultural community and, in its early days, was subject to attacks

ker, with about fifty men, was here encamped, when a party of the thieving Apachus crept upon them in the night and stole a number of their horses. The Indians were not aware that Kurker's party were prepared for war, but supposed they were stealing from an encampment of traders, who would not dare to pursue them. The robbery had scarcely been committed when it was discovered, and in a very few moments more Kurker and his fifty men were in close pursuit of the Indians. Knowing that the thieves would endeavor to escape over the mountains, by ascending a ravine that opened into a valley near the spot where the robbery was committed, Kurker led his men quickly around a by-path up the mountain side, and as the grey light of morning spread over the valley, the pursuers found themselves upon an eminence commanding the ravine up which the Indians were hurrying, mounted upon the stolen horses. The marauders numbered about a hundred and twenty, more than doubling the force of the pursuing party; but although these vagabonds hold the Spaniards in great contempt, they are the vilest cowards when opposed by the Americans. Cunning as they were they did not discover their danger until fifty American rifles were levelled, each with deadly aim, at a separate victim. The first cry of alarm from the Indians was the signal to fire, and as the early sunbeam penetrated the ravine, echo started suddenly from slumber, bounding wildly from cliff to cliff, and away among the distant crags, like the spirit of fear speeding from death and danger. Twenty Indians fell from their horses at that fire, some with a single frightful yell expiring on the instant, while others with clenched teeth, and with the desperate energy of departing life, clung to the reins, and were dragged about and trod upon by the alarmed horses. The Indians ride like devils, and without pausing an instant they turned and fled towards the valley. Some that were wounded fell from the frightened animals while they were in full speed down the ravine. Kurker and his men followed with-

by marauding tribes. Saint Francis of Assisi Mission, with thick adobe walls, twin towers, and supporting buttresses, was built in the center of the *Ranchos*.

out reloading their rifles, and chased the Indians until they emerged from the ravine, and took refuge within the walls of the Ranch.

This town called the Ranch lies at the base of a gigantic mountain, and is watered by a swift stream that rushes from the ravine we have mentioned. It contains about three hundred houses, and these are built compactly together, forming a wall, and enclosing a large square, in the center of which stands the church. Into this square the Indians rushed and endeavored to force their way into the church, having been taught to believe that the sacred roof is protection against all danger. But Kurker's men felt no disposition to let the savages off so easily, and reloading their rifles they resumed the attack within the walls of the town. It was still early morning, and the inhabitants sprang from their beds in the wildest confusion and alarm. First was heard the thronging of the Indians into the town—their murmurs of fear and terror; then the shouts of the pursuers; children screamed within the dwellings, and there was a rapid closing and barring of doors and windows. Then came the report of firearms, followed by the most fiendish screams and yells from the victims, over which again rose the loud hurrahs of the Americans, as wild and savage as the dreadful war whoop of the Indian. The men seemed to grow delirious with the excitement, and to become inspired with the savage nature of their enemies. One man after discharging his rifle and pistols rushed madly among the Indians with his knife, and actually succeeded in taking a scalp before he was killed. The fight lasted but half an hour, when the Indians begged for mercy and were suffered to depart.

Kurker's men are mostly robust, daring fellows from Kentucky and Missouri, wagonners, speculators who yielded to the seductions of the Monte Bank and were ruined; men of rough, yet chivalrous and romantic natures, who love the wild life they are leading. Their pay from Kurker is a dollar a day and half booty, so that their interest as well as their love of excitement leads them to make battle whenever opportunity occurs. In this battle forty

Indians were killed, and of Kurker's party but one American and one half breed. The stolen horses were recovered, and all the other animals in the possession of the Indians were taken as booty. Kurker, himself, is as brave as a lion, and a man of great enterprise as well as skill in this kind of warfare. Having just commenced operations his force is small, but men were thronging to join him every day, and he will soon be at the head of a powerful army.

A Mexican Inn

The Battle of the Ranch, related in a former sketch, took place upon the very morning that we left San Fernandez for Santa Fé. Captain Branch, early in the morning, received a mysteriously worded note, advising him not to travel that day, but to remain at home, and be prepared for danger. This came from a friend in the Ranch, which town was scarcely two miles and a half distant from San Fernandez, where we then were. Our preparations had been all completed to start, and our leader, Captain Branch, was a man not easily turned from his purpose, so that in spite of this ominous warning he determined to proceed. He was removing to Santa Fé, there to reside for several months, and his wife and two children were of the party. The receipt of the letter he never mentioned to us, our inexperience in the country rendering us entirely unfit to offer counsel, and he presuming that, should danger appear, we would probably find it out as quick, and be as well prepared to meet it, without being subjected to any preliminary uneasiness.

Branch locked and secured his house, leaving it in charge of a faithful Spaniard, and we all rode off together from the little town of San Fernandez, toward the huge pile of rock that lay between us and Santa Fé. By noon we had left the Toas valley, and crossed the first ridge of mountains in our path,[86] descending

[86] This is a very general statement. Perhaps Matt is referring to the Picuris Mountains.

into a beautiful ravine, where we found seven Indians, men, women, and children, seated around a cool spring that was gushing from the rock. Our party consisted of nine; six men, one woman, and two children. Branch said to us hastily, "They are Apachus, ride up and shake hands with them." We did so, and choosing a spot some few yards distant, we dismounted and camped for noon day refreshment.

From daylight until that hour, a fierce and bloody conflict had been raging in the Ranch, and forty Indians lay slaughtered beneath the church walls, but of this we were then all ignorant. Presently a mounted Indian came at full speed down the mountain side, and rode swiftly forward to the little party of Apachus in the ravine. A brief conference followed, and confusion among the Indians was immediately discernible. Their habitations appeared high upon an opposite rock, and to this they made their way, from whence we soon saw them departing over a higher ridge of the mountain, and carrying away their tent poles, skins, and luggage. Then Branch became thoroughly convinced that serious danger was abroad, and he showed us the letter of warning he had received. It was plain there was extensive communication among the Indians in some quarter, and our only course was to press forward and complete our journey as soon as possible, though we could not tell but we were marching into the very jaws of mischief. We had scarcely got in motion again after our repast, when a mounted band of twenty Apachus met us at a precipitous turn in our mountain path, and passed us with gruff yet inoffensive salutations. They too were carrying their tent poles and luggage with them, moving from one location to another, but they, no more than ourselves, had yet heard of the war in Toas, as we would have been assailed beyond question, as Branch assured us. We pushed on through mountain scenery of wildest and most terrific grandeur, and it was on this afternoon that we passed along the frightful precipice the *"Fire Jump,"* the story of which we give in one of our sketches.

194

General Manuel Armijo

"Emphatically a self-made man, he served three times as governor of
New Mexico."

WAGONS AND TEAMS IN FRONT OF THE GOVERNOR'S PALACE
SANTA FE, NEW MEXICO

"The customhouse and barracks were joined to the palace—the barracks and guardhouse set at the west end—all being held together by the power of mud."

At nightfall we reached the Mexican Inn where we were to pass the night, and which was reckoned to be just half way upon our journey.[87] It was situated in a deep and narrow valley, the mountains soaring in the clouds above it on every side. It stood upon the banks of the Rio Grande, so near the mountain source of that noble river, that we could find no greater depth of water than four inches, and it was clear as the frozen fluid of a gem, cold as though the congealing fingers of winter had already placed an icy spell upon its motion. The host was a rosy, rotund, hearty old fellow of, perhaps, less than fifty, and save in dress, he exactly answered all modern descriptions of a thrifty old village tavern-keeper. He was reputed to be rich, and doing business only for occupation and amusement, which was doubtless true, for the inn was furnished with, and in all its appointments displayed more costly elegance and taste, than any other house we entered in this part of Mexico. We were served upon silver plates and dishes, which were laid upon exquisitely wrought Chihuahua blankets, and we sat upon the most luxuriant couches, around a table heaped with novel and tempting viands, while the attentive submission of the Spanish servants left us with scarcely the necessity of uttering a wish. One peculiarity, new to us, about this Mexican tavern was, that our plates were brought to us ready filled from the culinary apartment, and placed before us; and it seemed that we must eat, if we were hungry, whether we liked the dish, or not. The host knew nothing about such a question as "What will you have?" either in English or Spanish. We did like the dish, however, and so well that we all wanted our plates replenished; but, Oh no, no more of that; other varieties were brought in succession, but eating two plates of the same seemed to be quite at variance with the etiquette of the establishment. The appetite we brought with us from our long day's travel over

[87] Doubtless there was such an inn along the trail, but dependable records do not locate one adequately in that region. The Río Grande Valley is very narrow in several places south of Taos.—Velarde, New Mexico, Quadrangle (1953).

the mountains, was quite sufficient to make us well satisfied with our meal, even were it not, as it was, not only pleasingly novel, but truly delicious. After supper, the couches we had sat upon were spread out upon the floor for beds, and then, before retiring, our host regaled us with grapes, apples, and other fruit, together with an exquisite glass of the genuine rocky mountain *poteen*, or *Pass Whiskey*.[88]

In the morning early we took with us a piece of soap, and made our ablutions in the cold waters of the *Rio Grande*, returning with ravenous and devouring appetites for the queer dishes given us by the Mexican innkeeper. At breakfast we found that the news of a battle in the Ranch had arrived during the night, and so our reason for alarm the day before was now fully confirmed. But for this, we three companions, who had leisure to pause for pleasure, would have loitered a few days at this delightful inn, but our captain, Branch, not encouraging us in such a design, we all resumed our travel again after breakfast. The sun was just lifting his last ray from the point of our long pilgrimage, the little mud-built city of Santa Fé, when we came in view of it from the mountain side, and ere nightfall we rode into the great square of the place.

The Fire Jump

When crossing the mountains from Toas into Santa Fé, we passed along the brink of a frightful precipice, called the *"Fire Jump,"* about which our guide told us the following story. *Col. Tom* was a half-breed, well known a few years ago through all the villages in Toas—living at times with the Indians—a shrewd, cunning fellow, not brave, but exceedingly wicked. He was the son of an American trapper, who perished in the snow one winter

[88] Although "Taos lightning" was a famous whiskey distilled in the Taos Valley from native wheat and was profitably bartered with the Indians and consumed by Santa Fe and mountain traders, Matt's reference here seems to be to the brandy brewed at El Paso and shipped north to the Santa Fe–Taos country. "Poteen" suggests illicit distilling.—Inman, *Old Santa Fe Trail*, 114; Ruth Barker, *Caballeros* (New York and London, 1935).

night in the mountains, while Tom was yet an infant. Tom obtained the title of *Colonel* from the Americans, on account of a martial and commanding manner which he was fond of assuming. He spoke Spanish fluently, and knew enough of English to mingle with the traders, and be useful to them as an interpreter, being also conversant with the language of his Indian mother. Though known to be a great rascal, he was tolerated by Americans and Spaniards on account, partly of his usefulness when he chose to make himself serviceable, and partly for his reckless and humorous disposition, but the Indians hated him with deadly hostility. His superior intelligence made him feared among them, and they were jealous of the white blood that ran in his veins. Living under the rule of the Spanish government, they could not kill him without being punished for it, and this made their hatred the more bitter. He knew well the hostile feelings of the Indians with whom he mingled, and the delight of his existence seemed to consist in planning schemes of deviltry and rascality to aggravate them. He would steal from the whites whiskey enough to make a whole Indian town drunk, and in the midst of the carousal he would drive off the horses and sell them to the Spaniards. He would interpret for the Indians when selling their skins to the traders, and invariably contrived to make to himself half the advantages of the trade.

At length his depredations became so notorious and of so villainous a nature, that the Spaniards would no longer protect him, and the Indians commenced hunting him for his life. He had been chased a whole day through the valley and up the mountain side, by a band of the Apachu Indians, when his horse gave out just at this spot, now known as *"The Fire Jump."* The animal fell near the edge of the precipice, and to prevent the Indians discovering him by the fallen steed, he exerted his strength, and actually pushed the poor dying horse over the rock into the abyss below. A hollow log lay near the spot; he heard the approach of his pursuers, and jumping into the log, he turned it over and lay concealed, as he thought, beneath it.

But the Indians had seen the action, and a fiendish revenge entered into their heads. They came to the spot, pretending to believe that their prey had escaped them, and manifesting great vexation and disappointment. They dismounted, and seating themselves upon the log, rehearsed to each other what they had intended to do to Colonel Tom had they caught him. Thus the cunning savages sat till night was dark around them, when they gathered dry leaves and branches, and commenced building their fire close against the hollow log where their enemy was hidden. The wretched victim then knew but too well that his concealment was discovered, and a horrid death was designed for him. He peeped from beneath the log, and saw that each man had his bow in hand, and his arrows ready for use.

The fire kindled rapidly, and the Indians laughed aloud as the flames curled around the rotten log. Tom was not brave, but it would seem as if the miserable wretch formed the desperate resolution of dying by the fire, rather than give the Indians the delight of killing him with their arrows. This, however, was a feat not in human nature to perform, and after enduring the torture to the last moment, the doomed wretch dashed off the burning log, and sprang to his feet with his deer skin dress rapt [*sic*] in a sheet of flame. He threw himself upon the ground and rolled, but the fire still clung to him. The Indians yelled and danced with delight. He rose to his feet again, and rushing to the precipice, sprang over the brink; a dozen arrows pierced him at the moment, and with a frantic scream of agony, he sped like a lightning flash into the dark gulf below. The Indians threw themselves upon their faces and peeped over the brink to see the burning body dash from rock to rock, until it disappeared beneath a projecting crag, hundreds of feet down in the frightful ravine; after which, they calmly smoked their pipes around the still blazing log; and the terrible precipice, whose brink is almost the very summit of the mountain, has ever since been pointed out to travellers as *"The Fire Jump."*

A Duel without Seconds

The two opponents stood, with pistols cocked and pointed, looking, with firm and unwavering glance, into each other's eyes. There was not another thing of life, save the summer insects, to be seen around the far prospect. The smoking carcass of a newly slaughtered buffalo cow lay between the young men, and the last breath had scarcely escaped from the poor brute at the moment of which we are speaking.

It was noon day. Some two hours before, the scene had been enlivened by the passing of an extensive trading company, and the duelists were two young hunters who had remained behind in pursuance of their sport. They were close friends, had known each other from boyhood, and through long years of intimacy had reciprocated a warm attachment and esteem. They stood now, with deadly determination flashing in their eyes, each waiting for the other to speak the fatal word of destruction. Not a spectator was there to mark the indomitable bearing of the friends so suddenly and strangely turned against each other. There was a pause, in which the very insects and the motionless atmosphere seemed to join, and the dark, glaring orb of the dead cow stood open, as if its wrathful spirit was still lingering there to witness the bloody spectacle about to be enacted.

Let us return now and learn how trivial a cause brought about this serious disposition of affairs. The two young friends, in full chase of the cow, had fired at the same instant, one with a large horse pistol, the other with a shot gun charged with a rifle ball. Each was proud of his aim, and in the excitement of the moment each claimed the honor of having given the mortal wound. One ball was planted in the liver, as was proved by the beast spouting blood before death. The other was dug from the fleshy shoulder, several inches above the hunter's well known mark, and in a part where no mortal injury can possibly be given to a buffalo.

"It is your ball; own it," said the youngest of the two friends, as he stripped the skin from the yet breathing beast, and tore out the ball that lay flattened against the bone.

"It is a *lie,* sir," said the other, shame for the word he had spoken instantly heightening his irritation, while stubborn pride arose to forbid retraction.

They were youths of a fiery mould. Neither, to preserve the last ebbing drop of life, could stoop to suffer a degradation. It was a too chivalrous and subtle temperament that made them wanderers at this time in the wild regions of the west. The young hunter, still upon his knees by the bleeding buffalo, lifted the ball above his head, and swore to plant it in the heart of his companion unless the reproachful word was withdrawn.

"Load then," said the other, coolly, as he plunged his knife in the buffalo's throat, preparatory to extracting the tongue.

The young man shot off the contents of a pistol in the air, and then proceeded to reload, charging his weapon with the devoted bullet.

"Do you take back the word?" said the insulted youth.

"No," was the cool response.

"Then get up and fight, and don't compel me to murder you."

"It must be murder if either you or I should die here," said the elder of the companions, "for no witness is present to testify for the survivor."

"Coward!" muttered the indignant youth between his teeth. The epithet was muttered, but not with design to be unheard.

"Then I will kill you dead upon the spot, since you desire it," said the other, rising to his feet and deliberately drawing a pistol from his belt. Thus they stood at the opening of this description. After the pause we have mentioned, the elder companion spoke, with a sarcastic smile upon his countenance and said, "Take the word, and tell me when to shoot, youngster."

"Take better aim than you did at the buffalo," replied the youth, "or your shooting will do me no harm."

"Come and meet me breast to breast," said the other, "and that will improve my aim."

The high-mettled young men advanced to meet each other, and, each placing his right foot upon the slain brute, the muzzle of their weapons were pointed within thirty inches of the murderous aim taken.

"Quite as well that the distance should be short," said the young man "as I do not wish to live and be accused of your murder."

"Give me your hand and fire," said the elder; "kill me dead or my ghost shall haunt you—*fire!*"

The elder pointed his pistol in the air and fired, while the younger after a pause, dashed his instrument upon the earth and exclaimed, "you called me a liar, Jack!"

"Then why do you not shoot me?"

"Why!" replied the impetuous youth, "because here in the lone desert I see your mother's imploring hands uplifted, and my pistol seems pointed at her heart instead of yours. Instead of your blood I see her tears flowing, and I stand here a dishonored man, powerless of revenge."

Moisture dimmed the eye of the elder hunter, and a plaintive alteration was in his voice when he said, "Well, Tom, you called me a coward."

"*Then* I was a liar, Jack, and not till then. You have called me a liar, and a retraction now can do no good, for a liar you have made of me."

"Never, Tom, never," was now the exclamation of the other companion. "No, Tom, I did you wrong, and I ask your pardon. By long years of our friendship, whether it was your ball or mine that killed the old cow, I was rash and wrong in what I said. Forget it, forget it, and let us just cut out the cow's tongue and be off after the waggons, for the sun will drop down the west before we reach our companions."

A few moments more saw the reconciled friends riding forward together, exchanging exclamations as warm as their quarrel was brief and rash, and the buffalo's tongue furnished them a supper over which the sudden difference was as speedily forgotten. Neither was ever satisfied, however, as to which killed the buffalo.

Santa Fé

We had wasted a few days in the Toas valley before we paid our visit to Santa Fé, consequently our first view of the mud built city was from the mountain side, as we descended after crossing from the distant valley. There, within half a mile of the base of the mountain, a small spot of the vast green plain that spread away before us was dotted with low one story buildings, reminding us irresistibly of an assemblage of mole hills. As we approached the city and the houses began to shape themselves more distinctly to the eye, the church in the centre, soaring above the surrounding dwellings, attracted our attention.[89] It was built as high and quite as large as any of our ordinary sized meeting houses, and upon after examination our surprise was not a little excited to find that these mud walls could possess such strength and durability. It would be perfectly practicable for the inhabitants to build their houses two or more stories high as far as strong walls are necessary for that purpose, and the reason why they are not so built is not, as one would at first imagine, because mud walls are inefficient, but because ground is cheap, and the people prefer half a dozen rooms in a row to as many apartments piled one above another. They think it is easier to go through a door way than up a pair of stairs, which is certainly not a very unreasonable conclusion to arrive at. Besides, although timber is plenty carpenters are scarce, and a boarded floor is a luxury for which they entertain not the slightest ambition.

The apartments are of various lengths but never exceeding

[89] The Church of Our Lady of Light (*Nuestra Señora de la Luz*) was a beautiful structure on the south side of the plaza, opposite its center and facing the Governor's Palace on the north. Constructed between 1717 and 1722, it was the church of the Santa Fe garrison (*La Castrense*), and its twin towers were a familiar landmark to American visitors.—Prince, *Spanish Mission Churches*, 126; Ralph Emerson Twitchell, *Old Santa Fe* (Santa Fe, 1925), 50, 154.

twenty feet in width, (the church alone is an exception,) and across the walls from side to side are stretched, sometimes good hewn timber, sometimes rude branches, according to the means of the builder. Over these is laid a thick covering of grass and straw, and upon this earth is piled from one to two feet deep, which forms the roof. A very pleasing effect is produced by the grass growing on the tops of the houses, and as all the dwellings are connected it is not uncommon to see children chasing each other the whole length of a street along the house tops.

The sun was just setting when we rode into the large square of Santa Fé and shook hands with the American store keepers. Here we were after our two months pilgrimage, arrived at last in the strange place to which our wild love of novelty had led us, and as we gazed round upon a race of beings

> *That seemed not like the inhabitants of earth*
> *And yet were on it,*

as we saw the dark eyed *Señoritas* peep at us from door and casement, and from beneath their shawls, worn like hoods, a buoyant excitement tingled through our veins more delightful than the exhilaration of the wine bowl. To meet here brothers with whom we could exchange greeting in our native tongue was another charm to heighten our satisfaction, for what delight is dearer to the heart or half so

> *Welcome as the hand*
> *Of brother in a foreign land?*

To the house of Don Louis Rubideau [*sic*],[90] an American and

---

[90] Louis Robidoux, the third of six sons of Joseph Robidoux II and Catharine Rollet, was born in Florissant, Missouri, in 1796. When he was thirteen, he and his family returned to their earlier home in St. Louis, where his father died and his mother remarried. Louis decided to build his career in the West. In association with his brother Antoine, he settled at Santa Fe and handled fur shipments and general business affairs connected with his family's trade in Colorado and Utah. He married Guadalupe Garcie, a member of "one of the old aristocratic families of New Mexico." In 1844, Louis, with his wife and children, moved to

first *Alcaldé* of Santa Fé, we were duly escorted; and after a delicious meal of roasted sheep ribs, eggs, wheaten cakes, and coffee, we spent the evening in satisfying the enquiries of the *Alcaldé* about St. Louis and all the old friends he had left there; receiving from him in return all the information we desired about Mexican Spaniards, Mexican Indians, Santa Fé, and the surrounding neighborhood.

The interior of one of these mud built houses, particularly when arranged with the assistance of American taste, forms a very comfortable and by no means inelegant dwelling. In winter it is warm, in summer cool; and in these respects indeed a Santa Fé dwelling is even preferable to an American brick or frame residence. In some of the better houses you will find an apartment set apart as a parlor, this invariably being also the sleeping room; during the day the beds are folded close up to the walls, and covered with the handsome (sometimes really beautiful) Spanish blankets, forming a succession of sofas all around the room. The walls are well whitewashed, and papered only high enough to keep the wash from rubbing off upon your clothes, while mats and sometimes blankets are made to serve the use of carpets as well as table cloths and bed covers. These blankets are the chief sign of wealth among the people, and their elegance and number forms the pride of every housekeeper; the best of them are so closely woven that they can be used for holding water, and the bright colors that never fade are mingled through them generally with very tasteful and ingenious disposition.

This fashion of making sofas of the beds, and covering floors and tables with the rich blankets (in the city of Mexico where

---

Southern California and took up farming on a large land grant near Riverside. He accumulated a sizable fortune in ranching and was active in politics until his death. Mount Robidoux, overlooking Riverside, bears his name and is the site of an impressive annual Easter service.—William S. Wallace, *Antoine Robidoux, 1794–1860* (Los Angeles, 1953), 3–6, 13; Oral M. Robidoux, *Memorial to the Robidoux Brothers* (Kansas City, 1924), 209, 223, 282; Cleland, *This Reckless Breed of Men*, 246; Reeves (ed.), "The Charles Bent Papers," *New Mexico Historical Review*, Vol. XXX, No. 2 (April, 1955), 160.

these blankets are manufactured they are sold as high as seventy-five dollars,) has not merely an agreeable but really an elegant effect, but an American eye can never reconcile itself to the wall decorations of a Santa Fé drawing room. Coarsely engraved and colored pictures; rude images of saints; religious charms; broken looking glasses (every bit of looking glass is a treasure); broken flower vases; any little shattered ornament brought from the States; such things are arranged about the walls with ostentatious display, and only where some resident American prevails over the taste of his Spanish wife are they removed.

A description of *Señora Toulous,* the great lady and rich monte dealer of Santa Fé, and her residence, shall form the subject of our next sketch.

Señora Toulous

We arrived in Santa Fé on Saturday; we received intimation from the Governor that he would be happy to make our acquaintance on Monday; so that on the intervening Sunday our introduction to fashionable society took place at the house of Señora Toulous,[91] the supreme queen of refinement and fashion

[91] The puritanical condemned Doña María Gertrúdiz Barcelo; those who better appreciated Latin society did not. To some she was Lona Barcelona, to others she was Madam Barcelo of Santa Fe, but to most she was La Tules. According to tradition, she was born in Spain, lost her mother in New York, lived briefly in Taos, and moved on to Santa Fe where gambling prospects were better. At the capital she made a fortune in her gambling salon, was accepted by the best society, is credited with aiding the United States occupation forces in the Mexican War, and died in 1851, an honored member of Spanish New Mexican culture. Many Anglos, however, took a dim view of her activities. Susan Magoffin credited her with "that shrewd and fascinating manner necessary to allure the wayward, inexperienced youth to the hall of final ruin." G. Douglass Brewerton, visiting Santa Fe when La Tules was at the end of her career, discovered a woman "whose face . . . bore most unmistakably the impress of her fearful calling, being scarred and seamed, and rendered unwomanly by those painful lines which unbridled passions and midnight watching never fail to stamp upon the countenance of their votary." Gregg noticed that "she was richly but tastelessly dressed—her fingers being literally covered with rings, while her neck was adorned with three heavy chains of gold, to the longest of which was

in the republican city of Santa Fé. After dinner, while strolling through the streets with our *cicerone*, the *Alcalde*, a light and somewhat gaudy four wheeled vehicle dashed past us, drawn in tandem style by three well fed and spirited mules with a driver seated upon the leader. Out of this vehicle the Alcalde received a bow from a middle aged lady and a smile from a young dark eyed beauty by her side; he told us that the former was the celebrated Señora Toulous, and the latter her beautiful niece,[92] an adventurous belle lately arrived from the city of Chihuahua; adding that we might appropriate the bow and smile to ourselves, as he was not in the habit of receiving such courtesies. He proposed to conduct us to the house of the great Señora, considering the condescention [*sic*] just received as an invitation to that effect, and we of course at once acceded to his proposition.

Allowing the ladies time to take their ride we accompanied the Alcalde to the Señora's house, and anticipated our introduction to Governor Amijo [*sic*][93] by finding him there surrounded by his

---

attached a massive crucifix of the same precious material." Blanche Grant, writing in 1941, concludes (and Matt would have agreed with her) that "they have maligned" the name of La Tules, since they could not understand her.—G. Douglass Brewerton, "Incidents of Travel in New Mexico," *Harper's New Monthly Magazine*, Vol. VIII (April, 1854), 588; Gregg, *Commerce of the Prairies*, 168–69; Bernard DeVoto, *The Year of Decision, 1846* (Boston, 1943), 321; Ruth Laughlin, *The Wind Leaves No Shadow* (New York, 1948), 320; Blanche C. Grant, *Doña Lona: A Story of Old Taos and Santa Fe* (New York, 1941), *vii–viii*.

[92] According to legend, she had adopted two daughters, possibly her nieces.— Grant, *Doña Lona, viii*.

[93] Manuel Armijo was "emphatically a self made man," who taught himself to read and write while herding sheep and did his ciphering with "a soft stone such as he could pick up in the prairie or coal from the camp fire . . . upon the knees of his buckskin breeches." From such obscure beginnings, he rose to make a fortune in illicit sheep trading and served three times (1827–29, 1837–44, and 1845–46) as governor of New Mexico. He invested in the overland trade to Santa Fe, was subject to bribery, and was known to be corrupt in office. His reputation as a tyrant, however, must be tempered with the realization that many of his detractors were Americans. In 1846, he retreated from Santa Fe before the oncoming U. S. Army and was, in turn, accused of treason by his own government. He was acquitted, nonetheless, and lived to retire to New Mexico until

officers and several of the young bucks of Santa Fé, admirers of the Señora's beautiful niece. We had just learnt enough of Spanish to create pleasant merriment by our blundering obeisance, and as all parties were predisposed to be pleased with each other, any breach of etiquette on our part, or any action of the Spaniards differing from our notions of good breeding, served only to create laughter and make the interview both interesting and agreeable. We were served with wine and we initiated the Governor and ladies into the mysterious American refinement of touching glasses, over which we all laughed as heartily as though something irresistibly witty had transpired.

Alcalde Rubideau had told us that not a solitary word of English would be understood by our Spanish friends, so that we could make what remarks we pleased in our own language; and being a set of very wilful youths, we exercised this license to its fullest extent, with little regard to the rules of American or Spanish good breeding. Thus we kept our interpreter, the polite Alcalde, in an absolute torture of laughter by requesting him to put to the Governor and ladies whimsical questions which he could well understand but which sadly puzzled him to express in the Castilian, and when successful in an attempt to interpret our odd conceits, the side-splitting merriment of the good natured Governor and the dark eyed ladies bounded back to us again, causing the tears to start from our eyes with a novel and singular delight.

But our sketch should describe the Señora and her house, and our limited space will not admit of minute detail. The apartment in which we were received was about fifty feet in length by twenty in width, one end of it only being carpeted. The beds were folded up against the walls to serve as sofas, and covered with costly Mexican blankets; and here we found less of the gaudy wall decorations mentioned in a former sketch. At the end of the apart-

his death in 1853.—Ralph P. Bieber (ed.), "The Papers of James J. Webb, Santa Fe Merchant, 1844–1861," *Washington University Studies,* Vol. XI (July, 1923–April, 1924), 274–75; Barker, *Caballeros,* 61–65; Gregg, *Commerce of the Prairies,* 79.

ment where we were seated was a large window latticed with wood; glass is rarely seen in this country, it being so difficult a commodity to transport safely from the States, and so easily destroyed when put into use. A very rich clock of American manufacture hung on the wall, completely out of order, and the hands were pointing with great constancy one at twelve and the other at six, they having been placed so probably to look uniform. The Señora told us facetiously that she was economical with her clock, it being too handsome to work, and not wishing it to grow old too fast, she only let it go on holidays.

Señora Toulous was not handsome, her only pleasant feature being an eye of shrewd intelligence, lit up during our interview with that expression of mischievous brightness which can make any countenance agreeable. Her figure was neat, her manners free and not ungraceful, and, on an after occasion, when she moved through the waltz with one of the young American visitors, the really elegant ease which she displayed would have made her an object of attraction in a *soirée dansante* at Washington.—This fine lady had become wealthy by dealing *monte*, a kind of game differing slightly from *faro*, and her bank was open almost every evening, (not in her own house but in another part of the city,) herself superintending while an assistant dealt the cards. We found the Alcalde on several occasions acting the part of dealer, his passion for the game leading him still to finger the cards although he had been three times stripped of accumulated property by unfortunate luck. Monte and the fandango are the only amusements of the place, and the people spend the evening in strolling from one to the other. Traders often lose the profits of a whole season in an hour's play, and when the last dollar is gone they walk off to a fandango, choose a partner and dance away care, never dreaming of curing misfortune by suicide.

By this business has Señora Toulous amassed a fortune and made herself a person of no small distinction. She selects who she will patronize, and her presence at a fandango is sufficient to render it a fashionable affair. It is not often, however, that she condescends to shed the light of her presence abroad, but when she does she appears in a blaze of rich jewelry and silk, calling contrast to her aid in producing effect, for at the monte table she sits in a common loose dress without any ornament of any kind about her, seeming to study negligence. The highest court her favor, and the lowest look at her with wonder. Such is the fine lady of Santa Fé.

The Monte Bank

One night a crowd of men sat, betting with intense earnestness, at a monte bank in Santa Fé.[94] It was late, and an immense amount of silver and gold was piled upon the table. A female was dealing, (the famous *Señora Toulous*) and had you looked in her countenance for any symptom by which to discover how the game stood, you would have turned away unsatisfied; for calm seriousness was alone discernible, and the cards fell from her fingers as steadily as though she were handling only a knitting needle. But the man who sat opposite to her exhibited the full reverse of this. His fingers trembled, as, with an affectation of unconcern, he drummed upon the table; and his eye watched each card as it fell with searching and intense scrutiny. He was betting largely, and losing, and the other gamesters had ceased their own play to be spectators of the exciting contention. Again and again the long fingers of Señora Toulous swept off the piles of gold, and again were they replaced by the unsteady fingers of her opponent.

Those around looked on in silence, and scarcely even a whispered remark was heard. The slip, slip of the cards, and now and then the jingling of coin, as the stakes were removed and re-

[94] The term *monte* is derived from the "mountain" of cards left after a certain number had been dealt. The game was played with a Spanish deck in which each suit—clubs, swords, suns, and cups—contained ten cards. The cards were numbered from ace to seven, plus the jack (knave), horse in place of the queen, and king.—W. H. H. Allison, "Santa Fe as It Appeared during the Winter of the Years 1837 and 1838," *Old Santa Fe*, No. 2 (October, 1914), 180; Magoffin, *Down the Santa Fé Trail*, 120.

placed, alone broke the midnight stillness of the apartment. Suddenly the man playing opposite the bank spoke to one who sat near him, who immediately rose and was let into the street by a stern visaged attendant guarding the door. The game went on, and a fluctuation took place in the gambler's favor. Ten minutes scarcely elapsed when a peculiar tap was heard at the door, which was immediately yet cautiously opened, and the man who had departed returned, bringing in his hand a bag, which he placed upon the table before the losing player.

Without speaking a word the player poured out a pile of large gold pieces beside him, and, doubling his former stake, commenced his play upon a new spot. The faintest curling of a smile —perceptible only to those searching the mind and not the game —flitted, like a thought conceived in dream, across the countenance of Señora Toulous. Slip, slip went the cards, with skilful precision, from the Señora's fingers, and the first award of the game fell to her opponent. Then a buzz of remark unsealed the observer's lips, which was instantly followed by a loud oath from the player, declaring his determination to double his bets on that spot until he was made or broke. Without even the faint changing of feature noticed before, the Señora continued dealing, and again and again the luck resulted in favor of the formerly unfortunate player. The stillness of the place, which had been broken a moment before by the startling oath of the reckless gambler, was resumed, and the hours of morning rolled on, while no clock gave note of time's passing, but the click of the pendulum found no bad representative in the constant slip of the monte cards.

Still the sudden change of luck continued in favor of the adventurous player, and still the beholders sat with their elbows upon the table and their chins resting upon their hands, watching the game, seemingly with all the interest, although with none of the hazard or hope of profit which gave excitement to the gamesters. The Señora paused and demanded a new pack of cards from one of her attendants.

"No," said the trader, (for he was an American, but addressed

From Harper's New Monthly Magazine, *April,* 1854

La Señora Toulous

"A great lady and rich monte dealer of Santa Fe whose favor is courted by the highest, she is a woman of deep policy and shrewdness."

From Harper's New Monthly Magazine, *April,* 1854

Gambling Saloon in Santa Fe

"Traders often lose the profits of a whole season in an hour's play."

Santa Fe Plaza

"The Church of Our Lady of Light (Nuestra Señora de la Luz) was a beautiful structure on the south side of the plaza. Its twin towers were a familiar landmark to American visitors." From a painting by Gerald Cassidy, in the possession of the New Mexico Historical Society.

the lady in Spanish) "No, Señora, we have played so far with this pack, and they are good enough for the rest of the game."

Toulous smiled as courteously as though she had received a compliment, although the abrupt objection and the tone of its delivery, evidently betrayed a suspicion of foul play. Yet, although even the victim might have fallen in love with that polite expression of feature, to a reader of hearts there was in it the dark designing of one who despised both her fools and the tools by which she ruled them.

Without speaking she waved back her attendant who presented the new cards, and went on dealing the former pack as composedly as one might lounge upon an ottoman reading the latest novel.

The trader's bet had now doubled and doubled again, over and over, and a pile of thousands lay upon the new spot selected at the changing of the game.

The player's companion said in a whisper "Break off."

"No!" shouted the now lucky winner, and again the uncurbed oath of an excited gambler burst, like a slumbering volcano, upon the breathless silence of the scene. "No, I double on that spot until I make or break."

At this moment Toulous lifted a fresh bag of gold to the table, and spread out a pile of glittering coin before her.

"Yes, pour them out, old lady," said the trader, in a loud voice, as he lifted his newly filled tumbler of *Pass Whiskey* to his lips, "Pour the yellow rascals out; we may as well make one job of it before morning!" and he set the glass down with a burst of that kind of laughter which causes the face to grow grave and the blood to chill.

The next card fell to the dealer's side, and Señora Toulous, with the same unchanging serenity, motioned to an attendant to sweep the dazzling heap of gold into the lately emptied bag.

"Good again for you!" said the trader, and, handing his tumbler to be refilled, he deliberately counted his remaining gold, and placed it all upon the spot which had just been cleared.

Slip, slip went the cards, and the new bet was counted out and paid by the losing dealer.

"Go on again," cried the gambler, without altering or dividing his bet, and the next card again doubled the amount in his favor.

A step was now heard passing in the street, and the next moment the "herald of the morn" lifted its voice in greeting to the Eastern glimmerings of day.

The now accumulated bet upon the table was sufficiently large to have covered all the player had lost during the night, and it would seem that his companion, either by pressing his toe, or pulling his sleeve, or some other sign, had given him an admonitory hint to this effect, for he suddenly broke out, even louder than heretofore, swearing that he would make or break before he left his seat; concluding with an imitation of the cock that was crowing outside, and drinking the health of the Spanish lady in the again refilled glass which was at the moment handed to him.

Twice again the game resulted in his favor, and when daylight was peeping through the door cracks, and the candle light began to contrast strangely with the dawn, Señora Toulous once more swept the table, and the reckless trader was left without a dollar.

"Wake snakes!" shouted the sturdy Kentuckian, as he jumped up from the table and commenced dancing about the apartment, "Wake snakes! Hail Columbia! I'm off for California to-morrow! and, I say, old lady, I'll see you again in the fall!"

The Señora curtsied and disappeared through a side door with the dignity of an Empress and the same skilfully modeled smile, followed by her attendants with the heavy bags of gold and Mexican dollars.

That man is now fighting under the Mexican Government against the dreaded Camanches,[95] and this was the third time he

---

[95] By 1840, Comanche raids on southwestern settlements were increasing in frequency and destructiveness. That year they raided as far south as the Mexican state of Zacatecas, and to the east they attacked Texas settlements and were attacked in return by Texas forces.—Rupert N. Richardson, *The Comanche Barrier to South Plains Settlement* (Glendale, 1933), 113–16, 196.

had hazarded the earnings of years, and sacrificed them at the Monte Bank!

Santa Fé—Its Ladies and Shops

A large square, comprising about three hundred square yards, is situated in the centre of the town of Santa Fé. The row of houses on one side is occupied entirely by the public offices, the custom house, and armory, and quarters for the military. The other three sides are used for shops for the sale of merchandise brought from the United States, and are kept by Americans. The houses are built of clay, and with very few exceptions are but one story high. Shops are rented to traders in this square, the best situation in the place at from ten to twenty dollars a month. The store keepers, in dull times, sit at their doors all day smoking cigars, cracking jokes with the Spaniards, and peeping under the veils of the Señoras and Señoritas as they pass. The ladies invariably wear either a veil or shawl thrown over their heads. They wear no hat or other covering for the head, but are never seen, in doors or in the street, without their shawl or scarf. They are all dark complexioned, some of them pretty, but many of them plain, and most of them ugly. Generally, they are but slightly removed from the Indians, and these paint their faces like the Indians, with vermilion, by way of ornament.

The Americans, who trade to the country, acquire the Spanish language very speedily, but the Spaniards seldom learn a word of English, and when an American remains long in the place, and obtains a facility in the language, he becomes a man of great importance. The first alcalde of Santa Fé, at this time, Don Louis Rubideau, was born in St. Louis, of a French family, and has spent fourteen years in the country. He shares the rule over the people almost equally with the Governor and priests. He was appealed to one day by a store keeper, who accused a Spaniard of defrauding him of five dollar[s] in the trade of a watch. The Spaniard was indignant, and the parties grew into high words, upon which the alcalde, whose principal was

Though justice be blind she is not deaf,

told them to look somewhere else for redress, for if they dared come to him again, and talk loud in his presence, he'd put them both in jail.

A Trader's Shop

Around the door, outside, sat upon the ground some half dozen ragged Mexicans, men and women, with baskets before them, containing grapes, melons, peaches, and other fruits for sale. Stepping over the bare legs of these fruiterers, we entered the store, and found ourselves in an apartment of about fifteen by eighteen feet dimensions. Two sides of the room were covered with shelves, upon which calicoes and domestics, and a variety of dry goods and nic-nacs were disposed in much the same manner as is customary in the States. A plain counter stood in front of these shelves, serving to show the goods upon and keep off meddlers, and upon the counter we found our friend, the trader, seated smoking a cigar.

We had scarcely exchanged civilities before a young *cavallero*, on a remarkably large and well fed mule, with saddle and other gear gorgeously decorated with silver, and little bells and ornaments jingling as he approached, rode up, dismounted, and came into the house. This young Spaniard was the fine gentleman of Santa Fé, the very pink of the aristocracy; we had met him before in company with Governor Amijo, and found in him a courteousness of demeanor which showed that he had been educated in the more civilized part of Mexico; therefore his appearance must be described.

His *sombrero* was an enormous, heavy, broad brimmed beaver, with a thick cord of gold wound round it several times in place of the simple ribbon used by Americans. Beneath this his dark and raven locks (for he had them in perfection, and was a fine handsome fellow,) shone with dazzling effect, and a painter would have chosen him for a model to paint a Macaroni from. His jacket of black cloth was covered with frogs and braid, and fitted him with exquisite neatness. He wore a shirt of American make, or at least not differing at all from our fashion, and round his neck a very elegant black silk handkerchief. He wore no vest, two breast pins glittered in his bosom, and a long silken sash was wound in many folds around his waist. Suspenders they never wear, and they express for such things a very hearty contempt. The sash, folded tightly round the top of the pantaloons, is the only support given to the habiliment. These pantaloons have more peculiarity about them than any other part of a Mexican's dress. The outside seam of each leg is left open from the hip down, for the purpose of exposing the white drawers beneath, which are made extremely wide, and this, together with the short jacket and sash, reminds one forcibly of the Turkish style of dress. His boots, too caught our attention; they were made to lace on the outside of the foot from the sole up, but were left flying open, and thus the white stocking was exposed. The long silver *espuelas* [spurs] were attached to the heel of the boot, buttoned across the instep with a broad strap, and hanging below the foot, so that it was always necessary to remove them upon dismounting.

His business showed him to be a lady's messenger, for he wanted silk for a dress, and other things for female use. Besides which he suffered himself to be seduced by the store keeper into the purchase of sundry new handkerchiefs and other matters just received from the States.

Having spared as many golden pieces from his net purse as he thought prudent, he took leave of us with much politeness, and mounted his noble mule. The mule was indeed the finest we ever saw, seeming to possess all the strength and capacity to endure peculiar to its breed, yet exhibiting the beauty and intelligence of the horse in an unusual degree. Off rode the *cavallero*, lifting his large hat to us with graceful ease as he departed, and the little, bright silver and steel ornaments jingling as he passed, attracted all eyes to the fine gentleman of Santa Fé.

He had scarcely departed when a little bare footed girl came in, with a dozen most bilious looking candles hanging together by a string. These she sold to the shop keeper for an old rusty steel thimble for her *madre*. The thimble cost the trader about the forty-ninth part of a cent, and he sold the candles before we left the shop for a good Spanish shilling, which was making, certainly, a small trifle above first cost. The old women all understood making candles, and one of them will often spend half a day boiling grease and dipping a dozen, only to realize sixpence worth of tobacco from a shop keeper.

Two rough fellows with long beards now came in, flinging their tattered blankets over their left shoulders with that free swagger which the action is apt to impart. This, with their slouched hats and rather hang-dog expression of features gave the new customers an appearance picturesque indeed, but by no means enticing. Old descriptions of Spanish assassins and Italian brigands instantly rose before us, and the best melo-dramatic murderer upon the stage might have taken a useful lesson in costume had he been upon the spot. Their naked toes were peeping through old Indian mockasins, which were strapped around the foot with many a string of deer skin, and their dark brown legs appeared naked beneath their blankets. Yet, though these were two most rascally looking fellows, there was something pleasant, something humorous about them, something of that devil-may-care manner which is rather agreeable than repulsive, (except when carried to excess) because, even when assumed, it denotes the absence of hypocrisy and deceit. They stared about a moment or two, when the trader told them, in a polite Spanish phrase which they seemed to understand, to walk out, and they very contentedly obeyed, without seeming to take any offence at their abrupt dismissal.

As these queer customers were stepping out, three *señoritas* and an old *señora* came tripping in. They were clothed entirely in black, and most impervious long black veils were thrown over their heads, giving them every appearance of nuns, but we afterwards learned that this was the aristocratical female dress, and these ladies belonged to the family of the ex-Governor. They looked at some goods, bought some, and were departing, exhibiting every indication of modest well-bred females, when their exit was retarded by the appearance at the door of a drunken American driver.

Here a ludicrous scene occurred. The fellow had been one of our own drivers, and we knew him for an excellent hearted humorist, so that we were willing to laugh at what fun he could make, feeling confident he would give no really serious offence to the ladies.

"Ladies," said he, pulling off his hat, from which tumbled three dozen cigars and a quantity of grapes, "ladies, I'm a man of fashion and a gentleman, from the great United States, and I want to ask what you will take for this town of Santa Fé."

The girls huddled round the old woman, and drew their veils close, while Charlie (for that was his name) stooped to gather the grapes and cigars; still keeping between the ladies and the door, for there was method in his madness, and he had no disposition to let them out.

"I'll give a heap of *paysos* for Santa Fé just for your sakes, though it's a monstrous *low* place. Your houses are all *in one story*, like a pack of thieves; built of *mud*, too, so they ought to go as cheap as *dirt*. Madame, will you have a cigar? Miss, I beg pardon, I don't know your name—O, I remember—*seen-yora*— Miss *Seen-yora*, these grapes are not sour, I assure you. Look here, galls," said he, and after pausing a moment, and peeping beneath one of the veils, he gave one loud Kentucky yell, which instantly drew a dense crowd around the door.

"Six months since I've seen a gal, so help me Cupid, and I'll marry are a one of you—I'll marry the whole bunch of you right off!"

The trader now interfered.

"Look here, Captain Branch," said Charlie, "do you call that perlite to interrupt a gentleman when he's popping the question

217

to a lady?" Three of the ladies had now escaped, and the youngest was following, when Charlie started after her, and with a low bow proffered his arm. To our utter consternation the girl took his arm, and Charlie straightened up his back and walked off with a tall strut, knowing that we were all staring after him.

Whether the young creature was so frightened she didn't know what she was about, or whether she had really taken a notion to Charlie (for good natured impudence has won more girls than ever sighing did) we never learned, but this is the true history of a merry half hour spent in a trader's shop in Santa Fé.

An Arrival

The arrival of [*sic*] Santa Fé of a caravan from the States is, both to the natives and the transient residents, an affair of much enlivening interest. The coming of a trading company is generally heard of full ten days before the loaded wagons reach the town, and this interim is all occupied in anticipation, curiosity, and speculation. Those interested in the new merchandise are all anxiety of course, while others, not connected in the enterprise, look for letters and news from home. The Señoritas who figure at fandangos, look for new faces and new beaux, while the customhouse officers grow more important in their bearing, and are constantly on the alert, ready for the most jealous scrutiny of the new comers.

After visiting Toas and spending a few days in that romantic valley, we proceeded to Santa Fé and were there five days before the wagons, which we had left some two hundred miles away in the prairie, came in. It was about noon-day, when, having been informed that the caravan was entering the town, we proceeded to the great square to witness the arrival; and we had scarcely whiled away fifteen minutes when whips were heard cracking round a distant corner, and we recognized the well-known voice of one of our noisy drivers. He had a name for every one of his mules, and an invariable manner of talking to them continually with loud and furious oaths. When crossing marshy places and difficult creeks, it would freeze the blood of an ordinary swearer to hear this man curse his animals. He seemed to employ his invention in framing the most frightful maledictions, and, from our own horror we could almost imagine that the poor mules understood them too, for, with ears erect, starting eyes, and straining limbs, they would force the ponderous vehicle through places where other wagons would remain stalled for hours. His method was in crossing these places, just at the moment when the wheels met a difficulty, to break out suddenly with these loud curses, screaming, yelling, and applying his long whip with furious vigor, and he scarcely ever failed in making the terrified mules jump the huge wagon out of the dangerous spot.

His leading mules he called "Pomp" and "Nell," and we now heard him, still out of sight in a distant street, astonishing the natives with his singular accomplishment. "Hey! You Pomp! you Nell! gee! gee! (whip crack) Pomp! (one of his patent oaths, the startling effect of which upon the mules could be likened to nothing else but the sudden explosion of a sky-rocket) Pomp, I say! you Pomp!—Haw! haw! Will you get out of that? Haw! You Nell, where are you going there? Now then, get up there!" (whip crack.) And this brought Pomp and Nell, and the eight mules harnessed behind them, the driver himself, handling his long whip with ostentatious flourishes, and making every tender part of poor Pomp and Nell quiver with scientific touches of his lash, driving at the same time his long Spanish spurs into the sides of the left wheel mule which he was straddling, this spectacle appeared now in full view approaching the square. Then behind appeared another wagon, another, and another, until the first had reached the customhouse door and the last had not yet turned the distant corner.

On they came up the long street, and old and young, American and Mexican, all sorts and sexes, assembled at doors and windows and in the street, to witness the procession. The drivers, reckless and insolent fellows, cracking whips and jokes simultaneously as they moved along, were as happy as sailors just stepping upon land. Indeed these prairie adventurers resemble no other class of men but the honest hearted and improvident Jack Tars. The travel itself is just like an ocean journey. There is the long absence from the sight of fellow-creatures—these wagons had been upwards of seventy days from Missouri—the wild and trackless region you traverse, its only difference from the ocean being that you have green beneath you, instead of "the blue above and the blue below"—and the near horizon bounding the prospect around you precisely as you view it on the ocean. No wonder that men who engage in such a trade should resemble the wandering, care-for-nothing sons of Neptune.

A few moments more saw the wagons halted and ranged in the square, and one after another they were emptied and the goods deposited in the customhouse. Then the trunks and baggage were submitted to examination, the officers simply ordering them open and handling one or two of the upper articles, but had they been more particular they might have detected in some of the trunks several hundred dollars worth of fine silks snugly packed away beneath the usual stock of personal garments.

This business gone through with, the empty wagons were driven away, the poor mules turned out to pasture, to rest and feast for six long months, and evening scarcely darkened over the town before the pass whiskey began to operate, and groups of noisy American drivers were heard singing, shouting, and rioting in every street. The sound of the fiddle and guitar soon succeeded, however, and this drew the rowdy customers from the streets into the fandangos, half a dozen of which are sure to be put in operation upon the evening of a caravan's arrival. Some *monte* dealers, too, commenced initiating the new comers into the Mexican game; but these are bankers of small capital, as the fashionable *Toulous* seldom condescends to show herself, either at the monte table or the fandango, until the strangers have had an opportunity to hear all about her and have their curiosity set upon a proper edge. She is a woman of deep policy and shrewdness, and the common people look upon her with almost as much reverence as they pay to the Governor and priests.

Thus each new arrival makes a kind of holiday in Santa Fé, and the thoughtless drivers generally keep it up as long as they have a dollar left to spend. The next day the goods are released from the customhouse, and the owners having duly engaged themselves to pay five hundred dollars for each wagon;[96] having undergone a scrutinizing cross-examination before the Governor to ascertain that no goods have been *cached* or otherwise secretly disposed of; and having laid a *douceur* of some kind before his eminence—proceed to open their shops and arrange their merchandise for sale.

In the meantime, if any visitors have come with the traders to see the country, they are received with much courtesy and distinction and particularly if they are possessed of the *lengua Castilliano*. Such travellers are looked upon as people of high birth and affluence, and the Governor, himself, is eager to pay them respect. Señora Toulous will mix with them in a waltz, and open her bank to relieve them of any superfluous pieces which may encumber their pockets. In short they are lions while they stay.

As we remained in Santa Fé but a fortnight, we witnessed but one arrival of this kind.

The Smugglers

Owing to the enormous duties imposed upon American merchandise, smuggling, to an immense extent, was for a long time carried on by the acute traders who brought goods from the States to the far Mexican settlements under the mountains. The

[96] "From 1839 to 1844 . . . Governor Armijo . . . without regard to the prevailing national tariff or to the manifested value of the merchandise . . . imposed a flat rate of $500 per wagonload on all imports. As the average legal duties amounted to from $1,000 to $2,000 per load, this arbitrary rate was hardly disadvantageous to the traders, and, as a matter of fact, it led to further reduction of their payments through the importation of more expensive goods and the transportation of them in oversize wagons."—Moorhead, *New Mexico's Royal Road*, 127.

plan used was to conceal valuable and contraband articles in *caches*, at a safe distance from the town, before entering, and there suffer them to rest until suspicion was no longer feared, when they were dug up, conveyed from the cache on mules, and quietly placed upon the trader's shelves during the night. Thus the Yankee trader *cached* his goods before he sold them. A vile pun, but we have knocked our head against the wall for having written it, and being now busy scratching a newly developed phrenological protuberance, and a little vexed, withal, between ourself and the wall, we shall not scratch it out.

The authorities soon became aware of this trickery, and guards were stationed nightly on the principal avenues to the town, for the purpose of detecting and intercepting smugglers. This proved of little avail, for the soldier who happened to wake up and pounce upon a transgressor of the law, was easily put to sleep again with a small roll of silk stuff or a bale of domestic. Bribery was all powerful with high and low among the government officers, and this was a matter publicly understood, at least among the Americans, but the Governor exacted higher fees than the poor, poverty-stricken night-guard. Thus things continued, until the higher powers, finding themselves duped, adopted measures of greater severity and watchfulness. Then great hazard and danger began to attend the secret operations of the traders. The simple Mexicans became initiated into the cunning tricks practised upon them, and soon learned to set traps, place spies, and discover the rich goods secretly deposited in the ground. Contraband merchandise of great value was seized, and the Governor, having his appetite thus whetted, pursued the unfortunate traders with still greater vigilance, enforcing his measures with an unbending determination strongly marked by jealous animosity to the Americans.

One night as the whirling waltzers were moving through a fandango in Santa Fé, an American entered the door with anxiety and alarm depicted in his countenance, and hastily plucking another, who was dancing, by the sleeve, he whispered two or three English words, and again hurried away, followed instantly by the man to whom he had spoken, he without ceremony leaving his partner, the Señora, to get through the dance as best she could.

"How many?" enquired the man who had just left the dance, as the two hurried round a dark corner, keeping in the middle of the unpaved and irregular street.

"There are twelve of them," replied his companion, "some have mules, some horses, and little Hernandez is their leader."

"Why do they think they have discovered our cache?"

"I don't know—the idea struck me, and it grows stronger with me every minute, I don't know why."

The two men now turned the corner of the great square in the centre of the town, and at the same instant a party of mounted men were seen to ride off at a quick pace from before the custom-house door.

A few hasty words passed between the two Americans, and they parted hurriedly in different directions. As they disappeared, the sound of drum and fife was heard, signifying, however, no warlike preparation; 'twas but the two soldiers who every evening at eight o'clock march round the square three times, playing a sort of demi-barbarous music, any thing but agreeable to ears polite. This is the custom in Santa Fé, and serves the purpose of a curfew or evening gun.

Dark clouds were floating about the sky, and now and then, as the moon rode into a blue place, her beams glanced upon the dark mountain—upon cliff and crag, and rifted tree, and splintered pinnacle—and gap and gorge, that lay in shadow, showed like the dwellings of storm-spirits and tempest-fiends. Then again the vapoury veil closed over the face of the night Queen, and the huge mountain appeared only one vast mass of black, as if it was the rendezvous where all the clouds of the sky were gathering.

It could not have wanted half an hour of midnight, when, as the moon spread transiently her light over the landscape, two men emerged from the dark gap of a mountain torrent, and spurred their horses with furious speed over the broad stretch of prairie that lay between this and the next mountain. Twenty minutes scarcely elapsed when the clattering of hoofs told of a larger party pursuing the same track, for now the sky was clouded again, and the riders pursued their way in darkness.

Let us follow the two men in advance. They dashed through a creek which crossed this prairie valley in its centre, without pausing an instant to suffer their panting animals to drink, and soon gained the foot of the opposite mountain. Here they seemed to be at some uncertainty.

"It is impossible," said one, "even with the moon we could scarcely find the place, and now 'tis as dark as pitch."

The men had scarcely spoken when a flood of silver light fell upon the scene, and the speaker instantly sprang from his horse, exclaiming—"Here we are—this is the very spot!"

The man [*sic*], still holding their horses, advanced to a small scrubby oak, which stood about twenty yards from where the thick, wild brush commenced at the foot of the mountain, and, with their united strength, they plucked it from the ground, and carefully filled up and covered the hole left by the root. They then moved away with it about a hundred and fifty yards, and selecting a place nearly as possible resembling that they had just left, they fell upon their knees and commenced digging up the earth with their large bowie knives.

A few moments saw the dwarf oak planted again as firmly as before, and the two men with their horses hastily disappeared in the brushwood and up the mountain side.

"*Vamos, Vaminos, soldados!*" was the exclamation now heard, followed by the sound of trampling hoofs swiftly approaching the spot. The whole party of *Teniente* Hernandez was soon at the foot of the mountain, galloping about in all directions, and confusing themselves by each leading the other astray.

The two Americans had concealed their horses deep in the brushwood, and were now ensconced quite at ease in the fork of a tree which projected from a cliff above, listening to the excitement and confusion among the Mexican soldiers, and now and then catching a sight of their glancing forms when the moon peeped out.

Presently a broad, blue space opened in the sky, and a steady sheet of light fell upon the wild scenery around. Then a loud shout of triumph was heard, and the two Yankee smugglers sat choking with suppressed laughter at seeing the eager Spaniards fly to the newly discovered shrub oak, tear it from the earth, and, with loud exclamations of delight, fall to digging for the concealed treasure.

Long after daylight the work continued, while the two Americans lay concealed among the branches of the tree, where they learned from the curses and exclamations of the disappointed Spaniards, that a treacherous driver, who had assisted in making the cache, had betrayed it to the Governor. But the best joke to the concealed Americans was, that the Spaniards at last gave up their fruitless search and departed, fully believing that a hoax had been played upon them by the rascally American *carrero* [teamster], whom they afterwards found means to punish severely.

But for the prompt action of the two smugglers in removing the dwarf oak from the *real* cache, and drawing off the pursuers on a false scent, they would have been ruined; and, profiting by the warning, they, by a further exercise of Yankee ingenuity, contrived to smuggle the whole contents of their cache into Santa Fé before the following midnight; and Lieut. Hernandez believes to this day that he was hoaxed by the driver, instead of being outwitted by the Yankee smugglers.

A Wedding

We were invited to attend a wedding. The bride was a dark-eyed Mexican brunette of about twenty; the groom was an American, who five years before had made his first trip to Santa Fé. When we entered the apartment, the colloquy which we had heard when passing the windows instantly ceased, and we began to feel the disheartening sensation experienced when knowing that our presence is a restraint. Not being sufficiently familiar with Spanish, we could not exercise the usual polite means of removing this difficulty, but we had a companion with us who could handle some instruments, and among the rest he could thrum the guitar very pleasingly, guided by an ear which took its lessons from the heart, for he could not read a note of music. He was a merry fellow, and making a boast that in five minutes he would remove the awkwardness of our situation and make all parties sociable, he, with great confidence, took the guitar from a musician in the corner, and played, sung, and danced "Jim Crow,"[97] in imitation of the great American original. The *señoras*, however, had not yet imbibed a taste for the refinement of American music, or were astounded by the remarkable musical qualifications of our companion, for they became even more inanimate than before at witnessing this exhibition. It served the purpose, however, for though our friend was completely chop-fallen, his discomfiture started our risibility, and our peals of laughter soon wrought a greater effect upon the Spanish girls than this extraordinary display of musical ability.

The bride was pointed out to us. There she was smoking her *chupar*. She would pass for handsome among all who do not consider a fair skin absolutely indispensable to beauty. She was well formed, had the glossiest raven hair, a graceful neck and bust, her complexion was not dark enough to prevent the lighter tint of the rose from showing in her cheek, and her eye was of that wild, dark, dazzling lustre which has a something of the fearful in it even while it enchants. She was a creature to love—just such a creature as was calculated to win the impulsive and adventurous young American—and there she sat with a cigar in her mouth! It would be curious if we could express the odd sensations we experienced at seeing a pretty girl, and a bride, smoking. We were half inclined to laugh, half disposed to be angry; one of us

[97] T. D. Rice, a famous minstrel, popularized this Negro song and dance in the 1830's.

was on the point of requesting her as a favor to throw away that cigar, and would have done so, had she not at the moment handed it to her mother, who sat behind her, and the old woman smoked up the cigar which her daughter had commenced.

Our friend the bridegroom now entered, and a little attempt at ceremony, in the way of introduction took place. Nothing is more awkward and ridiculous than a display of etiquette in places where it is not known or understood; and we could with infinitely more grace and ease have gone through a presentation to Victoria, than an introduction to this little Spanish girl who smoked cigars. Without taking a thought of where we were, the low bow, the smile, and the behavior most habitual with us, marked our obeisance to a lady; and instantly we became conscious that the women were all staring and the men laughing at us. The *señoras* and *señoritas* of Santa Fé were not accustomed to see lordly man bowing before them, and this extraordinary exhibition of politeness afforded, no doubt, great amusement for the rest of the season, through all circles, vulgar as well as fashionable.

Politeness, however, makes few enemies, and if there is no aphorism to this effect extant, it is very plain there ought to be, and no doubt there is, though it may very easily have escaped the notice of the present writer, whose readings are, if possible, more unconsidered even than his scribblings. We soon found ourselves favorites both with men and women, and the restraint which had attended our entrance to the wedding party, gave place to a free and sociable understanding.

Observing the bride about to roll up a fresh *chupar*, our jovial associate pulled a genuine, ready-made roll of the weed from his pocket, and with the best Spanish he could muster, (which must have been ridiculously foreign to his purpose, as we should judge from the laugh it caused,) he tendered an American cigar. Though made in Mexico, and by us properly termed Spanish cigars, here among Spaniards and Mexicans they were called *American*, which, though certainly strange, will be easily explained by a glance at the map.

The priest came in, and *he* had a cigar in his mouth. Next a dance took place, after which the bride and bridegroom walked up in front of the reverend minister of hymen, she presenting him with a glass of *Pass Whiskey*, and the groom tendering a neatly folded *chupar*. Then about ten minutes were occupied in ceremonies, similar in form, but differing materially in spirit, from our own, and the dance was again resumed.

Just as this ceremony concluded, three merry little children came bouncing into the room, the oldest a girl, and the other two dark haired and dark eyed boys, bearing a strong resemblance to the bride. They flew to our American friend, the bridegroom, and he seemed to receive their caresses with every mark of paternal solicitude and delight, which exciting our surprise, we made enquiry, and were told, to our no little wonder, that the children were his own, and that for five years he and the bride had been man and wife in all but the ceremony.

The young fellow was of good family in the States, and having quarrelled with his professors in a Western College, he, instead of returning home, went off upon this adventurous travel to Santa Fé. There he resided for a long time, partly enchained by the Spanish girl, and partly withheld by pride from returning home. At length, after sojourning two years among these strange people, he sought the States again, intending to abandon his dark eyed enchantress and join his relatives; but the next season found him again in Santa Fé, unable to violate his first attachment.

Nearly three years more he dwelt away from home, and at the time that we attended his wedding, he had just returned from another visit to the States, having bidden farewell forever to friend and relative, resolved to give his wife a husband and his children a father.

When made acquainted with these circumstances, we very naturally experienced a lively interest in our new friends, and upon calling on them we found our young countryman in a situation which we were far more inclined to envy than to commiserate. The Mexican girl, it was evident, stored up the whole treasure of her young affections in her American husband, and he seemed to love his children the more for possessing the dark eyes of their mother.

Clime has no control over happiness, and, though home ever holds a chain around the heart, love can fling charms around a habitation in the desert, and brighten a lot cast far from early kindred, in the strangest lands and among the strangest of men.

The Dying Murderer

A man was confined in the prison for murder.[98] We were admitted to see him. His mother, a ragged, tottering, grey-haired woman, sat by his side as he lay upon an old buffalo robe that was spread in one corner of the room. The face of that old woman haunts the writer at this moment. She sat upon the bare floor of the prison room, with her skeleton hands clasped in each other, and her glassy eyes fixed with intense vacancy (if such an expression is allowable) upon her wretched, dying son. The miserable prisoner noticed our entrance with a dark scowl, but she seemed wholly unconscious of our presence, and indeed of everything. Eighty years sorrow had furrowed double as many wrinkles, and left little room for expression in her countenance, yet the very absence of every thing like meaning in her face, made her appearance more strikingly impressive. In that fixed and vacant stare we read a doting fondness of a mother's heart, clinging still to her wretched boy, when branded by crime, and scorn, and misery, and marked for death by the law and by disease—that horrid and loathsome disease which is the terrible punishment of vice.

The unhappy wretch had murdered a girl, his own niece, a young and innocent creature, who reproached him for a robbery

[98] The Governor's Palace on the plaza was a medieval-looking structure, one end of which was barred and used as a jail. The customhouse and barracks were joined to the same palace—the barracks and jail (guardhouse) set at the west end—"all being held together . . . by the . . . power of mud."—Benjamin F. Taylor (ed.), *Short Ravelings from a Long Yarn* (Santa Ana, 1936), 146; Garnet M. Brayer (ed.), *Land of Enchantment* (Evanston, Illinois, 1954), 46.

he had committed upon a priest. He feared the artless girl would, in making her confession, expose his crime, and exasperated that he could not force her to promise secrecy, he plunged his knife into her heart. He fled to the mountains, and would have escaped but for the vigilance of the girl's lover, who hunted the murderer alone for days after the officers of justice had given up the pursuit, until he succeeded in capturing the wretched creature. Hunger, and the frightful disease which was consuming him, had made the miserable being weak, and he would probably have perished alone, among the mountains, had he not been found; for it was in January, and even had he possessed strength to hunt animals for food, he could not have lived through two nights, exposed in the snow to the freezing winds which howl in the winter months around those giant hills of stone. His pursuer found the most wretched man, exhausted and fainting, concealed in a hollow tree, and, bent firmly on a just revenge, he hunted game, kindled a fire, and with his own hands fed the murderer of his betrothed. A more extraordinary thing than this could not be conceived. The young man never exchanged a word with the criminal, but with an iron firmness, born from blighted hopes and the prospect of a life of sorrow, he fed him, restored him to strength, and drove him back to Santa Fé.

We spoke to the unhappy man, but the very kindness of our tones seemed to offend him, and he answered only with a dark frown. He took no notice of his mother, but lay brooding in sullen and gloomy despair. His features were handsome, but the expression of his eye made us shrink and shudder. The paleness of death was already visible in his dark sunken cheek, yet if his countenance was to be believed, wicked passions were still raging fearfully within his breast. He neither looked at us or at his mother, but with his dark brows contracted he gazed constantly at the ceiling of the dungeon. Now and then a more transparent paleness would visit his cheek, and the firm closing of his lips and teeth told that the pangs of disease were torturing his frame, but still he uttered no moan nor sound of any kind. And that poor old woman sitting upon the ground beside him!—she was the very impersonation of sorrow and despair. Her appearance awed us until we also became mute, and an oppressive silence that made the blood run cold in our veins, reigned around the death couch of the murderer.

An alcalde entered, leading a priest who carried a crucifix and prayer book. The criminal maintained his fixed stare at the roof, yielding no attention to the solemn greeting of the churchman; but the old woman instantly changed her position, and knelt beside her son. Still no expression appeared in her countenance, and no sound escaped her lips. Her white hair was rudely tied with a string of deer skin, and a coarse blanket and tattered undergarment was her covering. When the priest appeared she drew from her bosom a small crucifix of wood, attached to a string of beads, which she passed mechanically through her fingers, still with her faded and lustreless eyes fixed upon the form of her dying son. The priest knelt also, and offered to take the hand of the criminal, but the hand was snatched nervously away, and the dark, sunken eye of the murderer gleamed with a terrible look of hatred and defiance. Again the deadly whiteness stole over his countenance, and we heard his teeth grit as the pangs of death were raging through his vitals. Suddenly he sprang up in a sitting position, and opening his mouth for the first time, he gave vent to a succession of screams and yells that caused us to start back in terror. We hurried from the prison, for the sight was too terrible, and as we passed through the low door way we saw that the poor old woman had fallen upon her face, and was laying seemingly insensible upon the floor of the dungeon, while the priest was stooping to assist her. The miserable man died that night.

Timotéo

One day we were lounging on the wooden benches outside of a trader's store in Santa Fé, when we observed a boy of about six years of age seated near us upon the ground and watching us seemingly with great interest. We did not think this strange, as we were subjects of curiosity with young and old, but presently the stump of a cigar was thrown down, and the little fellow instantly rose, picked it up, put out the fire, rolled it away in a corner of his blanket, and resumed his seat. We were all smoking and in a few moments another stump fell upon the ground, which was immediately seized and disposed of in like manner. Seeing this, we soon gave the little fellow an opportunity of picking up our last stump, which he had not sooner done than he hurried away from the place, and we concluded his intention was to initiate himself into the fashionable accomplishment of smoking. The next day, when again indulging ourselves with cigars, we were attended by the little dark-eyed Mexican as before, who picked up our remnants of cigars and hurried away when he had gathered them all, like one who had secured a treasure of some value. The little fellow interested us and we rose up and followed him to see what use he had for the old cigar stumps. After following him round two or three corners we saw him enter a dilapidated dwelling, and upon arriving at the door we witnessed a mark of youthful affection as touching as it was simple. The boy was placing the stale remnants of cigars in the lap of his old blind grandmother, a woman of not less than eighty years, who, muttering blessings upon her grandchild, was crumbling the tobacco between her fingers and filling her pipe with the powdered leaves. And the little boy with his round laughing eyes sat at the old woman's feet looking up at her sightless orbs, and asking her how rich the young Americans were who could throw such good tobacco away in the street.

It is very true we were an impulsive set of youths, and our unsophisticated feelings were easily touched, yet there was something in that picture of the bright-eyed boy and his sightless grandmother which might furnish a noble theme for a better pen than the one which makes this simple narration. We entered the dwelling and threw some loose bits of silver and the remainder of our yet untouched cigars into the old woman's lap, and the large laughing eyes of the boy danced with delight as he told the poor old woman that the great Americans had come to see her and had brought her money and cigars. The childish and half oblivious grandmother sat muttering prayers and blessings in Spanish, and filling her pipe mechanically with her fingers, seemingly conscious of little else save that she was to enjoy a smoke. We called the boy to us, but although he seemed delighted to be noticed, he would not come until he had brought a light for the old woman's pipe, and then he came bounding upon our knees, and putting a thousand childish questions to us all about the Americans and the great United States. He told us that his name was *Timotéo*, (Timothy) and that his grandmother had been blind many years; she had dropped her eyes, he said, into the grave of his grandfather when they were burying him; she was weeping very much and did not know of her loss until the grave was closed up, and then she found that the sight of her eyes had been washed away in tears. Whether this was the child's fancy or whether he had been taught it, there is some poetry if no truth in the story.

Timotéo was filled with a remarkable enthusiasm touching every thing American. He asked us questions about the cities, and what he had before learned must have been from some facetious Missouri waggoner, for he spoke of the little town of Independence, the farthest away in Missouri and the starting place of the traders, as if it was the great city of the Union, in fact he seemed to think it was the great United States all in itself from its name being Independence. He was interesting, intelligent, and very handsome, which caused him to be noticed and petted by the traders, and was the more remarkable as the children are generally ugly and in fact really repulsive. His eye was of that brilliant black more characteristic of fierce passion than of affection, but in a child there was a sufficient softening of milder expression to give it the character of the latter emotion. His hair was the night gloss of the raven; and his eye lashes and brows of glittering jet seemed to catch brilliancy from the glowing orbs which they covered. Then his complexion, the soft breaking forth of the red through the shaded, yet hardly darkened skin; his round cheek would remind you of the mellow, melting, delicious, and nutritious peach, and the mantling glow of childhood spoke health more strongly than if contrasted by opposing white, for delicacy of complexion would have given his almost too handsome face a girlish character, from which his passionate eye only could have redeemed it.

In little Timotéo one might see not a "sucking Hamlet," but a childish Romeo—the making, the beginning of a Romeo—not a stage imitator of the character, but the character itself, growing up in real life, a breathing evidence that the mind of Shakespeare in studying nature

> *Felt through the dim wrapped mystery, and plucked*
> *The shadows wild forth with his reaching fancy,*
> *And with form and color clad them,*

making his pictures for all nations and for all time. And here was the "picture in little" of a Romeo. A few years would show him a being all heart and impulse, and passion swift as the lightning yet generous as the day. What is to be his story? Sure as he lives to manhood romance will be mingled with his history—romance, adventure, whirling excitement, crime perhaps, for, also, how often does heaven's own fire burning within us, acting upon mortal mould, destroy instead of blessing us.

He asked us to take him with us to see our great city of Independence. He said he would take care of our horses, watch for us while we slept in the night, and kill the Camanches; he would hunt buffalo and deer for us and we would have nothing to do because he would do every thing. We told him he should come with us and be a young American, and the energetic little fellow sprang upon the floor, dancing about and laughing with delight. Suddenly he paused and his face changed like the April sky. Large tears were rolling from the sightless eyes of the old woman as she sat before us, and the pipe had fallen from her fingers. The little boy flew to her, placed his arm around her neck, kissed her fondly, and with the corner of his little coarse blanket wiped away the tears that were rolling down her wrinkled cheeks.

Timotéo shook his head—he could not go with us—he could not leave his poor blind grandmother! Noble boy! In the breast of that ragged, barefooted, untutored Mexican child, who picked up our cigar stumps, dwelt a heart and spirit worthy of the God-like days of Rome.

Evening

Beauty and repose are attributes of evening in any clime; but here, at the mountain's foot, when the sun is hid beyond the tall peaks above, and a thin grey shadow falls over Santa Fé; while the blue sky is still illuminated with slanting sun-beams, and floating clouds are bathed in golden radiance; here, in the little mud-built Mexican town, beauty and repose seem folded away from the world, like flowers smiling in the desert, like young genius shrinking from the very admiration for which it pants in secret. To the contemplative traveller an evening scene in this place presents every material to excite interest and pleasure. The town itself, to the eye of an American, is as novel a spectacle as could be found upon the face of old mother earth, and to this novelty is added that peculiar charm pertaining always to evening, but in this place seeming to strike the senses and awaken admiration with greater force.

We were lounging upon an old bridge, which crossed a creek—a shallow, rippling stream of mountain water—dividing one section of the town from another. We were watching the broad red disc of the sun pass over the beetling peak above us. We were curiously observing the grey twilight settling and deepening upon the earth and creeping up the mountain side—From the green pastures surrounding the town, flocks of sheep and goats were coming, to be enclosed and secured for the night, while behind them, sportively singing and playing with each other, came bare-footed boys and girls, some skipping along on foot, others mounted on those shaggy animals with long ears, which are found so useful and plentiful in this region. The old bridge was in a condition so loose and ruinous that it seemed to be entirely in disuse, for young and old preferred jumping from stone to stone over the creek, rather than pick their way among the tottering logs and planks. It was pleasing to notice how eagerly the flocks, upon catching view of the shallow water, hurried forward to drink, giving the young shepherds and shepherdesses infinite perplexity in properly restraining and dividing them. So gently pleasing was the influence which the scene impressed upon us, that even the harshly screamed ejaculations of the youngsters guiding the flocks sounded musically in our ears, and a tranquil pleasure absorbed us, such as elaborate efforts of art, aiming at the same effect, may often fail to produce.

Deeper shadows were fast closing around us, and fainter glories appeared in the sky, as the flocks were driven slowly from the creek, and the tinkle of bells reached us from separate herds of horses and mules that now come galloping in from the pasture. These also drank at the creek before bounding forward again toward their different enclosures, and the buoyant motions of the well fed animals, as they dashed into the stream and tossed their nostrils in the air after drinking, gave to the evening scene a newer and more spirited glow of interest. Now a light appeared and soon another, glimmering from distant windows, and as we left the bridge the scraping of a fiddle and preparatory tuning of a tambourine announced an humble fandango about to commence somewhere in the neighborhood. Juvenile equestrians, riding juvenile mules and asses, were coming in from the fields, bestowing the usual curious glances and side remarks upon the Americans, as they jogged past us. One little jinny scarcely over two feet high, a more than ordinarily stupid looking, sleepy-eyed beast, came stepping lazily along, with two bare legged girls and a boy mounted upon its back. The little dark-skinned Mexican who was behind, sat upon the very rump of the animal, with his face to the tail, carrying a piece of plank in his hand, which he was using like a paddle to get his sluggish Rosinante forward. Asses loaded with wood, others carrying bags of grain, some with panniers of fruit, and others wholly unencumbered, were slowly moving before their drivers into the town. Girls with stone pots of goats milk upon their heads, blotches of vermilion upon their cheeks, and neither shoes nor stockings upon their feet, were entering the low doors of the one story dwellings, where they were soon engaged in busy preparation for the evening meal. Night now was closing rapidly over the scene, and in the eastern sky the stars came peeping out, catching brighter radiance as the golden flood of light sank fading behind the mountains. The vast prairies were folded away in a heavy mantle of gloom, tinkling bells were heard no more, a crescent moon came smiling from the far horizon, and starry night succeeded. Santa Fé never slept beneath a lovelier night, and night never followed a more beautiful evening.　*Buenas noches　A Dios*

A Fandango in Santa Fé

All dances or balls in Santa Fé are called *Fandangos,* at least by the Americans. Scrupulously republican in their amusements as well as their dealings, the Mexicans never enact a charge for admission into the ballroom. There is generally an extra apartment where sweet-breads, Pass whiskey, and wine are sold at double prices, and this is the landlord's or landlady's remuneration for the use of the ball room. The population of Santa Fé is estimated to be between seven and eight thousand,[99] and in the whole town there is but one house that has a boarded floor; all the others are wholly independent of art, and the inhabitants compliment nature by having the floors of their dwellings composed of nothing but pure and original mother earth. This apartment with the boarded floor is the fashionable ball room although

[99] The census of 1827 gave Santa Fe a population of approximately 5,700 or 5,800. In 1840, Governor Armijo counted 55,403 New Mexico settlers in his census. The Santa Fe proportion of the 1840 total would be about 7,300.— Twitchell, *Leading Facts,* II, 146; Bancroft, *Works,* XVII, 343.

the señoras entertain a decided predilection for the native soil on the ground of old use.

In compliment to the American strangers then in Santa Fé, Governor Amijo gave a ball in this grand boarded saloon during our visit. All the beauty and fashion attended, and also all the rabble, for, true to their republican principles, none can be refused admission. The night was warm, the windows were open, the Americans threw down their hats carelessly, and the Spaniards walked off with them cautiously. The Governor's lady, Señora Amijo, led off the dance with one of the young American guests, and another young American followed with the ex-Governor's daughter, a young lady who had been lately married, and was then the belle of Santa Fé. The Governor's lady would have weighed scarcely less than three hundred pounds, and her delicate and sylph-like figure would find a fit simile in a tobacco hogshead. She sailed through the waltz like an elephant dancing "Nancy Dawson" in the ring of a menagerie,[100] while her American partner, (who could speak what he liked in English with perfect freedom, as the natives of the place scarcely ever acquire a word of our language) amused himself and his friends with ludicrous compliments to his fair assistant in the dance.

The señora before mentioned as the beauty of the town was indeed a young lady of surpassing charms, and as pretty a little figure as ever graced the dance in our gay saloons. Her face was purely Grecian, and her complexion not dark enough to conceal the rich blood mantling in her cheeks. Her eyes were of that piercing black which makes you wonder how such light can live in things so dark, as though diamonds were embedded in jet. Her teeth were the sweetest little nest of pearls imaginable, sleeping in a ruby cavern, while her hair was the glossiest raven, and her

---

[100] "Nancy Dawson" was an eighteenth-century English melody inspired by a delightful dancer who appeared at both Sadlers' Wells and Covent Garden in the time of George II (1727–60). The tune is familiar to us as "Here we go round the Mulberry Bush."—S. Baring-Gould (ed.), *English Minstrelsie* (8 vols., Edinburgh, 1895–96), VIII, *vii.*

lashes the longest curtains of silk that ever shaded the eye of beauty. Our companion who danced with her was fairly smitten, and when he had led her to a seat he pulled from his pocket a little blank book where he had taken down a few gallant Spanish phrases. While he turned from the lady to study the compliment he wished to utter, the dark eyed beauty was rolling up a *chupar*, (which is a thimble full of fine tobacco folded up in a bit of corn shuck) and when the gallant American addressed her with "Señorita á las pies de vind.;" which is equivalent to "Fair lady I am your servant," she replied, after puffing a volume of smoke through her beautiful nostrils, "Servidora de vind, Señor," or, "Sir, I am your servant." Our friend's sudden passion for the young lady evaporated in that puff of smoke, and he never afterwards would acknowledge that she was at all pretty. The dances, as well as all the manners and customs in Santa Fé, are of a demi-barbarian character. The only music is a guitar and violin, and the same instruments are used for sacred music in the churches. Although there is little of elegance in their dances, yet about them there is a wildness and novelty truly enchanting to such young enthusiasts as we were. One waltz which they seemed to be very fond of, and which they perform with great spirit, represents a battle. The party on the floor separates in two divisions to the opposite ends of the ball room, and after singing a few words of defiance, they clap their hands, stamp the ground, and whirl off towards, round, and through each other, accompanying the music with short yells and other sounds vividly descriptive of a deadly contention. The effect is exciting and delightful. Few Americans can partake in this dance, as it requires a rapidity of movement which they find by no means easy to acquire. When the dance is over the Spanish beau hands his mistress a *chupar*, or when he chooses to be expensively polite, a glass of whiskey and a plate of sweet bread. When the refreshments are partaken of, and the segars smoked, another dance begins. The Americans have endeavored to introduce cotillions, but although the señoritas submit to them in compliment to their American beaux, yet they dislike them very much, and are always dispirited until the waltz begins again. Fandangos and the *monte* bank, which is a game that differs in some points from *faro*, but is very similar, are the only amusements of the place, and any person who chooses to bring a pack of cards may open a game of *monte* in the ball room. A Spaniard will often lose his last sand dollar at the bank, turn away whistling from the table, make his bow to a señora, and away he'll whirl through the dance as if nothing had occurred.

With all this unrestrained freedom of manners they seldom quarrel, and the harmony of an evenings amusement is seldom broken unless by some imprudent conduct of the Americans themselves. Scarcely an evening of the week passes without a fandango in one part or other of the town, and the same faces will be seen at every one. It would seem as if the people could not exist without the waltz.

A Night Row

We sat in a trader's store, and an old trapper, with a long iron-grey beard, was telling us his exploits in the mountains.

The monotonous and unmusical tune, played upon the drum and fife, by the two soldiers who parade the great square, announcing eight o'clock, had ceased nearly an hour, and all outside was still even as midnight.

Suddenly loud screams and yells reached us from some street in the neighborhood, and we had scarcely time to spring to our feet before several pistol shots were heard in rapid succession. We darted into the street, and met a dozen soldiers rushing in confusion from the custom house. They inquired the direction of the noise, and we all ran together down the dark street toward the vicinity from which the noise had proceeded.

It was at a time when the Camanches had been committing bold and bloody depredations between Santa Fé and Chihuahua,[101] and in other parts of the country. The daring American,

[101] See article footnote 95. Small Comanche parties made sorties into populated districts by day and night to carry off property and hostages. They laid

Kurker, had just completed his exterminating contract with the Government, by which he promised to pursue every red enemy on the soil to death, or bring them to such a treaty of peace as they would find impossible again to break. The state of the country was discussed at every corner and in every shop, every man had his suggestion to make, and all agreed in a strong feeling of determined hostility to the Apachu and Camanche Indians. Some declared that the Government ought to offer a reward for each red man's scalp that was taken, and half price for the squaws and children. Other equally desperate measures were suggested and warmly maintained, for the purpose of crushing speedily the Indian foe. So that in fact Santa Fé was

> *a town of war,*
> *Yet wild, the people's hearts brim full of fear,*

and yet this was only one year ago.

The soldiers soon outstripped us in running round the dark corners, for they knew something about the ground, but we were in constant fear of being thrown upon our noses as we hurried along. Thus we were left completely behind, but were soon guided to the spot by a loud and confused uproar of voices, uttering angry exclamations in Spanish and English. Still we neither heard or saw any sign of Indians, and, arriving at the place, we found a crowd of some ten or twelve young American drivers disputing furiously with Spanish guards. Such of the Americans as could speak Spanish were endeavoring to make themselves heard in that tongue, while those who could not, kept up an incessant fire of round English oaths at the heads of the customhouse soldiers. This was a most laughable part of the affair; to hear the wild American youths, (who were highly excited with pass whiskey, which they had been drinking at some fandango) utterly incapable of understanding what was said, either by their

Mexican towns under tribute, and the settlers fled to the protection of walls and barred adobes in "great terror" of even the smallest number of Indians.— Twitchell, *Leading Facts*, II, 31–32.

companions or the Spaniards, roaring away in English, as if by bellowing loudly they could make the Spaniards understand what they said.

The matter was, these young fellows had grown exhilarated at a fandango, and had sallied into the street to whoop and yell and fire off pistols. One of them was expostulating very seriously with a soldier, telling him that Santa Fé stood much in need of regulation, and he wished to show him how such things were done in St. Louis. Now, it happened that the only word of English with which this soldier had ever made acquaintance, was the affirmative, *yes,* and to every thing the American said, no matter what, he very contentedly answered "*yes, yes.*" This the young fellow no sooner observed than his mischievous spirit detected the fun that might be drawn from it, and calling two or three of his companions around him, he commenced putting the most absurd questions to the Spaniard.

"I say now, *Seen-yore,* did you ever feel of the back of your neck and find out what a Judy Fitzsimmons you are?"[102]

"Yes, yes," was the immediate reply, and questions began to pour upon him from all quarters.

"Parley vou Españole, *Seen-yore?*"

"Yes, yes."

"Well, does your mother know you're out?"

"Yes, yes."

"I say, old Monsure Don Bag-o-nails Spanish, aint you the ugliest ring tail monkey in Santa Fé?"

"Yes, yes."

"Well now, what do you want out here? do you want to know how we knock down Charlies in St. Louis?"

The simple fellow gave the answer as usual, and instantly

[102] To make a "judy" or a "Judy Fitzsimmons" of oneself was to be a fool or a simpleton. The term was known to American slang by the mid 1820's, having been derived, evidently, from the use of "judy" in reference to one (a girl particularly) of loose or low morals.—Eric Partridge, *A Dictionary of Slang and Unconventional English* (New York, 1950), 446.

went staggering across the street from the effect of a tremendous blow which took him under the chin.

The whisking of blades hastily drawn from their scabbards was now heard in the dark, and several bright instruments were seen glittering in the hands of the soldiers. This at once lifted the excitement of the young Americans into a perfect phrenzy, and, despising the poor soldiers for cowards, they made no hesitation in rushing upon their swords.

The facetious fellow, however, who was busiest with the fun, didn't seem to entertain quite so strong an inclination for the fight, for he now slipped back out of the way, and commenced popping off his pistols in the air. This valiant movement, strange as it may appear, secured the victory, and perhaps saved some bloodshed, for the Spaniards, supposing themselves fired upon, took to their heels and ran as fast in the dark as they could have done in clear daylight with ten thousand red Camanches after them.

The young rowdies now shouted and yelled more furiously than ever, until the drum was heard beating in the great square, when the whole party made a hasty adjournment, thinking, no doubt, that the victory already achieved was sufficient glory for one night, and not caring to risk a reinforcement of the enemy. We concluded to hasten away from the battle ground also, lest the exasperated soldiers should happen to mistake us for members of the offending party, and perhaps revenge themselves for their defeat by providing us with other lodgings than we looked for. It was perhaps well that we lost no time, for we had scarcely been admitted inside the gate of the first Alcalde (whose hospitality we were enjoying, he being a Frenchman, from St. Louis,) when a crowd of soldiers rushed down the street, with loud and furious threats of vengeance, and we knew, too, by the rattling they made as they passed that they had now their *escopétas* along with them, as well as the short swords which they usually carried.

At breakfast the next morning we told the Alcalde of our

adventure, and he laughed over it with as much glee as though he himself was one of the rowdy peace breakers. He was a jolly old fellow, and he remembered when he was a St. Louis boy, foremost in nocturnal mischief, and doubtless he was chuckling over many a midnight row, called up again to memory by this incident.

These young drivers are now nearly all fighting under Kurker, as, between the fandangos and the monte bank, their Mexican shiners soon disappeared; and they were eager enough to join a service, however dangerous, which promised them what most they loved, high excitement and rich booty. Kurker gives them a dollar a day and half spoils, so that they will seek battle upon every occasion, and doubtless they will get enough of it from the red marauders of Toas and Santa Fé.

The Rancheros

A knight in complete steel with poised lance, spurring to the combat in sight of his lady-love at a tournament of the olden time, formed not a more spirit-stirring or pleasure-inspiring spectacle than does a Mexican *Ranchero* in pursuit of a buffalo calf to ensnare it with a *lariat*. The *lariat* is a rope, sometimes twenty feet in length, and even thirty, made of hemp generally, but frequently formed from plaited strings of buffalo hide, softened well to obtain the necessary pliability; one end is turned into a slip-noose, and the use of both hands is required in throwing the rope. The Mexican springs upon his horse, caring little whether there is any thing more than a blanket upon the animal's back, and with the lariat coiled and divided, (the noose end and two-thirds of the rope in his right hand and the other end firmly secured in his left) he claps knees and spurs into his steed and darts away like an arrow, often with the bridle in his teeth. The buffalo cows are far swifter in flight than the bulls, and always keep the lead when pursued. The calves never lag behind their dams, but strain their tough young limbs into full as swift speed and keep ever close by the parent's side. During a hunt the calf seems almost under the cow, and so continues, scarcely varying its gait so as to advance or fall behind by any perceptible difference.

Thus they run as the *Ranchero* advances, until his position is about ten feet behind the flying cow and calf, when he suddenly bears away upon the side where the calf is running, at the same instant hurling the *lariat* and catching the young buffalo round the neck with the rope which tightens instantly and tumbles the victim over. This is a moment of glorious excitement to the Mexican hunters. They scream with delight as the animal is jerked over on the grass and separated from its dam. Then a kind of sport commences, which seems to an American traveller more exhilarating than any thing else of which he could have any conception. The angler with his hooked fish knows nothing to compare with it, and it beats even "cock fighting." The poor calf is no sooner down than up again, and scarcely up before he is again tumbled over, or suffered to run a short distance, according to the whim of the hunter. The Mexicans sit and laugh at this until they roll in their saddles; as for falling from their seats it seems to be a thing impossible. The young buffalo makes little effort to free itself from the rope, but rises after every fall, still pressing headlong after its flying dam until she disappears beyond the verging horizon. Here the fun ceases, for when the poor calf sees no longer any of its own kind it becomes tame at once, and will place itself by the side of a horse and run with it as formerly with the cow. The rope may then be taken from its neck, as it will never leave the horses unless it should again fall into trail and sight of its kind, so that the creature may be reared with the utmost facility by assistance simply of a domestic cow.

At Fort William we saw two buffalo calves grazing with the domestic cattle, and displaying no indication whatever of discontent at the situation. The poor cow, however, was obliged to be tied before the little buffalos could get nutriment from her, for they had an ungentle fashion of handling the udder which she considered somewhat unusual.

A method of highway robbery somewhat singular is also practiced in Mexico by means of this skill in throwing the lariat. The robber pursues the traveller in precisely the same manner as a hunter rides after the young buffalo, throwing the noose in such a manner as to pinion and tighten the victim's arms down to his side, at the same moment jerking him from his horse to the ground, by which action he is rendered powerless and the robbery is easy.

An incident slightly romantic in character, connected with this kind of plundering, occurred some short time previous to our flying visit to Santa Fé, and of course we heard of it. A rich Mexican was proceeding with an extensive caravan to Chihuahua, and he was in the habit of carrying a large amount of gold belted around him beneath his clothes. This fact became known to a daring and desperate gambler, whose character, among these people, was no obstacle to perfect freedom of intercourse with all classes. He travelled with the caravan, as it soon appeared, for the express purpose of making himself master of the golden girdle. His opportunity occurred when about half the travel was completed. The Don rode one day out of sight of the caravan in search of water, and the gambler, whose eye had been upon his victim through the whole journey, was instantly off to execute his scheme. He sought and came up with the Don, entered into conversation with him, and soon had the rich Mexican unhorsed at his feet. But to get at the 'yellow boys' it was now necessary to release the arms, which were tied down over the girdle, and this was not to be thought of. The robber dared not fire lest he should be heard by the passing caravan, and he seized a buffalo's skull which lay near, with the intention of dashing out the victim's brains. The Spanish desperado stood over his conquered prey, holding the tightened *lariat* in his left hand, his horse's reins around his left arm, and with the huge, white skull raised in his right hand ready to dash upon his prostrate victim.

"Don't kill me, and you shall have my gold!" exclaimed the helpless merchant; and the gambler paused.

Though the gambler had secured his own horse, the other had taken fright and galloped back to the moving caravan when its rider was thrown on the ground.

"I know you want my gold and not my life," said the merchant. "Cut the rope that binds me, and place your knife instantly upon my neck; and if I do not give you the gold, you may drive the blade into my throat."

The gambler did so, for in his flurry he had forgotten the frightened horse, but the merchant had not, and was playing a cool and cunning game.

"The gold, the gold," said the gambler, "or the knife sinks in your neck!"

"Instantly!" said the merchant, as he endeavored to gain all the time he could in releasing the belt of gold.

Another moment, and rapid hoof steps were heard, followed immediately by the appearance of a dozen approaching horsemen.

The robber turned pale, but his eyes flashed in desperation, and gritting his teeth horribly, he swore he would kill!

"Kill me," said the merchant, "and you are shot down instantly; release me, and I will never betray you; quick, put away your knife!"

Such a superiority has cool courage over the most daring wickedness! The gambler sheathed his knife and stood trembling, while the brave Mexican trader sprang to his feet, adjusted his dress, met his friends, said he had been by some accident thrown from his horse, and rode back to the caravan side by side with his enemy by way of warding suspicion from him. He promised not to betray the gambler, and he did not. But the guilty man succeeded soon after in another depredation; and fled. Then the story was told.

The Sacred Fire

Within forty-five miles of Santa Fé stands a dilapidated town called *Pécus* [*sic*], which in its flourishing days must have been inhabited by not less than two thousand souls.[103] The houses now are all unroofed and the walls crumbling. The church alone yet stands nearly entire,[104] and in it now resides a man bent nearly double with age, and his long silken hair, white with the snow of ninety winters, renders him an object of deep interest to the contemplative traveller. The writer with a single American companion once passed a night in this old church,[105] entertained by the old man with a supper of hot porridge made of pounded corn and goat's milk, which we drank with a shell spoon from a bowl of wood, sitting upon the ground at the foot of the ruined altar by the light of a few dimly burning sticks of pine. In this situation we learned from the old man the following imperfect story, which is all the history that is now known of the city of the Sacred Fire.

The inhabitants of Pécus boasted that they were the chosen people of Montezuma,[106] and in a deep cavern, whose mouth yawns in the hill side behind the church, the sacred fire was kept burning from generation to generation, watched and fed with unwearied vigilance through day and night by the faithful descendants of the great chief. He had said when he left them, "Montezuma does not die, my children, he goes to wander through happy regions and will again return to bless his people. Take from him this torch of flame, and so long as you suffer not the sacred blaze to expire so long hope to see your chief again, who will then make you a great and happy people and your enemies shall perish; but should this holy fire die, then dies Montezuma and you shall behold him no more!"

[103] As parties journeyed east from Santa Fe, they passed the Pecos ruins on the left of the trail between Glorieta and Rowe, New Mexico. The ruins, in the valley of the upper Pecos River, are approximately two and one-half miles south-southwest of the modern town of Pecos.

[104] The original Indian pueblo at Pecos was built in the fourteenth century. About 1617, the Spanish placed an adobe mission there (*Nuestra Señora de los Ángeles*, or Our Lady of the Angels); but, about 1838, the mission and town were abandoned entirely and fell rapidly into ruins.

[105] See journal footnote 43.

[106] See article footnote 83.

Thus spoke Montezuma before he disappeared, and through hundreds of years the sacred flame continued to blaze in the cavern of Pécus. Man, woman, and child shared the honor of watching the holy fire, and the side of the mountain grew bare as year after year the trees were torn away to feed the consuming torch of Montezuma.

At length a pestilential disorder came in the summer time and swept away the people. Pécus became a city of mourning, and death with conquering steps strode from dwelling to dwelling. Forms wasting with disease were seen to fall and expire while conveying the dry branches from the mountain side to feed the holy fire. The dying drew forth the dead from the deep cavern, and the last feeble breath of many a victim was given to kindle again the fast expiring flame.

Gualupeta was the daughter of a grey haired chief, and the betrothed of Josenacio. When the streets of Pécus became silent, and the voice of wailing was no more heard; when the ghastly and unburied forms of the dead outnumbered the beings yet alive; the aged man crept from his bed of pain, and descended from the hollow rock to watch the fire. For the children of Montezuma were passing away, and the sacred flame was almost extinct. Of all Pécus there were now but three to watch the sacred fire, and these were Gualupeta, her father, and lover. Josenacio brought wood from the mountain and sat beside his betrothed feeding the holy fire, while the old man grew weaker hour by hour, until in the deep midnight he expired. Then the heart of the lover failed and he urged Gualupeta to fly from death and abandon the sacred cavern. He was answered by a look which told him that Gualupeta had resolved to die rather than to leave the fire of Montezuma to be extinguished while she had strength to watch it.

"No, Josenacio," she said, "let us die with our people, and be faithful to our sacred trust, and though our race be extinct upon earth, Montezuma will forgive us and we will be happy with him in heaven!"

249

Josenacio kissed the faithful girl and sat down by her side to die; and the lovers looked into each other's face to watch the icy fingers of death tracing the pallid colors of the grave. Still midnight was around them and by their side lay the cold form of Gualupeta's father. The red light of the holy fire tinged the cold features of the corpse and with a healthful smile the old man seemed to gaze upon his child. Gualupeta was fast growing faint, and laying her cheek against her lover's, she said.

"See, Josenacio, my father smiles; he has already seen Montezuma in heaven. Are you not glad that you were faithful?"

Gualupeta started, for her hand which rested loosely in that of her lover, was clasped with sudden energy. She looked in her lover's face and exclaimed,

"Josenacio, what thought moves you? Why has the lightning kindled in your eye, and why do you press my hand so earnestly?"

"Gualupeta, the fire of Montezuma shall not yet expire!" exclaimed the youth, and starting to his feet he repeated the words, which were returned distinctly by the hollow echoes of the cavern, sounding like the sacred confirmation of a prophecy.

"We are dying," said the maiden, "how, what can we do to preserve the sacred flame?"

"We will fire the dry grass of the valley, and the forest that covers the mountain!" exclaimed the youth, "and over the mighty hills and the far prairies we will spread the destroying flame that shall tell the world how Montezuma's children have passed away!"

"It is good," said the maiden.

"Kiss your father, and let us be gone," exclaimed the lover, and snatching a brand from the fire he caught the maiden to his breast and rushed from the cavern.

A light then rose in the sky which was not the light of morning, but the heavens were red with the flames that roared and crackled up the mountain side. And the lovers lay in each other's arms, kissing death from each other's lips, and smiling to see the fire of Montezuma mounting up to heaven.

That summer passed away, and the winter, and when again the grass was green around the desolate city, two skeletons were found mouldering at the mouth of the cavern. These were Gualupeta and Josenacio, the betrothed lovers, the last watchers at the now extinct fire of Montezuma.

This is the substance of the old man's story. He told it in glowing words and with a rapt intensity which the writer has endeavored to imitate, but he feels that the attempt is a failure. The scene itself—the ruined church—the feeble old man bending over the ashes, and the strange tones of his thin voice in the dreary midnight—all are necessary to awaken such interest as was felt by the listeners. Such is the story, however, and there is no doubt but that the legend has a strong foundation, in truth; for there stands the ruined town, well known to the Santa Fé traders, and there lives the old man, tending his goats on the hill side during the day, and driving them into the church at night. He took from a niche in the wall a small burnt stick and a little clay bowl full of cinders, which he said he had himself brought from the bottom of the sacred cavern. That these were actually as he said remnants of the sacred fire there is not the slightest doubt, for from after enquiries we found the history he gave us fully confirmed, and the same story was current among all the Americans residing in Santa Fé. It was imperative upon us to leave the place before day light that we might reach our destination (San Miguel)[107] early the next morning, so that we could not gratify our curiosity by descending the cavern ourselves, but we gave the old man a few bits of silver, and telling him that the story with which he had entertained us should be told again in the great United States, we each pocketed a cinder of the sacred fire and departed.

A Sunday in San Miguel

It was past midnight, and a drizzly rain was falling when we

[107] *San Miguel del Bado* (St. Michael of the Ford) is located on the Pecos River where the Santa Fe trail crosses that stream some forty miles due southeast of Santa Fe. The original settlers, Christianized Indians, were served by San Miguel del Bado Mission.

rose from our two hours' slumber in the old church at Pécus, to resume our travel, in hopes of reaching San Miguel before the Spanish traders would leave it in the morning. Though travelling at a swift pace, our Spanish attendant and guide went fast to sleep upon his mule, which in fact was quite an easy matter, for in the high Spanish saddle and heavy wooden stirrups you can take a doze as securely as in an armed rocking chair after dinner, with your feet on the fender.[108] A blind man, however, is a better guide than a sleeping man with a pair of good eyes in his head, and daylight found us in a wrong track, several miles out of our way. Our attendants *Mula* had displayed some regard for her own convenience, but very narrow foresight as regarded the journey in selecting her path, and instead of reaching San Miguel at daylight, the bells, or rather the bell, (for there was but one, and the sound of that made us think it was a shame to exact duty of so crippled and superannuated an old second hand servant) was ringing for high mass.

Finding that the Spanish caravan did not intend to start until the next day, full time was allowed to witness the religious ceremonies in the church, and the writer mingled with a heterogeneous crowd that was moving toward the sacred edifice. Doubtless in that old church there were hearts as purely devoted to God as could be found in the cushioned pews of our own splendid tabernacles; for virtue is a thing that falleth as "the gentle rain from heaven" as well upon the rudest as the most cultivated spot of earth; and though we are prone to place crime with poverty

[108] James O. Pattie, the fur trader, observed that the Spanish saddle "looks as ours would, with something like an arm chair fastened upon it." Another American, Richard H. Dana, who spent many months in Spanish California, remarked: "The stirrups are covered or boxed up in front, to prevent their catching when riding through the woods; and the saddles are large and heavy, strapped very tight upon the horse, and have large pommels, or loggerheads, in front, round which the lasso is coiled when not in use." Both men were careful observers.—James O. Pattie, *The Personal Narrative of James O. Pattie, of Kentucky* (ed. by Timothy Flint) (volume XVIII of Thwaites, *Early Western Travels*), 74; Richard H. Dana, *Two Years before the Mast* (New York, 1936), 85.

and ignorance, yet we know that the evil which sullies the polish of refinement is as hideous and glaring as that which flourishes weedlike and without a check among uncultured men. Yet, though pure religion may have existed in that motley congregation, it was an offensive libel on sacred things the manner in which the ceremonies were conducted.

There were no seats of any kind in the church, and the worshippers were all either standing or kneeling. The mud walls were whitewashed, and a few wretched daubs of paintings, actually frightful to look at, were fastened up, some to rude frames, others hanging in rags with no frame at all. Among these was one piece of rotten canvas, with a little paint still lingering in it, but so completely demolished by time that it was impossible to discover what could have been the subject or design of the artist. It was probably some Madonna or saint, brought from Spain long enough ago to have passed through the wars. In a recess at one side of the altar, stood two men, one playing a fiddle and the other a guitar, and on these instruments the musicians seemed to be studying what kind of an extravagant and fantastic discord they could make. The noise made by two quarrelsome cats was quite as much like music. These musicians composed not only the church choir but also the ball room orchestra, and it may be supposed that they felt a necessity of making as broad a distinction as possible between the dancing and the sacred music.

In a few moments a priest appeared from an apartment at one side of the altar, and with great precipitation commenced his duties; he went about his sacred functions as though something of much more importance was awaiting his attention, and he had very little time to waste in performing the ceremonies of the mass. After bending one of his knees at the altar, he descended the steps, with a long brush like a musquito flapper in his hand, followed by a lank, uncombed figure, in a long black gown, bearing a large bowl of holy water. He kicked open a door in the wooden railing of the altar, and advanced among the people, who opened an aisle for him to pass, and dipping his brush in the sacred fluid he sprinkled the congregation, flirting his brush about and muttering blessings, much more like an angry housewife, hurrying about and scolding servants, than a man of God. This operation performed, he returned to the altar, and contrived to get through the whole ceremony of the mass in about half an hour, and in fifteen minutes after the writer found him smoking a *chupar* in the shop of the only American trader in the town.[109]

So much for the priest of San Miguel; now for the Alcalde, these being the two great potentates of the place, which, it is to be remembered, contains about fifteen hundred inhabitants. An important looking personage entered, and after exchanging with him a few words, the shopkeeper brought forth pen and ink and commenced making out a paper, observing, aside and in English, that this was the Alcalde, in whose education chirography had not been included. Thus any American who chooses to be a great man over such people may here have his ambition fully gratified, for the people fear and reverence the priest and the Alcalde, and these in turn pay great respect and homage to any one from the United States.

A beautiful crystal stream rushes through this town,[110] at no part more than four feet in depth, and so clear that the white pebbles can be seen glittering at the bottom and skipping along with the force of the current. Here in the afternoon, when the heat of the day had passed, groups of girls and children were

---

[109] Thomas Rowland was the sole resident American trader in the town in 1839. Born in Pennsylvania, he had married in New Mexico and established his store in a promising location at San Miguel. In 1841, when his brother John was accused of complicity in the Texan Santa Fé Expedition, a mob, under the *alcalde* of San Miguel, entered Rowland's store and in retaliation seized stock valued at $1,000. Rowland protested to the American consul at Santa Fe, and his protest was sent to Washington, D. C.—Letter of Thomas Rowland to Manuel Álvarez, October 28, 1841, and of Manuel Álvarez to Daniel Webster, February 2, 1842, Register and Despatches of the United States Consul at Santa Fe, 1830–46, in General Records of the Department of State, Record Group 59, National Archives; Gregg, *Commerce of the Prairies*, 162.

[110] The *Río Pecos* or Pecos River.

seen plunging their bare feet into the refreshing stream, and arousing echo with screams of laughter and delight. The writer joined one of these groups, at once to partake of the same luxury and to observe more closely the bathers. Sociably following the old principle of "when in Rome," &c. he pulled off his stockings and prairie "sandal shoon"[111] and sat down with his feet in the water, experiencing a refreshment so delightful that he longed to imitate the happy children, and laugh and shout aloud. But he was alone, and a stranger in a wild and strange place, and happiness only finds voice when kindred voices are near to yield the responsive echo. The children eyed the stranger curiously, and some remarks that were capital food for vanity, fell from the lips of the elder girls concerning the young American; "*el blanco Americano*," whose white feet excited the undisguised admiration of the young ladies. This might have been some gratification to the American had the young ladies themselves thought proper to wash their faces as well as their feet, and get rid of the dirt and red paint which sadly interfered with the effect of bright eyes, round cheeks, and the whitest and most regular teeth in the world. The simple *señoritas* are very fond of vermilion, and they daub it on forehead and nose as well as on the cheeks, showing that their ideas of beauty are in some measure derived from the Indians.

It io provoking to ooo really pleaoant featured girlo oo dio figure themselves, and the only bit of gallantry an American would think of offering them would be to dip their heads in the river or dash a bucket of water in their bedaubed faces.

The Lost Man

An unfortunate trader once strayed from his companions, and was lost for five days, suffering the keenest pangs of starvation and distress. It was years ago, yet the story has only been told in

---

[111] *Shoon* is archaic—the dialectic plural of "shoe." Either Matt wore a sandal-type shoe, or he refers, with poetic license, to his moccasins.

oral repetition among old traders, and has never before, to our knowledge, fallen in the way of a scribe.

The man wandered away upon a sultry midsummer afternoon, oppressed to desperation with thirst, in search of water, while the caravan was dragging slowly along the dreary and heated prairie. Making his way to a cluster of timber that appeared at no very tedious distance, he was fortunate enough to find a small cool spring gushing and rippling at the bottom of a deep rocky hollow. The fresh water, the cool shade of the steep rock and the trees above, together with the knowledge that the waggons were still moving along in sight, induced the poor fellow to yield to his weariness and suffer his eyes to close. When he awoke the grey of evening was already deepening around the prairie, and rushing up from the hollow, his eyes wandered about in vain search of his companions. He was a raw adventurer upon his first travel, knowing nothing of how to direct his steps in the wilderness, and trusting entirely to the guidance and experience of those with whom he travelled. Hasty, impulsive, and rash as he was careless, and without possessing a single quality of character to assist him in such an emergency, confused terror now at once took possession of him, and starting, as he thought, in the direction where he had last seen the waggons, he ran with headlong speed, shouting wildly at every step, in hopes of being heard and answered by his companions.

The terrified man, bereft of all thought by the fearful nature of his predicament, could not even remember to fire the rifle he held, but continued tearing his lungs with wild and desolate cries for assistance. While rushing blindly forward in this manner, the night still deepening around him, the man met a violent fall and was stunned into insensibility for hours. We are giving now the substance of the poor fellows own relation. He came back to consciousness some time during the night, in the midst of a pack of howling wolves, and found himself lying by the side of a buffalo's skeleton not yet entirely stripped by the prowling dogs of the desert. A situation more appalling to heart and nerve may not be imagined. The man doubted not but that he was aroused prematurely from his state of torpor by the hungry creatures assaulting his own body, for his clothes were mauled and torn and the scratch of a claw was on his leg, though a tooth it seems had not yet touched him. He had tripped upon the skeleton and struck his forehead on a horn or some other hard and stony part, as he discovered a huge lump upon his head, which also ached distressingly when he came to his senses.

The poor fellow in the heat of his terror made out to scare the wolves from himself and escape from the spot, leaving the famished animals to return again to the buffalo's bones and give them a cleaner polishing. Just escaping from one frightful danger, perhaps took something from the keen horror of his desolate and wretched condition, but the unhappy man's sensations were harrowing and fearful in the extreme. He still pressed onward, with strength failing at every step, calling in harsh and broken shrieks to his friends, and changing his course again and again, in utter and miserable uncertainty of which way to turn.

Day-light came, the sun rose, noon approached and passed, and the lost man was alone in the wide desert, famished and faint, and without a solitary hope of regaining his companions or finding the track they were pursuing.

That night the unhappy wretch sank exhausted upon the grass and slept, to awaken in a state of fear and danger more appalling even than the night before. A compact and innumerable band of buffalo came moving slowly across the region of prairie on which he lay, and he started from sleep in imminent peril of being trodden to death by the huge monarchs of the plain. As these dense masses of buffalo move they emit sounds that rise on the air like a sea surge, and as the vast black herd came toward him in the deep midnight, the poor trader declared that a rolling ocean seemed about to overwhelm him. Utterly paralyzed with his danger, the unfortunate man could but start to his feet and stand confounded, fearing either to fire or use other means to alarm the buffalo, lest by exciting their terror he should but increase his own peril. From this critical position, however, he likewise escaped unhurt, for the animals separated, as is their custom when a strange scent is detected, and passed on in two divisions, keeping some two hundred yards clear of the mysterious intruder in the middle. Day-light was again appearing as the last of this innumerable herd of creatures passed him and the man was starving. He took aim with his rifle at a retreating buffalo, and missed fire, for his percussion cap was damp with the night dew. Still he was famishing, and his only hope seemed to be in the slaughter of a buffalo. He followed, crawling upon his hands and knees, and, after hours of weary watching and labor, wounded a cow at last with a successful shot, but the terrified creature limped away, and the whole band disappeared, while the poor trader fell prostrate, too exhausted and faint to make another effort in the pursuit.

The unhappy wretch lay groaning aloud, alone in the midst of the interminable waste, abandoned to desperation and despair, when the thin bark of a small prairie dog attracted his attention.[112] Once more he charged his rifle, for the little creature was in sight, with its nose lifted just above the mound surrounding its hole. The starving man, still prostrate upon the earth, took slow and cautious aim at the dog, and was fortunate enough to knock it out of its hole with a broken back; but before he could reach the spot the dying creature had wriggled back into its hiding place again and disappeared. With his ten fingers the desperate man raked the earth, and succeeded in dragging the dying dog out upon the grass, where, without waiting to finish its agony, he tore its warm flesh with his teeth, like a wolf, while the expiring creature was still biting impotently at his fingers.

This unnatural sustenance restored the drooping man, and he was enabled to resume his wandering, which he continued for three more days and nights, alone, desolate, and miserable, until he encountered a hunting party of Camanches, whom, so far from avoiding, he rushed to embrace as though they were kindred

[112] Most travelers agreed that prairie dogs barked or uttered sharp cries.

From Narrative of the Texan Santa Fé Expedition, *by George Wilkins Kendall*

Mexican Girls

Many of the Santa Fe señoritas smoked *chupars*—"a thimble full of fine tobacco folded up in a bit of corn shuck."

From Notes of a Military Reconnoissance, *by W. H. Emory*

RUINS OF THE AZTEC TEMPLE AT PECOS

"Within forty-five miles of Santa Fe stands a dilapidated town which in its flourishing days must have been inhabited by not less than two thousand souls. The houses now are all unroofed and the walls crumbling."

near and dear and the best friends he could meet upon earth. They were friends, as it turned out, for they set him upon the track to regain his comrades, with instructions to direct him, and buffalo meat to support him, paying themselves by stripping him of his rifle and every thing else of the slightest value he had about him.

After four days' travel the poor trader reached his friends again, and was welcome as one from the grave. Upon the evening of his loss search had been made in all directions and signal guns fired from the camp, which he would have heard had he not been lying insensible by the buffalo's skeleton. Search was also continued upon the succeeding day, as the caravan moved along, but his wandering had been so irregular, tending in a far and opposite direction, that it was impossible to trace him. The five days suffering of this unfortunate man may be but faintly imagined. Deserted and lost without hope in the interminable solitude; alone in a vast domain of sky and grass; famishing, and tormented with raging thirst; O, terms may not be found of nervous force sufficient to thrill the natural sympathies as should such a story as this of *The Lost Man*.

Trappers Trapped by Crows

A party of thieving Crow Indians came upon an encampment of trappers, and requested permission to rest and refresh themselves with the white men. The vagabond Crows had neither horses nor arms, while the trappers had both, and the poor Indians were admitted into camp without hesitation. The trappers were old and wary followers of their trade, and up to all the subtile tricks and pilfering propensities of their visitors. It was their boast to be superior as well in cunning as in bravery to any of the red stragglers who occasionally crossed them, and on this visitation they held the unarmed and ill provided Crows to be objects fitter far for mirth and ridicule than capable of the slightest harm or mischief. In short, they looked for amusement from the Crows, and with the utmost freedom invited them into camp.

There were ten trappers and just eleven Crows, so that the white men were in a minority by one. The Indians might have been genuine emigrants from Down East by the interesting occupation every man was engaged in, for there was not one of them without a knife and a stick, and they came in among the white hunters, whittling their bits of timber down "to the little end of nothing" with that same indomitable gravity so strikingly, peculiarly, and proverbially characteristic of the true sons of Yankee land—

Native here and to the manner born!

So far from this singular proceeding exciting the watchfulness of the white man, they only made it a subject of mirth, and many jests were cracked, and a great deal of loud laughter exploded there in the far prairie solitude, at what the trappers considered an innocent and accidental imitation of a simple Eastern custom that has almost assumed standard as a national feature.

The eleven Crows took the mirth of their white friends all in kindly part, and while the sport was going on seemed quite contented to be laughed at. They, however, in the meantime occupied themselves in curiously examining every thing about the camp, and the trapper's rifles, one after another, were handled and admired by the scrutinizing Crows.

The horses were grazing loosely around the camp, and these next came in for the Indians' observation. Leaving the rifles of the white man standing against the trees where they found them, the eleven Crows went off to view the horses, while the trappers remained unsuspectingly lounging upon the grass, each with his loaded rifle within reach as he lay.

Suddenly there was a rapid and simultaneous movement among the Crows, and the next instant the whole party were seen to spring upon the trappers' horses, the odd Crow jumping up behind one of the other ten. Ten rifles, with infallible aim, were instantly levelled at the robbers, and ten Crows would inevitably have fallen dead upon the grass but for the unaccountable accident of every one of the rifles missing fire! Off went the Crows, disappearing across the horizon with a rapidity that even their sable feathered namesakes could scarcely have excelled, while the deceived trappers jumped and stamped upon the grass with rage and fury at finding the priming knocked out of their rifles and the touch holes plugged tightly with the little sticks which the Indians had been whittling! The trick was worthy of genuine Yankee origin, and the hitherto despised Crows were highly respected by the trappers ever after.

The Drama among the Crows

There is a time-honored custom among the Crow tribes of a grand yearly feast,[113] at which the scattered people of the nation, from various sections, assemble; and a brief sketch here of their rites and observances on the occasion, will serve curiously to show, that the all-pervading drama lived, in a quaintly rude state, among the aboriginal Americans.

At these grand annual conventions, or feasts, the first most striking solemnity is the appointment and preparation of a consecrated spot for the priests, where, after a certain time spent in necessary attention to temporal affairs, they commence their mystic dances and contortions of frame, while the multitude around remains gazing in silent and reverential awe. The "Medicines" continue this singular exhibition sometimes for several hours, shouting, singing, dancing, yielding gradually to the advance of a wild and almost demoniac excitement, and creating within themselves, as well as their audience, full conviction in the preter-

[113] Either Matt's information on the "grand yearly feast" of the Crows was gathered secondhand and mixed with information on other tribes, or else he was not observing carefully the Crow Indians. They had yearly festivals, to be sure, but the two principal ones—the Sun Dance and Tobacco Planting ceremonies—were not of the type described by Matt.—Robert H. Lowie, *The Crow Indians* (New York, 1935); letter of Frank H. H. Roberts, Jr., quoting John C. Ewers, to John E. Sunder, January 16, 1959.

natural character of the proceeding. There is a strange and subtile essence about fanaticism that can lead the mind of an enthusiastic juggler at length to receive as truth what procures him the homage of others and exercises over them so solemn an influence.

Yielding, no doubt, to a conviction of this kind—or, at any rate, knowing that it is their business, and their power depends upon it, the Crow priests have from year to year increased the extravagance of this department of the great feast, until now, it is said, no other nation can boast of so holy and inspired a set of men. They go on from one pitch of astonishment to another, excelling the last at each new effort; while their very forms seem undergoing a hidious [*sic*] and superhuman change, as the painted figures assume new shapes, fading and altering as the steaming perspiration exudes. Increasing this unnatural *furor* to the last moment of human endurance, the Indian expounders of Manito's will[114] at length (one after the other, mustering up their last modicum of strength, to appall the spectators with a final effort) spring furiously in the air, pointing wildly at the sky, and fall prostrate upon their faces, in utter exhaustion, with their heads turned to the east.

Then commences the solemn communion of the priests with the Great Spirit, and in motionless torpor they remain through the whole of three days, without food or water, while the other ceremonies go forward, in which the true spirit of the drama may be as clearly discerned as though a stage and all modern appliances were also in actual use among the Crows.

As soon as the priests are quiescent, and after a pause in singu-

[114] Matt also takes liberty with Crow religion. Broadly speaking, *Manito* was an Indian name given to any object of reverence, good or bad. Actually, there is no equivalent to *Manito* or its variants in the Crow tongue (the term is Algonquian). The old Crow term most closely resembling the Christian supreme being is *Isakawvate* (Old-Man Coyote) or *Axace* (Sun). The Crow tendency was to regard the Sun and Old-Man Coyote as one and the same.— Robert H. Lowie, "The Religion of the Crow Indians," *Anthropological Papers of the American Museum of Natural History*, Vol. XXV, Part II (1922), 315, 318.

lar contrast with the former uproar of the inspired men, a hum arises among the people, like an approaching gust from the sea. Gradually it swells, in wild and most extraordinary grandeur, until the ears are deafened with an incessant and prodigious din, like the roaring of a distant volcano, or the surging of an ocean against a rock-bound coast. Sports and revelry are now pursued with an eagerness sharpened by late restraint; but the great game, and that in which nearly all present enact either greater or lesser parts, is *a mimic representation in pantomime of the deeds, pursuits, and history of the tribe!* What is this, if not the drama? The vast mass of Indians separate and start out (in mimic show) as if on various expeditions. Here a party sets off to the great plains for game; another body of men is arming for battle, hurling their tomahawks into the trees, and swearing extermination to some distant tribe; a third party moves away, sly and cautiously, listening intently and crawling on the ground—the action intimating that they have discovered horses, and are going to steal them. Again, two parties appear, recognizing each other as enemies, and the warriors shriek out the blood-freezing war-whoop; knives, tomahawks, and arrows are seen darting through the air with harmless aim, but, to the eye of a white man, with mazy and dangerous impetuosity. A travelling trader would just as soon thrust himself into the middle of a real fight, as risk his person in the midst of one of these sham battles.

Then, others tell, also in action, the history of the nation. We are here—we are a great people—we slaughter our enemies, hunt the buffalo, ensnare the mustang, and steal the horses of bad Indians. We are here—we came neither from north nor south, east nor west; but we were here, and the land is ours. When the sun was a little star we were here. We have seen the sun grow, and the sun smiles while the eyes of the Crow warrior are open. The Crow chieftain opens his eyes in the morning, and the sun rises; he closes them at night, and the sun goes down. We are where we were born. The white men chase the bad Indians, and drive them over the hills of stone into the sea. The Crows shall never be driven. The arm of the Crow is strong, and the strength of his arm is very great. He was once a child upon the land he now treads; but the Crow nation has become a man. We are great— we are great! and our priests are talking for us to the Great Spirit! O-o-ha-huh-huh ha-ha huh ha, &c.

Again, the various parties will unite, and, with a sudden and simultaneous action, gather in one dense body, from whence a chief will move off at a quick step, but noiselessly, through the woods and over hills and plains, making an almost interminable tail of the whole nation, as they follow obediently after him in single file. The leading chieftain here has great scope for whim and caprice, taking whatever direction he pleases, and flirting [?] his long tail about in serpentine evolutions as he tacks and turns. This is supposed to be a grand expedition of the whole nation against a distant foe; and another still more interesting part of the performance represents their return, laden with scalps and trophies, and leading in their prisoners and horses taken from the enemy.

Then takes place a grand performance, explaining their conquest and the details of the fight to the women and children. A certain number lay down at a distance for those who were killed, and their wives and children take positions as if in grief for their bereavement,[115] while unlimited rejoicing, feasting, and merriment goes on among the victorious warriors.

On the third day the priests awaken, and the red men gaze with solemn awe upon the pallor of their hollow cheeks; but the greatest proof the Crows have of the spiritual communion of their priests, even beyond the secrets they tell of Spirit-land and Manito's will, is, that while in this sublime torpor they also possess a

[115] When a Crow Indian died of natural causes, his closest kin cut their hair, gashed themselves, or hacked off finger joints; then they left camp to brood in the wilderness for several months. If the deceased had been killed by an enemy Indian, he was mourned by the entire camp. Kin and friends alike pierced their bodies with knives and pointed arrows, "cried bitterly," and retreated for months to "miserable lodges." Until a member of the enemy tribe had been killed, they refused to indulge in "merriment."—Lowie, *Crow Indians,* 67–68.

sort of animal magnetic *clairvoyance,* by which they can describe every thing that occurred while they were asleep! They can relate every item connected with the sports and feasts of the three days, just as readily as if they had been on earth all the time, instead of far away, conversing with Manito in the sky.

Camanches

It was on the fifth day of our travel homeward, after leaving San Miguel, when the mountains were slowly lessening behind us, and far away before us stretched the great plains, that our attention was attracted at about eleven o'clock A.M. by the appearance of some three or four objects in motion at a great distance away to our right. A few indistinct spots appeared which would scarcely have been discernible at all had they not been in motion. We continued on our way with our eyes fixed upon the far horizon where these objects were seen, not apprehending danger, though being in a region much frequented by marauding tribes, we felt probably a sufficient mingling of apprehension to enliven our curiosity. It was soon evident that what we saw could not be buffalo, and a very few moments more brought us to the conviction that a band of wild horses was approaching us, for the swift and graceful lope of that animal became discernible, and as those in advance rose more distinctly into sight other spots appeared behind, and little knots of five or six were seen scattered about the same portion of the prairie, all seemingly moving toward where we were.

Suddenly one of the Mexican soldiers, who had ridden off to some distance for the purpose of scanning more nearly the advancing objects, was seen to turn and make back toward the caravan, seemingly in great confusion and surprise. When near enough to make himself heard he shouted to us, "Indios! Indios! Camanches! Camanches!" and instantly the wagons were drawn up forming a *corral,* into which all the loose animals were driven. Lieutenant Hernandez, who commanded our escort of twenty-five soldiers,[116] furnished us by the Governor of Santa Fé, gave us now a specimen of his military capacities, and set about arranging for defence with great coolness and deliberation. Some description of these soldiers is necessary, as also of the condition and strength of our whole party.

There were five leaders, each of whom employed from five to ten retainers or attendants.—The chief of these leaders is entitled to first attention. He always rode a more than ordinary sized mule, rather tough looking but very docile and very strong. His heavy saddle was ornamented with brass and silver headed nails, driven into the high pummel and back, and forming fanciful and unmeaning devices. The bridle—the wooden stirrups, with their thick and heavy leather guards—the Spanish bit, locking the poor animal's mouth up, and not suffering it to eat or drink, with the jingling ornaments hanging under the jaw—the skins hanging from the pummel, guarding the rider's legs from sun, and rain, and cold,—all these were more or less decorated with knobs and plates of fine silver, but so coarsely worked as to look no better than as many bits of tin. *Don José,* upon his mule, was a very formidable looking person for one who was so completely inoffensive. He was master of a very beautiful and very old double-barreled shot gun, and ditto broadsword. These were invariably every morning fastened securely to the pummel of

[116] American traders to Santa Fe petitioned Congress frequently in the 1820's and 1830's to establish military posts along the trail and to provide regular military escorts for trading companies. Congress refused to enact comprehensive legislation, although an occasional force of dragoons was sent to accompany caravans as far as the Arkansas. At times, the Mexican authorities sent military escorts with their trading groups as far as the southern bank of the river. The first U. S. escort was sent from Jefferson Barracks, Missouri, in 1829, under Major Bennett Riley. Other military units were on the trail in 1833, 1834, 1839, 1842, and 1843.—F. F. Stephens, "Missouri and the Santa Fe Trade," *The Missouri Historical Review,* Vol. X, No. 4 (July, 1916), 254, 257; Fred S. Perrine, "Military Escorts on the Santa Fe Trail," *New Mexico Historical Review,* Vol. II, No. 2 (April, 1927), 175, 177; Henry P. Beers, "Military Protection of the Santa Fe Trail to 1843," *New Mexico Historical Review,* Vol. XII, No. 2 (April, 1937), 113–33.

his saddle, and taken off again at night, by a servant; and the writer upon this emergency, finding *Don José* in some perplexity with his weapons, went to his assistance, and found that the shot gun was entirely useless, the nipples being broken and filled with fragments of caps, and the broadsword was so rusted within the scabbard that no effort could extricate it, and it was not actually drawn during the whole course of our travel. Such was *Don José* for a warrior, and such, with little variation, may serve as a description of the other Spanish traders and their servants.

The uniform of the soldiers was as follows:—A round jacket, and pantaloons open on the outside from the knee down, with cuffs, collars, and other trimmings of red flannel; leather leggings tied round the calves and ankles, and coarse shoes. Their weapons were—a short *escopeta* or fusil,[117] a long iron pointed lance, and a knife stuck in the belt. They were all mounted on mules, and each carried, hanging to his saddle, a long rope with a slip noose at one end, and a hollow gourd for transporting water. They were in truth as good a sample of

A tattered host of mounted scare crows

as were ever dignified with the name of soldiers, yet they manifested little alarm, and having been placed in the best defensive order by the lieutenant, and the brass cannon having been drawn in front of the encampment, ready for action, each man planted his lance in the ground, cocked his fusil, and awaited the approach of the enemy.

Five of the objects that we had seen were now swiftly approaching us, and the forms of the Indians were distinctly discernible, mounted upon their half-wild horses. Other groups were hurrying on behind, numbering in all something less than a hundred, though others were still rising into sight in the distance, and of

[117] The fusil was a light flintlock musket. In contemporary Spanish, *escopeta* means shotgun. In *The Scalp-Hunters; or, Romantic Adventures in Northern Mexico* (London, 1852), Captain Mayne Reid defined an *escopette* (p. 383) as "a short piece, used generally as a horseman's gun. They have straps and swivels, and many of them are merely razeed [cutaway] muskets."

course we could form no conjecture of how many were yet behind. Our lieutenant was undoubtedly a brave little fellow (a man of slender but sinewy mould, well traced features, deep, dark, flashing eyes, and an eagle nose), and to his spirited conduct on this occasion it is likely we were in a great measure indebted for our subsequent safety. After arranging the camp for defence, he took the bridle from his mule and placed it in the mouth of a swift horse, and jumping upon its naked back, he dashed off to meet the approaching Indians, ordering no man to follow him unless he should make signal for assistance by firing his *escopeta.*

In a very short space of time he was at such a distance as made it impossible for us to distinguish his form from those of the Indians, until presently we saw him wheel and ride along in front of the approaching enemy, flourishing his short broadsword above his head, the blade of which glanced in the midday sun, glittering defiance at the red marauders. Here the lieutenant took his stand, and a single Indian advanced to meet him. After spending a few moments in conversation, they advanced side by side toward the camp, and in twenty minutes more the whole scattered band of Camanches, numbering between three and four hundred, had advanced and completely hemmed in our camp, containing about sixty-five souls.

They were intimidated, however, by the bold and well prepared appearance we made (though indeed much of it was *but* appearance), but most of all, the sight of the cannon was most effectual in arousing their fears; and as one after another came nearer, to reconnoitre us, their eyes were instantly fixed upon the brass field piece. They sat upon their horses with as much carelessness as though they were lounging on buffalo skins within their wigwams. From men of sixty to boys of ten, all seemed equally at home upon horseback, and their whole appearance was entirely different from any Indians we had yet seen. There was no sign of civilization about them;—from head to foot they were *Indian*—close fitting jackets of deer skin, cut out in small crescents, which in a slight degree gave a resemblance of scale armour, long hair flying in the breeze; and not one of them was without a bow in one hand, and a bundle of barbed arrows in the other, while they held their slight yet strong deer skin bridles in their teeth.[118] Five hundred arrows might have been launched at us there before we could have fired one ball from our cannon, which conveyed such terror to our enemies. But, although of all the Indian tribes the Camanche is most warlike and dangerous to the trader, yet was this party that now crossed our path thoroughly frightened, and Lieutenant Hernandez understood their perplexity well, and knew as well how to profit by his advantage; and he talked to the savages as though they were all at his mercy, and he could, if he pleased, exterminate them all in an instant. They said they were in search of buffalo, and had no intention to molest us, upon which Hernandez told them they might depart, assuming an air as though he had magnanimously granted them their lives. They care little for the Spaniards, but they dread the Americans; and the first question these Indians asked of us was how many Americans were in our party.

Hernandez, still maintaining his confident demeanor, ordered the camp to be struck, and the Camanches, after hovering around us for two or three hours, at last went off in scattered groups, as they had approached us. They were covered from head to foot with vermilion; and as they dashed along the prairie upon their untamed horses, with their long hair streaming behind them, they seemed like mounted flames of fire, and the very horses seemed to spurn the ground, as though they were under the control of devils!

[118] The Indians did not ride bareback, as many people suppose. They made saddles patterned after Spanish ones or designed their own from pads of animal hair covered with leather. Their stirrups were of wood or rope, and their bridles, which tended to cut the corners of a horse's mouth, were made "by twisting horsehair into ropes" or improvising strips of hide.—D. E. Worcester, "The Use of Saddles by American Indians," *New Mexico Historical Review*, Vol. XX, No. 2 (April, 1945), 139; George W. Fuller, *The Inland Empire of the Pacific Northwest, a History* (3 vols., Spokane, 1928), I, 47.

The Snow Cliff

There is a high and precipitous rock among the great hills of the West known to trappers as the *Snow Cliff*. Once in the spring time, when the snow had fled away before the sunbeam, and torrents were roaring down the mountain side, the bones of a white man were discovered upon the summit of this rock. A small pocket liquor flask was also found, in which a bit of leather, which seemed to have been the lining of a shoe, was discovered.—Upon this leather was traced, seemingly with some sharp instrument, aided probably by wet powder, the following singular and at the time inexplicable memorandum.

> *Better to freeze than burn—D——n them I'll die like a man. It's a soft bed—I'll sleep in the snow till summer. Cold—Cold—Ice—Snow—It wont last long—I'll—good-by —good-by!*

This strange memorandum was carefully retained in the possession of a trapper for nearly two years, when a story was accidentally unfolded which is supposed to be the history of the unfortunate man who perished in the snow. Three trappers, belonging to a large party then scattered about in search of beaver, had spent some of the summer months upon one stream, setting their traps in company, but the game growing scarce, they agreed to separate and search for other streams where they might pursue their avocations singly. High up the mountain side above them, most prominent among the surrounding rocks, appeared the snow cliff, and the trappers agreed when the summer should depart, and the first snow should be seen upon the cliff, that they would ascend and meet each other there, and from that high point, from whence they could scan the country all around, they would mark their course, and journey together to join the main party.[119]

[119] Fur traders were not likely to select a cliff as a rendezvous site. A cliff might well be chosen as a landmark to direct trappers to a near-by valley (as

The three friends separated and one of them was never seen again. Fifteen months afterward two Americans met in a street in Santa Fé, and after a hesitating step, an incredulous stare, and a muttered exclamation of astonishment, they grasped each other's hands and laughed aloud with extravagant joy. These were two of the three companions; they had failed to meet according to appointment on the snow cliff, and after fifteen months of vicissitude and adventure, each believing the other dead, here they met and looked once more upon each other.

The story of the first trapper was as follows. At the first appearance of snow upon the cliffs he took up his traps and made his way to join his companions. He had not advanced far up the mountain side, when, as night was descending, the light of a camp-fire appeared above him, and joyfully thinking he had encountered his companions, he rushed imprudently forward and found himself seized by a party of Black Feet Indians. He was instantly stripped of every thing he possessed, bound hand and foot, and retained a prisoner, exposed almost naked to the cold and subjected to the most disgusting cruelty and insult. The Indians remained upon the spot about ten or fifteen days, when they were finally driven away by a violent storm of snow, which threatened to cut off their retreat from the mountain if they remained longer. When the whole of the Black Feet met together they numbered some ninety or a hundred, and from the barbarity with which he himself was treated, the poor trapper concluded that his companions were murdered. The Indians, he had observed, while encamped, were constantly watching the summit of the snow cliff, and even when they departed they seemed extremely loth to leave the spot. Though he could not divine the precise cause of this conduct on the part of the Indians, he knew it must relate to his unfortunate companions, and when leaving the mountain he sighed as fervent a farewell to his friends as though he had seen them fall beneath the scalping knives of the

Matt suggests), but not as the general rendezvous. Even a small trapping group preferred water, wood, and game to barren rock ledges for its annual gathering.

271

savages. During the whole of the winter the poor trapper remained a prisoner and a slave among the Black Feet, when he finally contrived to escape, and after a month of solitary wandering, he fell in with a party of Spanish traders in sheep, and with them journeyed to Santa Fé.

The other trapper related his adventure thus. When ascending to the cliff he became aware of the presence of the Indians in time to screen himself from observation, and by carefully reconnoitring the ground he discovered that the Indians were so disposed as to cut off completely his access to the summit above. From this he concluded that his companions had been observed and were hemmed in and besieged. He hovered about the spot, keeping himself well concealed, until the snow came on and the Black Feet departed, when he sought to find his friends, but found the precipitous rock so loaded with snow that ascent was impossible; and this was probably the reason why the Indians had not mounted the cliff and secured their victim. Knowing that if his friends were there they could not have continued alive, he left the mountain and sought the main party at their winter rendezvous, fully believing that his friends had perished, either in the snow, or by the cruelty of the Indians.

Many months after, as stated, these men met in Santa Fé and hailed each other as ghosts from the grave. Still the third friend was to be accounted for, and it soon happened that the finder of the bones and liquor flask fell into company with the two trappers, when the melancholy fate of their companion but too plainly appeared. He had perished in the snow; preferring to yield his life to the elements than to the fury of his savage hunters. That they sought his life was plain from the pertinacity with which they besieged his retreat, and as he was a man of valiant and daring spirit, it is probable that he had excited their revenge by killing one or more of the red devils who pursued him. And there he died upon the mountain top, smiling contempt upon his enemies beneath, while the chill of death crept slowly around his heart—*"Better to freeze than burn,"* he wrote in his dying moments, showing that he anticipated being tortured with fire if he was caught, and manfully did he keep his resolution. He went to his long sleep couched on a mountain throne with the winding sheet of the winter around him. The tempest whistled him a glorious requiem, and the earth was never laid upon his breast for the rude foot of the stranger to trample on. Upon the mountain he lay down to rest, and his noble spirit near to its native heaven parted from its tenement of clay.

An Alarming Rencontre

It was two hours past noon and two men were alone upon the prairie. Save these two human beings, the only things of life within view were a wounded buffalo cow in the next hollow of the prairie, and an old grey mare, that was *staked* (fastened by a long halter to a stick driven into the ground) in the hollow where the men were crouching.

"Don't waste another shot, Tom, the old cow is done for."

"Waste shot!—but you don't consider how much time we are wasting. It's four hours since the wagons passed us, and they are now fifteen miles ahead."

"Aint that your last charge?"

"To be sure it is, and here it goes plump into the old cow's liver."

"Stop, stop, Tom—now, for heaven's sake, keep that charge." The cow was seen to drop upon her knees. "There, you see the work is done; I am reduced to my last shot too, and if any of those Camanches or Pawnees should"—

The speaker was interrupted by a roar of loud and unrestrained laughter. "Well, Sam," said Tom, "I do despise a coward, and if you aint a perfect fenomenon of that genus I'm the handle of a tea-pot. Once, twice—going, going—look at the old cow roll over now, will you?"

"Tom, stop," said Sam, laying his hand upon his comrade's rifle and lowering the muzzle to the grass. "Now, you must keep that shot; the cow will be dead in ten minutes, and we'll have time to butcher and get the meat and reach camp before dark."

"*You* ninnyhammer! That buffalo will get up when she's done saying her prayers and be out of sight in a jiffy, if I don't pop her over. Let go."

"Sam, I ask it as a favor. Will you just remember where we are, and only two of us?—Good heavens, the Camanches,"—

"D——n the Camanches! How do they know whether a fellow's gun is loaded or not? Any ten of them will run from an American rifle if there never was a grain of powder in it. Sit down, Sammy, there's a good boy."

Tom was upon his knees, and using his ramrod for a rest, he took deliberate aim at the dying cow.

"Tom, you're a fool," said Sam.

"Sam, you're a Sammy," said Tom. "O Sammy, Sammy, think of your anxious mammy!"—Click—bang! and as the shot sped the hunter threw himself prostrate upon his face, and without looking at his companion, he exclaimed in a voice strangely changed from gaiety to alarm, "For God's sake, Sam, what is that?"

Sam gave a swift glance around the prospect and instantly dropped to the earth in imitation of his companion.

"Sam! Sam! What is that?" said Tom, in a voice so altered from its former merry vaunting tone that it scarcely seemed to belong to the same individual.

"Indians! there are five at least, and heaven knows how many more behind," said Sam, placing a fresh cap upon his rifle, and then adding, "Have you not another charge?"

"Gracious heaven, no," said Tom, "I have powder, but my last ball is gone."

"Take this," said Sam, taking a bullet from his mouth, where it had lain to create moisture for his parched throat. "Load."

"Father of Heaven, Sam, do you think"—

"Load!" said Sam, in an imperative yet calm tone; and Tom remembered that a minute before he had called Sam a coward.

274

From Commerce of the Prairies, *by Josiah Gregg*

"Dog Town," or, a Settlement of Prairie Dogs

"Upon the approach of intruders those out on the grass instantly rush to their holes, and those under the ground pop out their heads to see what is the matter."

MATTHEW C. FIELD IN FRONTIER DRESS

"A weary, wind-burned traveler from the plains stopped in Pollard's Hotel at Independence, Missouri, in the autumn of 1839, after spending the summer on the Santa Fe Trail and in the settlements of New Mexico." From a painting by James Carson.

While Tom proceeded to re-load Sam raised himself cautiously from the ground to reconnoitre the coming danger.

"Do you see them, Sam? Are they coming toward us?"

"Not precisely in this direction," replied Sam; "we might perhaps escape, but they must have heard your shot."

"O Sam, that shot! O, if I hadn't fired! I'll never fire another shot, Sam, never! Never!"

Poor Tom had a heart made all for love and kindness; any girl might have won a treasure in it and prized it greatly, yet was it now a thing of less value than five grains of powder.

"There is a large party," said Sam, still observing, "I can count fifteen spear heads glancing in the sunbeam."

Tom groaned.

"Yet they are not coming this way."

"What!" said Tom, lifting his head. "But the old mare! Ah, they will see the old grey beast and there's no avoiding it."

"Oh, the confounded old beast! O, Sam, must we be killed for an old horse! Well, now, d——n that old horse, it never was good for any thing either. O Sam, can't you coax it to lay down? Betsy! Poor old Betsy! Lay down, you d——d old horse, lay down!"

Poor old Betsy was innocently grazing some forty feet from where the two hunters were, and paid not the slightest attention to Tom's kind entreaties.

Suddenly Sam dropped again precipitately by the side of Tom.

"Are they coming?" whispered Tom in an unearthly voice, as he buried his face in the grass.

"Hush—listen!" said Sam, placing his fingers upon the lock of his rifle.

Hoof steps rapidly approaching were now distinctly heard beating hollowly over the level earth. Tears rushed from poor Tom's eyes the instant this sound reached his ear.

"Cock your rifle," said Sam, sternly.

"I can't—I can't Sam; shoot it yourself. O I'm a dead man! I haven't been married a year, Sam, and my mother loves me more than any of the other boys! O Mary, God bless you! you'll never see me again. To die, and be scalped, and shot, and killed by Camanches!—red devils!—where there aint a tree nor a drop of water! O mother, mother, if I was with you at home again I'd never leave you, never, never, never!"

Two or three shots were now heard, and poor Tom continued, never raising his face from the grass, "Yes, there they go—some big Camanche has got his gun levelled at me now. Good-by, mother! Good-by, Mary! Are you dead yet, Sam? Good-by! God bless you! Yes I'm a dead man, and my hair is gone. O Sam, Sam, how the wolves will knock our bones about!"

Tom was now completely alone, Sam having crept away into the next hollow to observe more nearly the horsemen, who he could now perceive were in chase of the poor wounded cow which had sprang up and ran toward them when pierced by Tom's last ball. Thus poor Tom lay in solitary despair, mourning and bewailing his fate, when a single rider came at full speed directly to the spot where he was lying. Tom heard the horseman rein in his steed, and his voice became mute, his breath seemed to leave his body and his heart to cease its action.

"Why, friend, are you dead or asleep?" said the rider.

Had the expected ball pierced his heart, Tom could not have changed his position more suddenly. He sprang from his face into a sitting posture, and after rubbing his eyes, wet with tears, with his hands, which were black with powder, he sat gazing at the horseman with a mingled expression of utter amazement and unbelieving joy.

"Wh-a-a-at?" was the only word he could make out to utter.

"Why, my friend, why aint you butchering that cow over there? Those Spaniards will have all your meat away from you."

"Spaniards!" almost shrieked Tom, as he sprang to his feet and looked in the direction pointed to by the stranger.

A glance was enough for Tom. He saw a crowd of men round the dead cow, but not one of them looked like an Indian. He turned to the stranger beside him and saw a man dressed in garments which betokened him from the States, and speaking his own language; and with a jump in the air and a loud shout of joy he rushed to the horseman, grasping his hands and embracing his legs and his horses neck with every extravagant demonstration of overflowing delight.

This little incident occurred somewhere between the crossing of the Arkansas and *el Rio Colorado*, when the writer was returning to the States with his party of Mexican friends. In the morning we had met and passed the large caravan of *Señores* Thompson and Cordero,[120] comprising more than one hundred wagons, on their way to Santa Fé, and these two hunters had lingered behind, having been out since daylight in search of buffalo. They of course knew nothing of our approach, and having been sixty-five days on their travel without seeing a soul that did not belong to their own party, their surprise at meeting strangers was natural, and equally natural was it that they should mistake the ragged soldiers of Santa Fé, who rode before us with their long spears erect, for Indians.

Sam, in a good humored way, gave the writer the history of Tom's cowardice, which Tom was very happy to laugh at himself, now that he was relieved from his overwhelming terror; and in a comfortable little log cabin in Missouri the writer afterwards related to Tom's mother and his wife Mary how he had seen Tom butchering a buffalo in the wilderness, and how Tom

[120] José Cardero was a wealthy Chihuahua merchant and a friend and money-lender to Americans in the Southwest. After the Mexican War, he served as governor of Chihuahua (1852) and was said to be the "richest man in the state." —Moorhead, *New Mexico's Royal Road*, 180. His partner in this 1839 venture was Philip (Phil) M. Thompson, an American merchant to Santa Fe who traded out of Independence. He is, possibly, the same man who returned to Independence early in June, 1839, with Andrew Sublette from the Rockies. In all probability, Thompson is also "P. W. Thompson," who was an agent for the St. Louis trading company of Powell and Lamont.—P. W. Thompson inventory and letter concerning inventory, 1837 and 1839, Santa Fe Papers, Missouri Historical Society, St. Louis; Union Historical Company, *Jackson County*, 170; Shortess, "First Emigrants to Oregon," *Transactions of the Twenty-Fourth Annual Reunion of the Oregon Pioneer Association for 1896*, 93–94.

had evinced for them the most affectionate feelings and sent them the kindest regards. Mary, the young wife, was nursing a fine infant, born since Tom's departure. When he returns he will probably know better how to love his home.

A Cool Greeting

Our present sketch has a close connection with our last, entitled "*An Alarming Rencontre.*" It was upon the eighth day[121] after our departure from the last Spanish settlement of San Miguel that about 10 A.M. we discerned before us an appearance which, after twenty minutes observation and conjecture, we rightly determined was an expedition from the States, travelling to Santa Fé. We were aware that a trading company, of which Señore Cordero was the principal, was expected in the Mexican country before the winter set in, and the appearance before us, which we could liken to nothing else but a line of white wagon tops, we naturally and rightly concluded must be the expected caravan.

The only point of interest which the writer has to notice in the present sketch is the strange want of warmth, the unnatural coolness with which these desert wayfarers actually met and passed each other without halting an instant or pausing for even a momentary exchange of civilities. It is true that the party approaching was chiefly composed of Americans, while our own contained but a single speaker of the English tongue, but would not any civilized being suppose that the common sympathies of man for man would irresistibly impel travellers, when meeting in the heart of a vast wilderness, to rush toward each other with joyful greeting, even though they were of opposite nations and speaking strange tongues? There could be no suspicion on the part of either party as to the design or character of the other. The Americans were travelling to Mexico with goods, and the Mexicans coming to the States to purchase merchandise; friendly

[121] September 29, 1839.

traders, visiting each the country of the other. Yet they passed with side-long, hesitating, and half anxious glances, short bobs of the head, and a few brief and inarticulate "How are you's?" from the Americans, and *Como lo va's?* from the Spaniards. A dignified "Good morning," passed between two politic citizens in the street, who hate each other, and yet feel the necessity of being civil, could not be half as cool.

We were three hundred miles from the last wild mud built settlement in this wildest part of Mexico, and about double that distance from the outer log farms of Missouri; we had been ten days out, and expected to be twenty or twenty-five more on the prairie without meeting another creature bearing the form of man, unless perhaps our dreaded enemies, the Indians, should cross our path; yet here we passed a body of our civilized fellow beings, exchanging no more notice than if it was an occurrence of every day, than might pass between two of the most distantly related sons of Adam, in the heart of a crowded community. The American caravan comprised over a hundred wagons, and these were moving in two divisions, along parallel tracks, the distance between being about twenty or thirty yards. Some of the drivers did not even cease their whistling or indulge us with a glance as we passed, carrying their indifference to an amount that seemed much like affectation.

The fact is, the Americans despise the Spaniards, and are jealous of seeing attempts made by the natives to share in the trade, hitherto monopolized by traders from the States. Not only will the extent of their business be thus contracted, but their chance of realizing extortionate profits will be cut off. This, however, is not much to be feared, for the simple Mexicans are subject to such disadvantages, and are so much exposed to imposition from their want of knowledge of our customs and method of dealing, that the probability is they will soon abandon the trade. The cost of a Spaniard's goods, when brought from the States and safely deposited in Santa Fé, exceeds those of an American by fifty per cent., not less, so that there is little fear of the American being undersold.

Yet the Santa Fé trade is not at this time, nor indeed has it ever been, as profitable as it is generally imagined to be.[122] None of the adventurers have become wealthy, and even the dealers, who by years of experience have secured all the facilities of which the trade is capable, complain loudly of the poor returns they receive.—When the advantages and disadvantages of the trade are well considered, it will be seen how just are the complaints of the traders. In crossing the Arkansas and many of the creeks, great risk is run of damaging the goods—wagons are often upset in the creeks and in other difficult places—then the danger of being attacked and robbed by Indians—the dreary journey—rain often falls incessantly for twenty-five days, and the prairie becomes in many places so soft that the heavy wagons sink to the naves of their wheels in the earth, and in such situations the utmost straining of the jaded mules will scarcely advance the wagons three miles a day. A trader by the name of Kelly,[123] who arrived at Santa Fé about a month before our party, was distressed in this manner during the whole of his journey, and was one hundred and nine days making his travel.

But the enormous duty is the greatest hindrance to the trade. One hundred per cent, is asked by the law, but *only* thirty-five is *exacted*. A great deal of successful smuggling used to be carried on, but the Government officers have now become so expert and vigilant that the smugglers no longer dare attempt the old game. This last spring a new arrangement was made, by which dealers were allowed to pay five hundred dollars a wagon instead of the thirty-five percent upon their invoices.[124] The chief article of

---

[122] Gregg's trade figures in *Commerce of the Prairies* reveal that many merchants found it profitable enough to trade to Santa Fe despite regulations and a smaller return. Trade was more profitable in the years before 1831, when the New Mexico market was a ripe plum for the intrepid. It might be well to consider also that American traders oftentimes had an exaggerated notion of profit to be gathered in the Southwest and were disappointed with anything less than an extremely large return.

[123] See article footnote 26.

[124] See article footnote 96.

trade is common domestic, and this was retailing at thirty-one cents a yard when we were in Santa Fé, although at times it brings forty and fifty. When leaving the country you are obliged to smuggle away specie and gold dust,[125] and these, with what furs you may be transporting, are in danger of being stolen from you by the Indians. The Santa Fé trade, however, a few years ago was much better than it is at present.

Las Tres Marias

It is not likely that any but such as have wandered over the vast wastes of the west, can conceive such sensations and impressions as are experienced by the traveller.—Nothing in nature can be compared to the prairie but the ocean, and the similitude is indeed most striking. The horizon bending to the land resembles the meeting of sky and water; the rolling undulations of the prairie are most like to the heaving of old ocean; and the flutterings of the silken grass imitate most exquisitely the ripples of the sea. Add to this the slow rising of an object in the distance, particularly the white top of a trader's wagon—ideas of the ocean are irresistibly forced upon you—the distant wagon becomes a sail; the green grass the green sea; and the wild roving herds, monsters of the deep. In the night one would suppose the scene would be most solemnly impressive, but it is not so; it is in the stillness of the noon-day, when the sun that we have looked on from childhood is shining bright as ever; when the sky is the

[125] Much of the New Mexico–Missouri trade was limited to the small amount of cash Santa Fe merchants received in trade with Chihuahua and the south; yet an estimated $150,000 to $600,000 in silver coins, brought from Mexico to Santa Fe, was carried away each year by American merchants returning to Missouri. Gold bullion from New Mexico mines, mules, buffalo rugs, furs, and wool were the principal exports, in addition to silver, taken to Missouri by the wagoners. There was, however, a high duty on precious metals exported to the United States; and, to avoid that duty, the American traders resorted to such deceptions as false axletrees, in which bullion and coins could be hidden until the customs agents were passed.—Inman, *Old Santa Fe Trail*, 60; Cleve Hallenbeck, *Land of the Conquistadores* (Caldwell, 1950), 317–18.

same, but the earth is changed; and deserted nature smiles upon desolation. Then do solemn feelings steal upon the heart, and then, like half-remembered dreams, do memories of other scenes flit before us—faces that are loved take shape in the space at which we gaze—tones that were dear to the heart, tingle again within the ear; the busy haunts that we before have trodden, are pictured again to memory, and we start from abstraction to look around the vast desert solitude and ask ourselves, "where exist the millions of men that people the earth, while here the whole earth seems silence and desolation."

The night is full of wildness and of beauty, yet it is not half so solemn as the day. The small band of travellers gather round the camp fire, and while jest and laugh passes round the idea of solitude is lost; or perhaps anecdotes of home are rehearsed until the wildness is forgotten, and the wanderers yield themselves to slumber that they may dream of kindred and kind ones far away, whom perhaps they may never meet again. Though it is difficult for the life-long tenant of a city to realize the impressions of the traveller, yet it may be easy to conceive what would be the feelings awakened by a star-light night upon the prairie; for the object of contemplation is the sky, and the sky is the same whether viewed from the city or the desert, the palace or the hovel of misery. This distinction is perhaps the only one that exists; upon the prairie your eye is attracted to the circling edge of the horizon where the "brave o'erhanging firmament" bends down to kiss the earth. In cities you look up at the stars above you, but in the waste you wonder to see the glittering gems of the sky touching the grosser earth.

On an occasion, when journeying only in the night, while crossing a district of country much infested by the Camanche, about an hour before day-break a star appeared just rising to the sight, so large, so flamelike, and seemingly so near, that we hesitated many minutes before we could determine whether it was an Indian camp-fire or a star of the sky. As we journeyed forward the beautiful star rose from the land, and it was long after the grey light of morning spread around the sky that the silver twinkler disappeared. The sky seems nearer to the earth upon the prairie, and a beautiful reflection may be drawn from this:— When human aid is distant divine benevolence seems to protect our steps, and heaven bends down to guard the wanderer. You may lay upon the ground and see the stars rise in the horizon, until you fancy that you feel the eternal motion of the planet on which you rest; and hushed stillness through day and night reigns in the airy-silence that is doomed to sleep upon the green desert from creation until the end of time, when merged in chaos its destiny shall be eternal.

One starry night, when musing somewhat in this wise, stretched at length upon the green bank of the beautiful Arkansas, at a part where the stream though wide is so shallow that the deer can bound across without swimming, one of the Mexican sentinels addressed the writer and requested him to observe two stars which appeared just above the verge of the horizon.—These, the sentinel said, were two of three brilliant stars which he called *"Las Tres Marias,"* or *The Three Marys*—the third would soon appear, and then his term of duty as guard would expire for the night. Thus the Spaniards in this country regulate their hours, such a thing as a watch being a curiosity among them. As he said, the third star soon rose, and indeed *"The Three Marys"* were most radiant and beautiful. It was a pretty idea of the Spaniards to christen them with such a title, for from their name, matched so admirably with their beauty, you can not look upon them without associating their appearance with that of some three of earth's fairest daughters–three Marys of earth—some three gentle beings born to be loved and enshrined forever in pure and pleasant thoughts.[126]

"Las Tres Marias" are the three stars which form the first joint of the tail of the Scorpion, and are seen opposite to the seven

[126] Matt overlooked the likeliest possibility: that *Las Tres Marías* were named by certain pious Spaniards in biblical reference to Mary the mother of Christ, Mary the wife of Cleophas, and Mary Magdalene.

stars, which the Spaniards call *el Carro*, or the *wagon*, but which has found a more appropriate name in vulgar phraseology among ourselves, as the *dipper* or *ladle*.[127] Other stars are quite as beautiful as the three Marys, but in this sweet name, given to them by the Spaniards, consists the charm that makes them seem more bright than all the others in the fretted firmament; and having once learned their title you cannot look upon the sky without your eye wandering in search of the starry three. If you have known a Mary that was beautiful, a Mary that was sad, a Mary that was loved and lost; if your mother or your sister was a Mary, there in the wilderness you see her in the sky. If your thoughts question the night to know the fate of the beings you have loved, those beautiful stars smile and answer, "we are here, come to us and smile as we are smiling, for here is happiness." Beautiful, most beautiful *"Tres Marias!"*

Dog Towns

One of the most striking peculiarities which rivet attention in the buffalo regions is the number of what are called 'dog towns.' These are spots of short white grass, growing exceedingly thick and fine, where the prairie dogs gather, dig their holes and live in communities.[128] They burrow in the earth, throwing up little mounds, in the center of which are the holes leading to the domiciles below. It is said these under-ground habitations are made to

[127] In July and August, the tail of Scorpion is very close to the horizon opposite the stars of the Big Dipper in Sagittarius; but they are not seen in that position in early October, when Matt was on the Arkansas and claims he saw them. Evidently he saw them on the way west in July and, when writing this article, placed the event on his return journey. The two conspicuous stars of Scorpion's tail are Lambda and Upsilon. The third star is probably Kappa, which barely touches the outside of the last link of the tail.

[128] If this is not dead grass, it may be prairie grass nibbled to the ground. The prairie dog lives principally upon green plants and grasses, eating roots, stems, and leaves. During a drought, the dog villages are "almost destitute of plant life, so closely is every living bit cropped."—N. Hollister, "A Systematic Account of the Prairie-Dogs," in *North American Fauna No. 40* (United States Department of Agriculture, Bureau of Biological Survey, Washington, 1916), 7.

communicate below, and the dogs are continually burrowing, meeting each other in all directions. Snakes and owls are said to dwell with the dogs in their holes, with the utmost harmony, but we had no opportunity of finding a proof of this, though the story is very generally believed.[129] They feed upon the short, silken grass where their dwellings are always located, and when their peculiar pasturage is exhausted, they emigrate and form settlements elsewhere.

The dogs are about the size of full grown rats, and they have a queer, shrill bark, which (if such a thing may be imagined) forms a sort of medium between the yelp of a cur and the squeal of a rat. They are generally white or grey, and we saw not one of a darker color.[130] The towns sometimes spread over a distance of several hundred square yards in circumference, spangling the darker green of the prairie in a manner that would doubtless be exceedingly picturesque could it be viewed from a balloon. The little creatures are exceedingly difficult either to catch or kill, and it is very seldom that travellers attempt one or the other, for upon the approach of intruders those out on the grass instantly rush to their holes, and those under the ground pop out their heads to see what is the matter. If one is shot it tumbles back immediately into the hole, and there is no getting at it, but there is never any telling whether a shot takes effect or not, for whether hit or not the creatures disappear instantly. On one occasion, however, we hit an impudent little fellow which sat barking at

[129] The legend is explained easily when we realize that a hungry snake will enter a prairie dog hole in search of food, frightening the dog to run and dig a new home. When the snake leaves, the small western burrowing owl, to avoid building itself a nest, moves into the abandoned underground dwelling.

[130] Since these animals are true ground squirrels, it is inaccurate to call them prairie dogs. There is great variation in the animal's color, caused by age, molting, and soil; but the adult summer coat is usually "dark pinkish cinnamon, finely lined with black and buff" on the back and "whitish or buffy white" below. Its tail has a black or brown-black tip. The particular animals Matt saw were *Cynomys ludovicianus ludovicianus* and range from northern Montana to southwestern Texas.—Hollister, "Systematic Account of Prairie-Dogs," in *North American Fauna No. 40*, 5, 13, 15.

us with its nose above the mound, and broke its back. The poor dog was knocked out of its hole, and the disabled creature wriggled and struggled pitifully in the grass. This was the only opportunity we had to observe the little animal closely, for during our whole travel we were never at any other time successful in a single shot, though we fired at the mounds repeatedly both with pistols and rifles as we rode along.

Those who have been compelled by necessity to eat the creature say that the meat is extremely tough and unpalatable. Two men whom we met returning home disheartened, told us they were preserved from utter starvation by a lucky shot at a dog, which, with a little flour, was their only sustenance for nearly three days.[131] When coming near a dog town your ears are assailed with a vociferous barking from the whole community, which gradually ceases as you advance, until, as you pass over the spot, the little animals all disappear, and the singular sound is no more heard. Dozens of them will be sometimes peeping and barking above the mounds, and at the report of a rifle they are gone like magic into the earth, and scarcely a sign of them remains. You may poke the full length of a walking stick into one of their holes and not find a bottom to the subterranean habitation.

Night on the Prairie

The following stanzas were suggested in the midst of a scene the most singularly wild and beautiful that the writer ever witnessed. The prairie was flat, not undulating as is usual, and covered with a growth of grass yet untouched by the buffalo. Not a blade grew higher than its fellows, and all seemed as regular as though measured off by the scythe of the husbandman. Not a single flower appeared around the vast carpet of green, and one solitary white buffalo's skull glittering in the moonlight was the sole relief to the eye.

[131] One traveler on the Santa Fe Trail in 1854 tasted prairie dog soup and pronounced it "not first class."—James A. Little, *What I Saw on the Santa Fe Trail* (Plainfield, Indiana, 1904), 34.

Night on the prairie! Lone and solemn night.
  Night on the desert waste, where howling strays
The hungered wolf, baying the silver light
  Of Cynthia, and the planets starry maze.
And O! how peacefully the moonbeam plays
  Upon the grassy carpet. Not a sound
Reaches the ear. Nought moves except the rays
  Dancing with unseen zephyrs upon the ground,
And rising stars which tell the world is rolling round.

How changed the earth! Yet heaven is the same.
  Those are the stars which smiled upon me when
A hundred leagues away I heard my name
  Spoken by brothers in the haunts of men.
  And shall those brothers greet me e'er again?
Ye silent stars, my sole companions now,
  For once reveal yourselves to mortal ken.
And here your solemn mysteries avow.
Why does man turn to thee when gloom is on his brow?

Ye beauteous heavens, bending so lowly down,
  Bounding my vision upon ev'ry side;
Thus have ye taught me in this moment lone
  The weakness of man's vanity and pride.
  A breathing atom on the desert wide!
This blade of grass as great a thing as I!
  Though to its spot of birth 'tis ever tied,
It knows no greater evil than to die—
  And better far its lot, it falls without a sigh!

Its death is useful as its life hath been;
  It carpets summer, till it dies to feed
The untam'd monarch of the prairie green,
  The lordly Buffalo. While man, indeed,
  Lord of the brute, the mountain, and the mead,
Great though he be in fame, and high in station,

Is doomed to fall that his proud flesh may breed
The vilest creeping thing in all creation—
The worm, the slimy worm. Ah! sad humiliation!

But hark? What sound disturbs the solemn stillness?
    Whence comes that cry so desolate and so drear?—
Checking the life veins with a frosty chillness,
    And piercing like an arrow through the ear?
    It is the wolf! Hark to the echo near!
Louder and nearer still! The hungry band
    Howl at the moon and at the starlight clear.
The wretched brutes prowling in vain the land,
Cry to the skies for food with desperate demand!

Kindred and home!—E'en like yon starving throng,
    Now yearns my bosom for your sympathies,
And like the music of a once-loved song
    My heart is teeming with your memories.
    Dear home! Your simplest joys seem ecstacies,
Even your *care* now seems a sweet delight.
    Thus never till we're plunged in miseries,
Learn we to love and cherish what is bright.
Alone! Night on the prairie! Lone and solemn night!

Fording the Arkansas

On our return travel from Santa Fé Governor Amijo gave us
an escort of twenty-five Spanish soldiers commanded by Teniente,
or Lieut. Hernandez. They were to see us as far as the Arkansas
and then leave us to our fate. We travelled by the Semirone
road,[132] a shallow stream which affords to the trader the advan-

---

[132] The Cimarron branch of the Santa Fe Trail (east to west) left the
Arkansas at any one of its several crossings in western Kansas and struck southwest. The trail crossed the north fork of the Cimarron and then followed the
north or right bank of the main channel of the river across a tiny segment of
Colorado into the far upper western part of the Oklahoma panhandle. There it
crossed the main branch of the Cimarron, entered New Mexico, crossed the

tages of water, but not a stick of brush or timber grows up on its bank. In dry weather this want of wood presents no serious inconvenience to the trader, as the "buffalo chips" are found in abundance, and make excellent fuel; but when rain overtakes travellers on this portion of the road severe privation is the consequence. Our party suffered this privation only for about eighteen hours. A cold wind came on, accompanied with heavy rain, soon after we started upon our afternoon travel. Night descended, and still the rain continued. We held on our course, for we had left the Semirone in the morning, and there was no chance now of either wood or water until we could reach the Arkansas. We continued travelling in the dark until the mules began to give out, and we had completely lost the track. Endurance was our only resource and we halted.

The Spaniards have a kind of fine sweet flour made of pounded corn, sugar, and stale crumbs, which they carry in bags to use upon such emergencies as the present. A little rain water was scooped up from hollows in the ground, and a cold porridge was soon made that was by no means unpalatable. We turned our animals loose and prepared ourselves to make the best of the situation. The Spanish soldiers kept guard during the night, and our only care was to make ourselves as comfortable as possible. We rolled ourselves in our buffalo robes, and after listening awhile to the dull moaning of the chill night wind; the dash of the rain, at intervals swift and heavy, and again dying away; the quick challenge of the sentinels from one to the other, "*Quien vive?* and the watch word in answer, *Mejico:* after listening to these sounds for a short time we fell into profound slumber, and did not awake until the Spaniards, in the earliest light of morning, had again prepared for us the dish of cold porridge.

We soon resumed our travel, for to reach the Arkansas was now an imperative necessity—Four mules had died during the night from fatigue, want of water, and the cold during the night,

North Canadian River, dropped southwestward to Las Vegas and San Miguel, and approached Santa Fe through Glorieta Pass.

and the poor dispirited creatures remaining could now scarcely crawl. After two hours travel we distinguished trees in the distance, and at eight o'clock A.M. we were camped on the banks of the Arkansas. We rested the remainder of the day, allowing the animals to graze and recruit, and the next morning after breakfast commenced fording the formidable river that crossed our path. Before starting, however, we had a little incident with a band of buffalo worth noting. A large herd came to the opposite bank of the stream to drink, and a little wooded island interposing our presence was not perceived. Our Spanish escort had with them a brass six pounder, which they levelled at the drinking herd and blazed away. The ball passed over the island, skimmed the water, and plunged into the opposite bank in the very center of the herd; but none of the band were hurt, or if they were, they managed to get away, and that in such a hurry that in two moments not a buffalo was in sight.

We had five wagons with ten mules to each. After choosing the most favorable place to cross, the mules, without much difficulty, were led into the water, dragging the lumbering wagons after them; and here was a scene for Hogarth. Some of the Spanish servants stripped off their clothing, and waded the stream with nothing on them but a cloth wound round their middles, in the common Indian mode. The wagons were drawn slowly through the water by the mules; the Spanish traders, folded closely in their blankets and mounted chiefly on mules, followed, driving their long iron spurs into the lazy animals, while the soldiers, who were now to leave us, remained upon the Mexican side of the river waving their hats to us and shouting *A Dios*, at the tops of their voices, as we arrived upon the opposite bank. We were now standing once more upon the soil of the United States. The Spaniards cast many longing, lingering looks behind at the land they were leaving, but our hearts were bounding with thoughts of home, and we cheered the Mexican strangers with *bienvenido* to the United States.

290

The Lost Track

The writer of these random, unpremeditated sketches returned to the States from the Mexican country the sole American companion of a party of adventurous Spaniards, who without possessing a word of the English language, or knowing aught of the manners of the people, had resolved upon a trading enterprise to the United States. A fortnight's sojourn in Santa Fé and the adjacent towns was sufficient to satisfy an impetuous yet aimless curiosity, and as travelling with the Mexican strangers afforded to the writer a new novelty, he readily, although ill fitted for the task, became guide and interpreter to the new speculators. With the assistance of a grammar and dictionary he soon became familiar with a language which he had never before studied, and which of all others is the easiest for a speaker of the English language to acquire, and thus his task of interpreting turned out nothing more than a pleasant recreation; but the office of guide, assumed by one who had but once, and then unobservantly, traversed the wilderness, seeking only excitement and trusting entirely to the guidance of others, soon proved a responsibility very difficult to answer.

From the Arkansas to *"el Rio de Pananas,"* or the point which the Americans call *"Pawnee Fork,"* there runs two tracks,[133] one of which has not been used for many years and is now almost obliterated. The new track is shorter by nearly a day's travel, and on it there is some certainty of finding water, which is not the case with the old one, and consequently it has been entirely abandoned since the more advantageous route was discovered. Of the existence of this old track the writer was wholly ignorant, until after having struck into and followed it for a day and a half, it grew fainter, fading away as we advanced, and at last disappeared completely in an ocean of fine, silken, white grass peculiar to the buffalo regions, which now spread away before and around us

[133] The regular trail closely paralleled the north or left bank of the Arkansas (going east) from Dodge City to Larned, Kansas. Inland, four to seven miles to the northwest and roughly parallel to the river trail, was the dry route.

like an interminable sheet of snow. The surprise, the consternation of the *guide* at this moment may be imagined! Without being familiar with a single rule by which travellers in these wild solitudes are wont to direct their steps, he found his only dependence vanish like an *ignis fatuus,* leaving him without resource and as completely lost as ever was mariner upon a wrecked vessel at sea. In endeavoring to shape some reason for the sudden disappearance of the track his mind only grew into greater perplexity, and all he knew was that he had not only lost himself but had also led a party of innocent strangers into the same helpless predicament; for the scene around him was not such as he had seen upon his former travel, nor was it possible that the mark of the wagon wheels could have been so completely obliterated in so short a space of time. To confess his ignorance, however, and excite the alarm of the Spaniards, would not merely bring upon him disgrace, but perhaps subject him to danger, and he was just wise enough to maintain an unmoved countenance and answer the questions of his somewhat uneasy companions by hypocritical assurances that all was right.

With the best imitation of confidence and unconcern that he could call to his assistance, (and being a runaway disciple of Thespis in this he found little difficulty) he continued to lead, or rather *mislead* the confiding Mexicans. Before night closed in we were fortunate enough to discover, by the hovering of some large birds about the spot, a stagnant pool or marsh, where we camped and dipped up sufficient ill tasted water to moisten our throats, parched by a whole day's travel under a sultry sun, and through a region so smooth and level that not a hollow appeared where a drop of water could rest had heaven benevolently lent us a shower.

The next morning the bewildered guide led off the caravan again, trusting only to fortune and the sun to get him out of his unfortunate dilemma. In the midst of this difficulty there was at least one consolatory reflection, we could not starve, for the buffalo were grazing about the plain in every direction. Their appearance, however, was another convincing proof that we were far from our proper course, for the absence of their usual wildness and alarm was a sure sign that they had not recently been disturbed by the hunter, whereas along the traders' path they continually manifest the greatest uneasiness and terror.

This day rolled away without producing the slightest variation in the desolate prospect, and at night we camped again at a stagnant pool, the water of which was so bitter and repulsive that we could not, though fainting with thirst, force it down our throats. Some whose desperation made them successful in this operation were tortured during the night with sickness and with languor, and headache during the whole of the next day. When the sun rose we resumed our travel, and at about 10 o'clock A.M. we caught sight of a line of trees stretching across the prairie and of course marking the course of a creek or river. Upon discovering this prospect, the writer, after in vain soliciting some of the Spaniards to accompany him, applied spurs to his horse and started forward alone, his anxiety to recognize some point which might help him to regain the lost track, and his impatience to swallow a draught of clear water, completely overcoming all fear of peril from the Indians. At two in the afternoon he reached the creek and found it *dry!* Some indications, however, induced him to think the water course was that known as "Pawnee River," and after riding a few more miles along its bank and from bend to bend, he at last with inexpressible delight struck again into the lost track and reached "Pawnee Fork,"[134] the well known crossing where water is always found.

As he dismounted to plunge his parched lips in the refreshing stream, three buffalo that were drinking dashed up the opposite bank, scattering dust and heavy stones behind them as they hurried away from the unwelcome intrusion.

[134] Pawnee River and Pawnee Fork are one and the same. The stream flows into the Arkansas from the west. Larned, Kansas, county seat of Pawnee County, now lies at the confluence of the two streams. Fort Larned (Camp Albert) was set up there in 1859 to guard the trail.

Col. James Bowie

We are in possession of a little anecdote highly characteristic of those remarkable men, Col. James Bowie and his brother Rezin,[135] which has never, we believe, yet appeared among the various printed relations of their battles, dangers, bravery, &c. that have met the public eye.[136] The incident we are about to relate occurring among the wild prairie regions of Texas, we shall here introduce it among the prairie sketches we have already made.

Col. Bowie was undoubtedly a man of vigorous intellect, as well as of firm and flintlike nerve. His character is one of bold and captivating individuality, and would form a magnificent study for some native novelist. We say "some," meaning only a few, and we will mention Simms as one; there are also "some" that we hope will never mar so excellent a subject. From the wild forest life to which his bold and daring nature led him, and the deeds and scenes in which he constantly appeared as the masterspirit, an untractable and coarse disposition is apt to be imputed to him, yet directly the opposite of this was one of Col. Bowie's most distinguishing traits of character. His manners in

---

[135] James and Rezin P. Bowie were two of the five sons of Rezin Bowie, Sr. About 1828, James left the southeastern states for Texas, took up Mexican citizenship, and went into land speculation. He served as a colonel in the Texas revolutionary army and in 1836 fell at the Alamo. Either James or Rezin first conceived the bowie knife, and both of them left colorful reputations.—W. J. Ghent, "James Bowie," in the *Dictionary of American Biography*, II, 509–10; Amelia Williams, "A Critical Study of the Siege of the Alamo and of the Personnel of Its Defenders" (Ph.D. dissertation, University of Texas, 1951), 189.

[136] Only a part of our voluminous Bowieana was available in print at the time Matt wrote this article. A newspaper account of Bowie adventures had been carried in *The* (Natchez) *Ariel* of October 19, 1827, and a letter written by Rezin on his brother's life appeared in both the *Planter's Advocate* (Donaldsonville, Louisiana?) and in *Niles' National Register* (Baltimore) in the late thirties. Mary A. Holley had carried accounts in her *Texas* (Lexington, Kentucky, 1836).—J. Frank Dobie, "James Bowie, Big Dealer," *The Southwestern Historical Quarterly*, Vol. LX, No. 3 (January, 1957), 337–38, 343, 346.

social intercourse were bland and gentle, so much so as to heighten materially the interest of his character. He spoke with slow and impressive intonation, nicely *ar-tic-u-la-ting ev-e-ry* syllable he uttered, and with strict yet easy politeness observing every form of delicacy and good-breeding. In society he was stared at as a lion; but acquaintance attracted a gentler interest toward him, and it was curious, as well as pleasant, to find how the lord of the forest had known the embrace of the lamb. The following anec- dote relates immediately to Rezin, but, being here giving [*sic*] as told by the Colonel himself, it will be found to convey a very vivid and just idea of both men's characters.

In one of the Texan wilds a brave little band, of which the Colonel and Rezin were, as usual, the leading men, fell into an engagement with a vastly superior number of mounted Caman- ches. Upon detecting his red enemies, Colonel Bowie so manoeu- vred his men as completely to conceal his inferiority of force, and, securing a position for defence, he very coolly awaited the mo- ment for action. A favorable chance for execution soon occurred, and a few American rifles began to blaze away upon the savages in such a manner as to convince them that the party told about double its actual number. Still the Camanches were appearing in all directions, flying about in great force, and the condition of the little American party became extremely critical; for, once knowing the possession of advantage, these Indians are sufficient- ly warlike and daring to be of very respectable consideration as enemies, even to Americans; though, until they obtain this con- fidence they will seldom venture upon much hazard. Now, every moment seemed to convey information to the Camanches of the miserable weakness of Bowie's party, and the Colonel disposed his men with the coolest caution, in expectation of an overwhelm- ing assault.

In such ticklish emergencies it is customary for a hunter to pat his good rifle affectionately, and say, "I'm sure of at least *one* man before I fall!" but it seems Rezin Bowie had made up his mind for *two*. Rezin possessed the best rifle in camp—a weapon which was considered by connoisseurs a perfect prince of shooting irons, and with which its owner was as sure of his mark as of lifting food direct to his mouth. At this position of the opponents the colonel observed his brother reclining behind a log, with his favorite rifle in rest across it, his eye to the sight, his hair trigger sprung, and his finger in place for sending out the well-directed leaden messenger.

Looking in the direction of Rezin's aim, the Colonel saw two mounted Camanches (important chiefs, as appeared by the gleaming of their ornaments in the sun) dashing about, farther, then nearer apart, and seeming to be a pair of the most daring warriors, endeavoring to learn the true condition of the American party. They were beyond the reach of any ordinary rifle, where they took care to keep, but the Colonel knew that Rezin's beautiful weapon was equal to the distance, and wondered why he delayed firing.

"Brother Rezin," said the Colonel, in the smooth and deliberate manner which we have attempted to describe—"Brother Rezin, do you not see these two red rascals wheeling about there, near each other? Why don't you pull one of them down from his horse?"

"Don't hurry me, brother James," replied Rezin, keeping his eye steady upon the sight, and speaking slowly like the colonel. "If I pull *one* of the red rascals down, brother, the other red rascal will get out of my reach; but wait till they *lap*, and then I'll pull them *both* down, brother James."

"They *did* lap, gentlemen," said Colonel Bowie,—and these were the brave fellow's own words, as he used to tell the story— "they *did* lap—Rezin pulled the trigger—and, as I am an hon-est gen-tle-man, they *both fell from their horses!*"

The engagement with the Indians terminated with some loss to Bowie's party, but the two brothers lived to pass through many perilous adventures after that.

Jim Rogers

Jim Rogers was a half-breed whom we met travelling alone far away in the prairies. He had with him two horses, one of which carried himself while the other transported his beaver traps, his skins, and the whole sum total of his goods and chattels, personal property, merchandise, and kitchen furniture. The load with which this horse was burdened was curious enough to the eye of a white man, and more especially to one who for the first time looked upon such a sight. The animal had passed his best days, but though his pace showed that he no longer possessed speed for the chase, yet the peculiar fire of the wild prairie steed still sparkled in his wandering eyeballs, as if kindled there still by contemplation of his broad native plains of green. And now he toiled slowly along, with his proud spirit bowed down by years of toil to the service of his lordly master, but still the characteristic of the free-born steed beautifully alive in his eye. A simple string of deer skin tied round his under jaw and passed round his neck was the bit and bridle by which he was held and guided. Upon his back was tied and strapped the whole worldly possessions and stock in trade of his master Jim Rogers:—a buffalo robe, a blanket, an iron pot, a newly slaughtered badger, half a dozen beaver skins, the traps for ensnaring his prey, a deer's head with the skin of the animal still attached to it, an old broken tin coffee pot, utterly useless, which had been thrown away by some passing trader, and picked up as a treasure by the half-breed, also a glass liquor flask with the bottom broken off, a bundle of dry branches for fuel, these and various other things of the same curious nature, were fastened upon the horse in dirty and careless disorder. Upon the top of the whole rested the iron pot, and in it some cooked meat and roasted ears of corn were seen.

Jim spoke English very well, and claimed kindred with us immediately. He said we must of course know his father Tom Brown, because he was an American and used to live, when a boy, in Philadelphia State, but afterwards he came to St. Louis, and from there he had gone trading among the Indians on the Upper Missouri. There he married Jim's mother, and lived in the village five years. Jim was very communicative and told us his whole history. He had two sisters, he said, and a brother, also children of Tom Brown, but none of them were as "smart" as him— couldn't speak American—married Indians, and disgraced their family. But Jim was "cute," he said, and knew how to catch beaver and sell skins to the whites—his father taught him.—He hadn't seen "Old Tom" for sometime, because the last time the old fellow was at the village he got offended and went away angry. Lewis licked him, Jim said. Lewis was Jim's younger brother, and Old Tom never liked him much, because he was lazy and was little better than an Indian. So Lewis and the old man quarrelled over a bottle of whiskey, and Lewis licked Tom so bad that he went away four years ago, and had never visited the village since. Jim said the last he had heard of his father was that he had started away with another tribe of Indians to go and fight the Seminoles, but he had never learned whether Old Tom had returned or not.

The horse on which Jim himself was mounted was in some respects a fair match for the other animal, but he was evidently not so far worn with service, and Jim assured us that he could "catch" with ease, which meant that he could pursue and overtake a buffalo. The same wild rolling eye, characteristic of the native tenant of the prairie, marked the animal bestridden by the half-breed, but a finer and glossier development of limb and muscle told of superior strength and activity. Jim rode bareheaded, and everything he had on in the way of clothing was composed of deer skin. A deer skin coat or shirt, deer skin leggings, moccasins, deer skin strings suspending his powder horn and pouch, deer skin stirrups, a deer skin bridle, deer skin sustaining his saddle, which was nothing more nor less than a buffalo hide rolled up into a seat on the horse's back, and his rifle was slung by deer skin over his shoulders. The greatest oddity about Jim was an old stock which he wore fastened around his neck, and which looked as though it had not come off his neck since the day it came into his possession. A few straggling bristles were still protruding from it, although its original shape was entirely gone, and it had curled or shrunk into a rope, encircling his neck so tightly that it almost conveyed a painful sensation, as though the poor fellow was choking. To add even to the oddity of this, the buckle of the stock was gone, or its use had never been understood, and deer skin strings were corded round the half-breed's neck to secure this fashionable ornament of civilization from tumbling off.

Jim Rogers was deeply pock-marked, and his skin was lighter by more than one shade than the complexion of a Mexican Spaniard. He seemed to entertain great affection for the Americans, and had become so versed in their manners that, had he not told us his history, we would sooner have taken him for some hardvisaged Canadian boatman than a half-breed.

Observing an old pipe stuck in his moccasin, we tendered him a present of tobacco, which he accepted, and instantly, by way of return, made us welcome to his iron pot, helping himself at the same moment to a lump of cold meat, by way of admonishing us that ceremony was needless. Finding us backward, he thought, perhaps some further solicitation was necessary, and commenced tearing the lump of meat to pieces and handing it round to us, but, finding his courtesy again declined, without seeming to conceive any idea of offence, he disposed of the meat himself, and then proceeded to fill his pipe with tobacco.

He seemed very much surprised that we did not know his brother Lewis, nor his father Tom. Tom was a regular white man, he said, and of course we must know him; and his brother Lewis had been down the Missouri to Fort Leavenworth twice, therefore he was certain we must have been great friends and associates. He invited us all to stay and camp with him, pointing to the deer's head and telling us what a feast we should have. Jim generally made one culinary operation serve him for one or two, and sometimes three days, he said, but if we would stay with him he would build a grand camp-fire and cook his deer's head. His old iron pot was a source of great pride with him, and he pointed to it with very dignified ostentation.

Among our own men we had before observed a method of cooking the deer's head, which they told us, was acquired from the Indians. The head, completely undressed and with the skin on, was buried in a hole under the camp-fire, and left all night beneath the cinders; the next day the skull was easily pulled apart, and the brains, to hungry travellers, coming off a night-guard, were indeed truly delicious.

We were on our return travel, and Jim was making his way to the mountains. He had been trapping on a wooded prairie creek, and assured us that he had not seen the face of Indian or white man for five months. Now he was going off alone over hundreds of miles of dreary land, to spend years away from companionship, and he seemed as cheerful about it as we were who were just beginning to rejoice in anticipations of home.

Buffalo Chase

It was when travelling homeward, and we were fast receding from the wild region tenanted by the buffalo—a few days more and we could no longer enjoy either the spirit-rousing excitement of the chase or the delicious fresh meat thus procured. The party was composed entirely of Mexicans, the writer forming one solitary exception, and the hunting was principally done by horsemen with lances, in a style entirely different from either the American or the Indian. The most skilful *matadore* among the Spaniards was a little fellow named *Jose Alexico*, and his admirable management of the horse and the lance was the wonder and envy of all the rest of the party. He sat upon an impatient steed with as much confidence and ease as though reclining upon a couch, and handled his lance with all the grace, dexterity, and elegance of a French fencing master flourishing his foil. For several days the buffalo had been rapidly diminishing, and it was now only at long intervals that small herds would cross our path or appear in view scattered around the prairie.

It was scorching noon when we discovered a band of about twenty grazing far away to our right, yet not so distant but we could plainly distinguish three tempting fat cows among the number. Twelve or fifteen of us instantly separated ourselves from the caravan, and were off in pursuit. *Alexico,* in less time than the swiftest pen could relate the action, jumped from his mule, caught with a noose the fleetest hunting horse in camp, clapped a bridle in his mouth, threw a blanket on his back, himself on the blanket, and in an instant, although we had started first, he was flying before us like an arrow from a bow. An instant more and a cloud of dust bounced up in the air from the spot where the buffalo were grazing, then the whole band were seen straining their ponderous limbs and tearing up the earth in their flight, and *Alexico,* like a pursuing devil, with his lance couched, full in the midst of them. We were all badly mounted for hunting, not having like *Alexico* stopped to change steeds for the sport; so that when we came up we found the expert Spaniard had wounded and detained a choice cow, and the rest of the band were dispersed and completely out of sight. *Alexico* had here a loud call for the display of his accomplishment as a *matadore,* and he performed a most curious and admirable exploit.

The day was more than half gone, the wagons were already passing us, and to kill the cow here, butcher it, and carry the meat after the caravan, would have imposed a weary burden upon the animals, and we should not have got to camp until after night. *Alexico* needed no prompter to teach him this, or how to obviate the difficulty. He had with the coolest precision just wounded the cow sufficiently to draw her away from her companions, not materially to diminish her strength, and he now, by aggravating and teasing his victim with the point of his long lance, contrived to make the huge brute chase him, he keeping just beyond reach of her sharp horns, and guiding his horse in the direction he wished to go. When the poor beast would grow weak and pause, *Alexico*

301

would prick the wound he had already made, upon which the angry cow would gather up strength again, toss her horns furiously in the air, and make another headlong rush after the laughing *matadore*. Once the cow stumbled upon her fore knees, and the daring Spaniard rode up and beat her over the head until she rose again, just as one might take a stick to drive away a sick dog. We trembled for *Alexico* when the cow rose then, for she sprang suddenly from the ground and passed her short curling horn within an inch of his horse's flank. The fine steed upon which the Spanish hunter sat seemed to understand every motion, not only of his rider but of the enraged beast with which he was contending, and he would charge, wheel, return again, and fly before the buffalo, seemingly without needing the usual guide of the reins. But for this superior intelligence he would certainly have been gored by that last desperate plunge made by the wounded cow.

In this manner *Alexico* drew the poor exhausted creature after him three or four miles in advance of the wagons, when he drove his lance deep into its liver, and, spouting thick blood from its nostrils, the slaughtered beast fell staggering to the earth. The Spaniards were instantly dismounted and at work with their knives, tearing away the reeking skin of the buffalo while it yet lay panting with life. Their haste was occasioned by the approach of night and a dark storm that was hurrying on, flashing and roaring from the far horizon. Still a single ball or another plunge of the lance might have stretched the animal cold, sparing it unknown pangs, and proving its butchers not altogether heartless.— They were both heartless and pitiless, and the cruelly-tortured cow actually breathed its last while its merciless butchers were chopping the ribs from its side. They were clustered so thickly round the cow that the writer could not use his rifle, or he would have sent a ball through the animals heart; but the horrid scene curdled his blood, and he turned away sick forever after of the cruel sport of buffalo hunting. It is not cruelty in these Mexicans, but a callous want of feeling. They seemed to have no conception of the tortures they were inflicting. On another occasion, when butchering a cow in the same hurried manner, the unfortunate creature rose to its feet and ran off a few steps, quivering with agony, with the warm skin stripped from its side and hanging about its legs.

Evening began to grow dark around us, and the storm rolled threatening over our heads before the cow was thoroughly cut up, but still the wagons did not appear in sight, and we could not account for the delay. A man was despatched to ascertain the cause, and before he returned, the pitch black mass of vapour that now spread all around the sky, bent lower and nearer to the earth, till at last the heavy cataract dashed upon the green like steel attracted by the magnet. The man returned and informed us that in consequence of the storm our party had ceased travelling earlier than usual, and camp was formed a mile and a half behind us, so that the labour of *Alexico* in bringing the cow so far turned out worse than useless.

The meat was packed on the animals and carried into camp, and the next day when we passed the spot of the butchering, not two bones of that huge skeleton we had left remained together. They were scattered far and wide, and polished clean and white by the sharp tooth of the wolf. The starving creatures had feasted during the night, and unsated had exhausted their repast; for not an ounce of red flesh remained, and even the bones were gnawed and scattered about as if tossed away in angry disappointment.

What a scene must have been there in the deep midnight, when the flood was pouring from the gates of heaven! Hundreds of starving wolves, prowling about the wilderness, caught scent of the buffalo's blood and rushed to the banquet, to

> *Hold o'er the dead their carnival.*
> *Gorging and growling o'er carcase and limb,*
> *They were too busy to bark*

at or listen to the rolling thunder above their heads, and still unsatisfied with their scanty meal, they left the white bones of the buffalo to howl hungrily and dismally at the dawning light of day.

The Burning Prairie

In the fall of the year the Indians set fire to the dry grass of the prairies, and the flames sweep over the vast plains with inconceivable rapidity. Their object is to drive the game to the edges of the creeks where they may be hunted with greater facility.

'Twas in the latter part of October that we first enjoyed the magnificent spectacle of a burning prairie. During the whole of nearly two days we had perceived far away on the horizon before us an appearance which we at first supposed to be a line of thin clouds floating along the sky; but as night was approaching on the second day, the red light which began to display itself in the contrasted darkness told us that the vast wilderness before us was on fire. We could form no estimate of the distance that lay between us and the raging element, as all we could distinguish was a line of faint light stretching along the circling edge of the sky and land like an expiring rainbow. Our travel the next day brought us slowly nearer to the fire that was hurrying on to meet us, and at night we camped upon the edge of a stream, which lay between us and the consuming grass, so that in case the fire should reach us before morning we would have no danger to apprehend.

The first guard was set and we were soon locked in slumber. The second guard was called up to duty, and as they lazily rolled out of their buffalo robes, various exclamations escaped their lips about the approaching fire. At length the third guard was called, which was at half past one in the morning, and there was no more sleep among us that night. The whole camp was generally disturbed at the changing of the guard, and our eyes now opened upon a scene of wild splendor that at once enchained us in boundless admiration. The fire had approached us to within four or five hundred yards, and we could hear the tall dry grass crackling in the flames and the dull roar of the night wind like an angry spirit hurrying on the work of destruction. The trees and brush that lined the creek added to the enchantment of the scene. As the fire swept on, the light seen through the trees appeared in all kinds of fantastic and curious shapes; and the flames (now raging steadily forward, and again darting furiously in side-long and eccentric directions, where beds of withered flowers and tufts of drier grass lay in its course) formed for a lively imagination things of phantasy and ludicrous grandeur, such as we are wont to see among tinted clouds when the sun is setting, or when we are gazing in abstracted musings on a sea-coal fire.

The night was just cold enough to afford us comfortable sensations while rolled in our buffalo robes; and, having chosen the most convenient logs and stumps on the side of the creek for pillows, we lay dozing and dreaming and gazing at the fire till morning. The creek made a wide bend at the point where we were camped, and as the flames closed up far along its opposite bank we were encircled by a vast crescent of fire. In the distance trees and shrubs seemed to be dancing in fantastic groups, and flocks of birds, burnt out from their grassy homes, would dart for a moment through the lighted sky and again disappear, screaming faintly in the distant gloom. Volumes of smoke, swept by fitful gusts of wind, would blind us for a moment, and roll away over our heads, a dark caravan of travellers through the sky. The fire at last seized upon the tall grass and shrubbery that skirted the opposite bank and raged with a fierceness that seemed to threaten destruction even to the trees. The heat became oppressive, and we screened ourselves behind fallen logs while we peeped through the clustering shrubbery at the fire. At one moment we almost expected to see the grass upon our own side of the creek burst into flame, so heated became the ground. The strong wind in places would sweep the fire completely out for an instant, till, as the gust died away the grass became again ignited, and the flames would seem to rage more furiously for their momentary suspension.

At length the fire hissed in the water of the creek and expired. We watched the flickering remnants of flame far along the distant winding of the stream, until the last blade of grass was consumed, the last spark extinguished, darkness again shadowed the scene,

And all was black.

Impressed with wonder at the extraordinary scene we had witnessed, we mused sleeplessly till light spread slowly in the eastern sky, and the day dawned.

The Burnt Prairie

We crossed the creek as the sun rose, and the "burnt district" lay before us. If the prairies are desolate when clothed in their garniture of green, how dreary must they be when robbed of their only relief, presenting nothing to the eye but a vast circumference of black. In mere wantonness we fired the grass behind us when we left the opposite bank, and as the flames spread away in the distance we hoped to enjoy an excitement similar to that which we had experienced in the night. But the spectacle was tame and spiritless. It wanted darkness to lend it splendor by contrast. We had travelled about a half an hour when we came upon a group of five buffalo. They stood and gazed at us without displaying their usual alarm. Their food had been swept away—they had been hunted by the fire instead of their usual foes, and a new terror seemed to have taken possession of them, which banished their fear of man. We continued approaching, and they still paused irresolute. When they did move from us, it was not with the headlong speed with which they usually shun the approach of man, but with slow uncertainty, as though they felt a vague consciousness of danger yet knew not what it was or which way to steer from it. They were probably starving. The vast plain was one black bed of dusty cinders; and as the wind swept over the prairie the sooty ashes rose in whirling eddies about us, and our faces were soon as begrimed and black as the ground over which we were travelling. Snakes were peeping fearfully from their holes. Toads, lizards, and horned frogs, remained passive on the ground, having no sheltering grass in which to hide from us. What surprised us most was the appearance of a mouse, a genuine little cheese nibbler, hurrying away from us as we advanced. The little animal must have smuggled itself out to these strange regions among some traders flour or biscuit bags,[137] and when discovered was turned out to grass.

We had missed our two dogs for a few minutes and suddenly discovered them chasing a raccoon, which they had found crouched in a buffalo wallow. The chase was the most ludicrous and laughable thing imaginable. The creature was very fat, and could not run fast, and in its attempts to get away from the dogs it would stumble and roll over and over again. The dogs would pounce upon it, and the three animals would be hid in the clouds of black dust which they raised. One of the Spaniards promised us more amusement with the creature, and dexterously throwing a noose around its body, he galloped off at full speed, dragging the unfortunate animal at his horse's heels. For fifteen minutes he kept his horse at full speed about the prairie, and when he returned to us the miserable raccoon was still breathing. We drove off the dogs and ended the poor creature's sufferings with a pistol shot.

This whole day we travelled over the long rolling prairies with nothing in sight but the blue sky, and the black earth stretching away to the horizon, with here and there a few blades which had escaped the fire, bending before the wind, and seeming to mourn over the ashes of their lost companions. Fire had swept away the natural carpet of the earth, and driven before it the things of life that were thus robbed of the provender prepared for them by nature.

All was black.

---

[137] This little fellow was probably a grasshopper mouse, although other varieties are found in that area. The grasshopper mouse is a creature of the plains and is abundant also in deserts.

We witnessed a spectacle that was

Seasonless, herbless, manless, treeless, lifeless.

The white skulls of the buffalo that ever strew the prairies, were now the only relief to the deep funereal blackness of the burnt earth. On we travelled, crossing the rolls, descending the hollows, still hoping at every rise to discover a tree or a speck of green, or a pond, any thing to relieve us from the depression which such a scene of desolation naturally threw over us. When the grass is plentiful and green, it seems like being cut off from humanity to be upon the prairies where man seldom appears, and woman never; but when fire has made the earth untenantable even for brutes, with what sensations must man view the scene!

Night approached, and still the same desolate prospect lay before us. Night descended, and darkness reigned above as well as beneath us. Nothing in the created world could so nearly resemble chaos. The moon rose, and never did she seem so beautiful. Though she did but again make visible the blackness of the earth, yet we knew she was shining on other scenes, on Christian habitations, and on spots where the green grass was still growing, and bright waters rolled. There was fellowship in the thought, and as our tired animals bore us slowly forward on that dreary night, we mused in silence about distant friends. Recollections that had lain dormant in memory for long years, broke upon us as lost diamonds sparkle in night when they would be passed unheeded in the day. How mysteriously are the ingredients of pleasure and pain mingled in the cup of life! In that hour's musing, on the burnt wilderness, and in the night, emotions thrilled us as delightful as the dearest blandishments of society could yield.

The Lost Dog

'Twas about five in the afternoon, when, as we were dismounting to camp on the banks of the Arkansas, the sentinel who had taken his station on an eminence near, called to us for the purpose of attracting our attention to a wolf that appeared near our camping place. Three of us took up our rifles again, mounted, and rode off in the direction of the animal, which we soon perceived to be a dog—a nearly starved, timid, domestic creature, which had been lost probably by some solitary trapper or wandering Indian hunter. We endeavored to coax the poor beast nearer that we might give it food, but its fear overcame its wish to make our acquaintance. It ran from us, swiftly, but not with the spirited speed of the wolf or the antelope; it still turned to gaze at us, and rather *slunk* than ran.

Finding our efforts to bring the dog into camp ineffectual, we gave up the pursuit, and the poor creature was forgotten. The next morning one of the night guards told us that a wolf had approached him within twenty feet during the night, and of course he could not shoot for fear of alarming the camp. That a wolf should prowl so near to us seemed strange, but none of us ever gave a thought to the poor lost dog we had seen, and this little incident was also forgotten. We had two dogs with us. The next night between ten and eleven we were awakened by the loud barking of the dogs, and every man was instantly on his feet, rifle in hand, in expectation of an Indian attack. No enemy appeared, and the cause of the alarm was traced to our dogs having discovered a strange cur in camp—the same poor starving animal had followed us, and crept into camp in search of food. The next morning we discovered it still following our trail, when we camped at noon it prowled about at a distance, and at night it remained crouched outside of the sentinels gazing at our camp fires. No solicitation would induce it to approach us, and the best we could do for it was to leave bones and scraps of buffalo meat behind us when we struck camp, that it might feed whenever we departed.

Thus for five days the poor dog followed us, crouching at a distance when we stopped, and travelling after us as we journeyed forward. It perhaps would have grown familiar with us, but our own dogs would not suffer it to approach, and invariably drove it back whenever it seemed disposed to become sociable. How strange that an animal, which towards men displays so many admirable traits, should to its fellows betray such want of sympathy. This poor dog had been wandering about the prairie evidently a long time for when it was at last brought into camp we could perceive it was dwindled almost to a skeleton, and its extreme shyness towards us sufficiently proved that it had endured much. Misery and luxury are equally potent in making cowards, and the rule applies to dogs as well as men. The animal had been lost perhaps from some former caravan, and in the unbroken silence of the vast prairies had wandered about days and nights in search of the familiar hand that used to caress it. It had felt the biting pangs of hunger when nought was in sight but the blue sky, and the boundless prairie carpeted with green. The hand of nature had strewed there a lordly banquet for the untamed buffalo, but there was no provision for the poor bewildered dog. It could not claim kindred with the wolves when they howled in the night; perhaps they would have hunted it down and torn it to satisfy their own savage hunger; and during the day nought crossed its path, save, perchance, roving herds of buffalo, from whom it doubtless fled in fear and terror. When we had succeeded in bringing it into camp, it crouched and crawled upon the ground before us, and seemed almost afraid to touch the food we offered it. Not a sound did it utter, neither bark nor growl, the dread stillness of the desert seemed to have struck the poor dog mute, and awed the starving creature into eternal silence.

There are many animals formed by nature to be usefully subservient to men, and some even draw from us kindly affections; among these are the horse, and next the dog. Among all the varieties of the dog, there is not one which does not possess either the quality of beauty or of usefulness, and many combine both. Few men despise dogs, most men appreciate their worth, and many almost feel for them the kindling sensations of love. The poor animal that we had picked up in the wilderness, followed us through the remainder of our travel, till we reached the first log house that appears among the far western settlements of Missouri. Here we gave him to a farmer, and as we sat beneath the hospitable shelter of the first Christian roof we had seen during five months' travel; while we were feasting upon a luxurious banquet of corn-bread, fried bacon, and rich milk unmingled with water, we told the history and adventures, and excited the good farmer's sympathy for our poor desert foundling, the lost dog.

Index

"Adam and Eve," painting by Claude Marie Dubufe: 137
Alarm, in camp: 164–66
Albert, Prince, of England: 180–81 n.
Alcalde (alcaldesa, alcalda), Spanish term for mayor: 179 n.
Alexico, José, Mexican in caravan: 300–303
Álvarez, Don Manuel, U. S. consul at Santa Fe: *xix*
American traders: *see* Santa Fe traders
Antelope: 3, 4, 5, 152
Apache Indians: 175, 190–93, 194, 197–98, 241
Arkansas, Choctaw Indians in: 104–105 n.
Arkansas River *(Nepestry)*: *xxiii*, 7 n., 8, 9 n., 16, 21 n., 25 n., 28–29, 30, 31, 35, 37, 38, 40, 41–42, 55, 57, 71, 72, 73, 75, 85, 87, 91, 92–93, 96 n., 99 n., 107, 112–13, 121, 127, 128, 129, 131, 136, 140, 141, 143, 145, 146, 149, 155 n., 162 n., 266 n., 280, 283, 284 n., 288–90, 291, 293 n., 308; Bernardo buried on banks of, *xxi*; Mexican military escort takes leave at, *xxiv*; caravan comes to, 13; "Pilgarlic" reaches, 27; Matt crosses, 56; crossings of, 71 n.
Armijo, Manuel, governor of New Mexico: *xix*, 205, 206–207, 214, 225, 288; criticized by Santa Fe traders, *xxiii*; puts tariff on merchandise, 221; counts population of New Mexico, 237 n.; gives ball for American traders, 237–40

Armijo, Señora, wife of Manuel: 238
Army (U. S.) protection of Santa Fe caravans: *xxiii*
Arapaho Indians: 133–34
Arroyo of the Ears: 55
Ash Creek: 21, 56, 72
Ash Hollow: 21 n.
Austin, Texas: 69
Axace (Sun), Crow Indian term: 262 n.

Bailey, Leonora, wife of James J. M. Valentine: *xxii*
Baird, James, digs at Caches: 129 n.
Barcelo, Doña María Gertrúdiz (Madam Barcelo): *see* Toulous, Señora
Barcelona, Lona: *see* Toulous, Señora
Barney: *see* Hicks & Barney
Bartlett Mesa, N. M.: 161 n.
Bayou dwellings of Choctaw Indians: 104–105
Bell, Mr., member of caravan: *xx*, 36
Bent, Charles: 143 n., 144 n.
Bent, George: 144 n.
Bent, Robert: 144
Bent, William: 72 n., 73, 143, 144 n.
Bent brothers, hospitality of: 73
Bent's Fort (Fort William): *xxiii*, 44–46, 72, 73, 107, 131, 140, 141, 142, 143–46, 149 n., 152, 155 n., 245
Bent's New Fort: 72 n.
Bernardo, cook with caravan: *xx*, *xxi*, 36–38, 126–28
Big Blue Creek: 70 n.
Big Cow Creek: *see* Cow Creek

312